3/24

For Indigenous Eyes Only

School of American Research
Native America series

James F. Brooks
General Editor

For Indigenous Eyes Only

A Decolonization Handbook

Edited by
Waziyatawin Angela Wilson
and Michael Yellow Bird

School of American Research
Santa Fe

School of American Research Press
Post Office Box 2188
Santa Fe, New Mexico 87504-2188
www.sarpress.sarweb.org

Acting Director: Catherine Cocks
Manuscript Editor: Ellen Cavalli
Design and Production: Cynthia Dyer
Proofreader: Sarah Soliz
Indexer: Ina Gravitz
Printer: Sheridan Books, Inc.

Library of Congress Cataloging-in-Publication Data

For indigenous eyes only : a decolonization handbook / edited by Waziyatawin Angela Wilson and Michael Yellow Bird.
    p. cm. — (School of American Research Native America series)
  Includes bibliographical references and index.
  ISBN 1-930618-63-8 (pa : alk. paper)
  1. Indians of North America—Ethnic identity. 2. Indians of North America—Politics and government. 3. Indians of North America—Social conditions. 4. Self-determination, National—United States. 5. Decolonization—United States. 6. Postcolonialism—United States. 7. Cultural property—Protection—United States. 8. United States—Race relations. 9. United States—Politics and government.
I. Wilson, Angela Cavender. II. Yellow Bird, Michael. III. Series.

E98.E85F67 2005
323.1'197073—dc22

2005017295

Contents

Figures

Standing (from left): Robert Odawi Porter, Michael Yellow Bird, James Riding In, T'hohahoken or Michael Doxtater.
Seated (from left): Cornel Pewewardy, Chi'XapKaid or Michael Pavel, Waziyatawin Angela Wilson, Suzan Shown Harjo.

Contributing Authors

T'hohahoken or Michael Doxtater was raised and schooled on the Six Nations Indian Reserve. Professionally, Doxtater's area of specialization is organizational learning, cultural education, and educational media. As a private consultant he produced communications and training projects for the Canadian Government Expositions Centre (CGEC), Indian and Northern Affairs Canada (INAC), and Health Canada. Doxtater headed Studio One of the National Film Board of Canada (1993–1995), the Native Business Summit (1986), and the Canadian Indian Pavilion at the Canadian National Exhibition (1981–1984). His practice includes facilitating group processes for dispute and conflict resolution in the Native community from 1989 to the present, at Kanehsatake (1990), Ohsweken (1989, 1991, 1992, 1995), Tutelo Heights (1995–1996), and the Red Hill Valley (2003). Doxtater has produced 20 films and videos including the award-winning documentaries *Forgotten Warriors, Laxwesa Wa: Strength of the River,* and *No Turning Back: The Royal Commission on Aboriginal Peoples.* Also, Doxtater has written for the Beachcombers and Spirit Bay children's television network series. He was a team member for the restructuring of the American Indian Program, Cornell University (1998–2000). Doxtater has taught at Mohawk College, Niagara College, Cornell University, and Laurier University. Currently, Doxtater is Director, Office of First Nations and Inuit Education (OFNIE), McGill University, Montreal, Canada.

Suzan Shown Harjo (Cheyenne and Hodulgee Muscogee) is a poet, writer, lecturer, curator, and policy advocate. She has helped Native Peoples recover more than one million acres of land and many sacred places, and developed religious freedom, repatriation, and culture and arts laws. President of The Morning Star Institute in Washington, D.C., and a Columnist for *Indian Country Today*, she also is a 2004 School of American Research Artist Fellow and Summer Scholar, a Founding Trustee of the National Museum of the American Indian, Founding Co-Chair of The Howard Simons Fund for Indian Journalists, and Past Executive Director of the National Congress of American Indians.

Chi'XapKaid or Michael Pavel is an enrolled member of the Skokomish Indian Nation in Washington. His research on American Indian and Alaska Native access to and achievement in higher education has resulted in numerous publications (journal articles, chapters in edited volumes, national studies, reports to major foundations and organizations, digests and project briefs, a book foreword, and book review essays). He represents one of the few higher education researchers in the nation engaged in a research agenda to fully explore and understand the factors that influence American Indian and Alaska Native K–12 experiences as well as postsecondary enrollment, retention, and graduation. His scholarly productivity has brought him national attention and has positioned him as a respected scholar in the field of higher education with publications in: (a) leading publishing houses—Jossey-Bass, Garland, JAI; (b) journals—*The Review of Higher Education, Journal of College Student Development, NEA's Thought & Action, Journal of American Indian Education*, and *American Indian and Culture Research Journal*; and (c) influential professional associations—American Council on Education, American Association of Community Colleges, American Association of State Colleges and Universities, National Advisory Council on Indian Education, and National Education Association.

Cornel Pewewardy (Comanche and Kiowa) is associate professor in the department of teaching and leadership, school of education, at the University of Kansas. He is the co-editor of *Counting Coups: A History of "Indian" Mascots* (Nebraska, forthcoming). His research agenda is studying the psychological impact on children's academic achievement caused by ethnic stereotyping. He serves as the key consultant for the National Collegiate Athletic Association's (NCAA) study for the elimination of "Indian" mascots from member institutions as well as educational consultant to numerous school districts across the country on improving the academic achievement of underrepresented populations in education and faculty curriculum development.

Robert Odawi Porter is a citizen of the Seneca Nation of Indians (Heron Clan) and was raised on its Allegany Territory in upstate New York. He is currently Senior Associate Dean for Research, Professor of Law, and Dean's Research Scholar of Indigenous Nations Law at Syracuse University. He also serves as the founding director of the Center for Indigenous Law, Governance & Citizenship. After graduating from Syracuse University with a Bachelor of Arts degree in political science and economics, he attended Harvard Law School where he received his Juris Doctorate

degree in 1989. Upon graduation, he joined the Washington, D.C., law firm of Dickstein, Shapiro & Morin. In 1991, Professor Porter was appointed as the first Attorney General of the Seneca Nation of Indians. Also during this time he served as an Adjunct Professor at the University of Buffalo School of Law and as a Visiting Assistant Professor at the University of Tulsa College of Law. Professor Porter's academic and personal interests focus on the decolonization and revitalization of Indigenous nations and peoples. His most recent publications include "The Meaning of Indigenous Nation Sovereignty," *Arizona State Law Journal* 34:75 (Spring 2002); "Pursuing the Path of Indigenization in the Era of Emergent International Law Governing the Rights of Indigenous Peoples," *Yale Human Rights & Development Law Journal* 5, no. 123 (2002); and "The Inapplicability of American Law to the Indian Nations," *University of Iowa Law Review* 85 (2004). He has also written for *Indian Country Today*, the *New York Times*, and several other national and local newspapers. His book, *Sovereignty, Colonialism & the Indigenous Nations: A Reader*, was published by Carolina Academic Press in 2005.

James Riding In is a citizen of the Pawnee Nation of Oklahoma and an associate professor of American Indian Studies at Arizona State University. His research about repatriation as well as historical and contemporary Indian issues appears in various books and scholarly journals. He is now conducting a research project entitled "American Indians and the Santa Fe Trail" on behalf of the National Park Service. He has served as NAGPRA consultant for the Pawnee Nation, the University of Nebraska, Lincoln, and other entities and he is a member of the Working Group for the Disposition of the Culturally Unidentified Human Remains.

Waziyatawin Angela Wilson, a Wahpetunwan Dakota from the Pezihutazizi Otunwe in southwestern Minnesota, is currently an assistant professor of Indigenous history in the department of history at Arizona State University. She received her undergraduate degree in history and American Indian studies from the University of Minnesota in 1992 and her Ph.D. in

American history from Cornell University in 2000. Her research interests center on decolonization and the recovery of Indigenous knowledge, oral tradition and Indigenous language revitalization, and historical trauma and memory. She is co-editor of *Indigenizing the Academy: Transforming Scholarship and Empowering Communities* (Nebraska, 2004), and author of *Remember This!: Dakota Decolonization and the Eli Taylor Narratives* (Nebraska, 2005).

Michael Yellow Bird (University of Wisconsin) is a citizen of the Sahnish/Arikara and Hidatsa First Nations. He is the Director of the Center for Indigenous Nations Studies (www.ku.edu~/insp) and Associate Professor of American Studies at the University of Kansas. He has held faculty appoint- ments at the University of British Columbia, Arizona State University, and the School of Social Welfare, University of Kansas. He teaches graduate courses in research methods and issues facing Indigenous Peoples. His research focuses on Indigenous Peoples, the effects of U.S. foreign policy, oral histories of Native Vietnam combat veterans, colonialism and methods of decolo- nization, and Native men. His most recent publica- tions are "Cowboys and Indians: Toys of Genocide, Icons of American Colonialism" published in *Wicazo Sa Review* 19, no. 2 (Fall 2004), and "Reservations: Spiritual and Cultural Implications" (forthcoming) in *American Indian Religious Traditions: An Encyclopedia*, edited by Suzanne J. Crawford and Dennis F. Kelly.

Beginning Decolonization

Waziyatawin and Michael Yellow Bird

A. Introduction

Congratulations! In opening this book you have engaged in an act of decolonization. We hope this will be one of many steps on your journey toward liberation. As Indigenous Peoples we have an inherent right to be free in our own lands. We have an inherent right to self-determination. Though these statements represent truths and they speak of rights we once possessed, these rights have been systematically stripped from us. When others invaded our lands and stole them from underneath our bodies, when they destroyed our ways of life and injured our peoples, they prevented us from living the way we were intended to live. Reclaiming our inherent rights will require tremendous struggle. It will require learning to meaningfully resist the forces of colonialism that have so detrimentally impacted our lives. It will require the decolonization of North America.

Since the relationship between the colonizer and the colonized is so deeply entrenched in the United States and Canada, most of us have never learned how to actively challenge the status quo. The current institutions and systems are designed to maintain the privilege of the colonizer and the subjugation of the colonized, and to produce generations of people who will never question their position within this relationship. Thus, no handbook exists to teach our people how to begin to challenge this oppressive relationship in our daily lives. Until now. This workbook is intended as a primer to help you to think more concisely about the meanings of colonization and decolonization, to give you a language to talk about them, and to assist you in developing strategies for decolonizing your life and your world. But first we must define some basic terms.

B. What Is Colonization?

Colonization refers to both the formal and informal methods (behaviors, ideologies, institutions, policies, and economies) that maintain the subjugation or exploitation of Indigenous Peoples, lands, and resources. Colonizers engage in this process because it allows them to maintain and/or expand their social, political, and economic power. Colonization is detrimental to us because the colonizers' power comes at the expense of Indigenous lands, resources, lives, and self-determination. Not only has colonization resulted in the loss of major rights such as land and self-determination, but most of our contemporary daily struggles (poverty, family violence, chemical dependency, suicide, and the deterioration of health) are also direct consequences of colonization. Colonization is an all-encompassing presence in our lives. The consequences of colonization are similar for peoples all over the world including, for example, the Maoris of New Zealand, the Aboriginal Peoples of Australia, First Nations Peoples of Canada, and Indigenous Peoples of Africa and Latin America.

C. What Is Decolonization?

First and foremost, decolonization must occur in our own minds. The Tunisian decolonization activist, Albert Memmi, wrote, "In order for the colonizer to be the complete master, it is not enough for him to be so in actual fact, he must also believe in its legitimacy. In order for that legitimacy to be complete, it is not enough for the colonized to be a slave, he must also

> **Decolonization is the intelligent, calculated, and active resistance to the forces of colonialism that perpetuate the subjugation and/or exploitation of our minds, bodies, and lands, and it is engaged for the ultimate purpose of overturning the colonial structure and realizing Indigenous liberation.**

ACTIVITY:

As your first community activity, create a term for both *colonization* and *decolonization* in your Indigenous language. This exercise will provide an opportunity for you and your community to think consciously and critically about the meaning of both these terms from your own cultural framework.

Colonization: _____

Decolonization: _____

What are the literal and figurative meanings of your translations and what does this indicate about your culture's view of these processes?

_____

_____

_____

accept his role." The first step toward decolonization, then, is to question the legitimacy of colonization. Once we recognize the truth of this injustice we can think about ways to resist and challenge colonial institutions and ideologies. Thus, decolonization is not passive; rather, it requires something called *praxis*. Brazilian liberatory educator Paulo Freire defined praxis as "reflection and action upon the world in order to transform it." This is the means by which we turn from being subjugated human beings to being liberated human beings. In accepting the premise of colonization and working towards decolonization, we are not relegating ourselves to a status as victims. On the contrary, we are actively working toward our own freedom to transform our lives and the world around us. The project that begins with our minds, therefore, has revolutionary potential.

Colonization and *decolonization* are words that should become a standard part of the vocabulary of all Indigenous Peoples, including the young people. Giving a name to our experience will add to our own empowerment. When you can use this language to speak for yourself, you are engaging in a form of resistance to colonialism. Furthermore, conceptualizing these ideas within our own Indigenous lens is a more advanced decolonization activity. In drawing on your Indigenous language you are not only recovering Indigenous knowledge that is in jeopardy of being lost as a consequence of colonialism, you are also making that language relevant to contemporary times. Because the colonizers attempted to methodically eradicate our Indigenous languages, our efforts to recover the language are also a powerful form of resistance.

D. A Gathering of Decolonization Activists

The topic of a decolonization workbook was initially proposed by Devon Mihesuah and Waziyatawin Angela Wilson, who believe strongly that scholars should engage in projects useful to Indigenous Peoples. Though, quite regrettably, Devon was unable to participate in the project, we hope that her inspiration and commitment are evident. To carry out the proposed topic, in February 2004 a group of nine Indigenous intellectuals gathered at the School of American Research in Santa Fe to address the topic of "Creating a Decolonization Workbook" in a short seminar. This handbook is the result of that meeting. The intellectuals who attended this meeting are all individuals rooted in tribal communities who are dedicated to helping Indigenous Peoples move toward freedom from the oppressive forces of colonialism. We are all what might be called practitioner-activists. That is, we frequently take political positions to challenge colonialism, practicing this in our daily life, at our jobs, in our children's schools, in our communities, and in the broader society. In addition, we are all writers who have engaged in the intellectual debate surrounding decolonization and we subscribe to the notion that decolonization is necessary to the well-being and liberation of our peoples.

In this handbook we do not intend to provide universal solutions for the problems stemming from centuries of colonialism. Rather, we hope to facilitate and encourage critical-thinking skills while offering recommendations for fostering community discussions and plans for purposeful community action. Therefore, we are not making recommendations for what Indigenous individuals and communities *should* do, but instead we are establishing starting points for discussions about employing decolonization strategies in daily life. We have constructed this in a workbook format to immediately encourage your active participation in the hard work of decolonization. We believe that as Indigenous Peoples we have the power, strength, and intelligence to develop culturally specific decolonization strategies relevant to our own communities. We all have the capacity to actively pursue our own emancipation from oppression.

We must also emphasize that this handbook is intended to prompt *beginning* discussions on decolonization. It is intended to rally a critical, and critical-thinking, group of Indigenous People dedicated to decolonization who will eventually help to mobilize a massive decolonization movement in North America. As Indigenous intellectuals concerned about the survival of our peoples, we have included exercises and activities here that we felt we could responsibly advocate as beginning decolonization strategies. We are not advocating the immediate taking up of arms or the organization of an Indigenous militia. Instead, we are advocating peaceful, intelligent, and courageous challenges to the existing institutions of colonialism as well as questioning our own complicity in those institutions. But make no mistake: Decolonization ultimately requires the overturning of the colonial structure. It is not about tweaking the existing colonial system to make it more Indigenous-friendly or a little less oppressive. The existing system is fundamentally and irreparably flawed. We hope the decolonization strategies we offer will help Indigenous communities become increasingly more sophisticated and fundamentally challenging to the current power structure as we strengthen and prepare ourselves for our long struggle toward complete liberation.

E. The Topics We Cover

The topics covered in this volume include the decolonization of Indigenous thinking: ideas about citizenship, governance and organizational structures, education, oral tradition, language, repatriation, images and stereotypes, and diet, as well as the role of truth-telling as an act of decolonization. While there are many other areas of our lives in need of decolonization, we believe this offers a solid basis for beginning the discussion. We hope that from these discussions, plans for action will be developed.

The first chapter discusses how to establish Tribal Critical Thinking Centers. All acts of decolonization require engaging the mind critically; thus, relearning this skill as individuals and as communities is central to the decolonization project. Michael Yellow Bird provides a step-by-step approach for transforming the world through the use of what he calls "criticality." Real-world change is what we are after, and he helps us to understand the connection between thought and meaningful action. In addition, he details what is required of critical thinkers as well as how to recognize and overcome the barriers to critical thinking. Yellow Bird then outlines how you can set up a Critical Thinking Center in your community so that you can begin to share this process with others and contribute your skills and developing knowledge to a growing tribal critical consciousness.

Suzan Shown Harjo demonstrates the importance of thinking critically about how Indigenous Peoples are represented so that we can take appropriate action against colonialist representations to prevent further harm to our peoples. In her chapter, "Just Good Sports: The Impact of Native References in Sports on Native Youth and What Some Decolonizers Have Done About It," she breaks down for us how the identity of the colonized is negatively affected through colonization. This, she argues, is most apparent in popular American culture's use of Native mascots in sports. She explains the various points of contention in the controversy as well as why these mascots are unacceptable. Harjo then provides several specific examples of how Indigenous individuals and their families have confronted this aspect of colonialism in their own lives. This allows us to not only see the importance of Indigenous People engaging in the struggle for human dignity, but it also provides us successful strategies for participating in that struggle.

The pursuit of dignity for ourselves and our

ancestors is the topic of James Riding In's chapter, "Decolonizing NAGPRA." Riding In characterizes the fight for the return and protection of the bodies of our Indigenous ancestors as well as sacred objects as a fight against colonialism. He states, "The perpetrators disregarded our views, beliefs, and rights because colonialism instills the colonizer with a notion of absolute entitlement—a notion that denies the colonized the respect and rights afforded other humans." While strides have been made in protecting some gravesites and in repatriating some remains and sacred objects, Riding In argues that this struggle is ongoing, particularly in regards to those remains labeled by the colonizers as culturally unidentified. He guides us through the various controversies surrounding the Native American Graves Protection and Repatriation Act and helps us to approach the issue from a strong, culturally grounded position. Thus, he lays the foundation for our organized and thoughtful responses to these attacks on our humanity.

The next chapter addresses the importance of decolonizing Indigenous diets. Waziyatawin begins this discussion by recounting health conditions of Indigenous Peoples both before and after colonization and by explaining precisely how colonization has detrimentally impacted Indigenous health. Once we understand how Indigenous health has been compromised and how we have often unknowingly participated in the decline of our own health, we can begin to decolonize our diet. This is achieved not just by eating healthier foods and exercising more; rather, it requires returning to Indigenous foods and lifestyles that will help promote not just nutritional but also spiritual, cultural, and mental health. Decolonizing our diets works to support the decolonizing of other important aspects of our lives.

The decolonization of our tribal governments is another project central to the broader decolonization project. In his chapter, Robert Odawi Porter explains how Indigenous forms of governance were affected by colonialism to the detriment of Indigenous Peoples. "The Europeans," he argues, "knew that destroying Indian governments was the key to controlling

Indigenous Peoples." He is concerned with repairing the damage caused by colonial domination by creating community-built and -supported governments that operate according to Indigenous values. In his analysis, Odawi also explains the complexities of attempting to return entirely to precolonization forms of Indigenous governance because of the extreme diversity of values and agendas among individuals present in our communities today. Because of his honest assessment of the current reality of reservation populations, Odawi is able to offer a useful and important process for decolonizing Indigenous governance. He further discusses the need to decolonize the United States Indian control laws that continue to impact our lives and make true self-determination impossible. Overcoming these barriers to the redevelopment of our sovereignty is crucial to our eventual decolonization as Indigenous Peoples.

From a cultural perspective, Indigenous language recovery is another essential component to the decolonization project. Because the vast majority of Indigenous languages are in a state of crisis, unless drastic and immediate steps are taken to recover those languages, many of them will be lost. Since languages are the key to worldview and the embodiment of Indigenous cultures, their loss would threaten all that makes Indigenous societies culturally distinct. In her chapter, "Defying Colonization Through Language Survival," Waziyatawin explains how Indigenous languages were systematically and intentionally brought to the edge of extinction by government policies and institutions. She then articulates strategies for Indigenous individuals and communities to actively work on recovering their languages by first establishing a critical mass of support for language revitalization efforts and then creating a sustainable tribal language movement. Saving Indigenous languages will require extraordinary amounts of hard work, but the results will contribute invaluably to Indigenous decolonization.

ChiXapKaid picks up this discussion on cultural decolonization in his chapter, "Decolonizing Through Storytelling." An accomplished storyteller, ChiXapKaid explains how Indigenous societies can decolonize themselves through education, particularly through the medium of Indigenous storytelling. Recognizing that shared knowledge of cultural concepts is a tool of Indigenous survival, ChiXapKaid explains how Indigenous Peoples developed a belief in story symbology to create sophisticated educational systems. In recovering those systems we are countering the damaging effects of mainstream colonizing educational institutions to which our people have been subjected. ChiXapKaid offers strategies for Indigenous Peoples to remember ancestral teachings and begin to recover the art of storytelling.

Cornel Pewewardy then addresses in detail how a colonial Indigenous education was created by whites to help foster the ideology of white supremacy and ensure European domination. In "Ideology, Power, and the Miseducation of Indigenous Peoples in the United States," Pewewardy explains how Indigenous educational systems prior to colonization functioned successfully and appropriately to meet the needs of Indigenous societies, and how those systems were suppressed and denied by the white architects of Indian education. In this chapter Pewewardy helps us trace how we have been subjugated by white educational systems and whose interests have been served by our uncritical participation in them. He then offers suggestions on how to decolonize Indigenous education by building our communities so that we can offer stronger opposition to domination and injustice while organizing ourselves for small- and large-scale action.

T'hohahoken is also concerned with community development and organization in his chapter, "Organizing Indigenous Governance to Invent the Future." He encourages Indigenous movement toward self-determination through the recognition and use of the unique intellectual estate offered by our ancestors. In using our inherited knowledge, we can problem-solve today. Using Kaniienkehaka (Mohawk) traditions as an example, T'hohahoken demonstrates the relevance of this knowledge in the twenty-first century for renewing or inventing missions that can guide our Indigenous clubs, associations, organizations, or agencies, wherever they are located. In particular, he offers

suggestions and helps us identify how we can balance power within our organizations for effective problem solving, how we can create interdependency and unity, and, ultimately, how we can work toward the idea of democracy as consensus building.

One of the most contested issues among Indigenous Peoples today remains the issue of tribal enrollment. When Indigenous nations were prevented from freely governing themselves and were instead made subject to the institutions and forces of colonialism, methods for determining who was an American Indian were dramatically altered. As a consequence, most Indigenous nations today rely to some degree on blood quantum to determine who is and is not a part of their nation. Michael Yellow Bird addresses this hot topic in his essay, "Decolonizing Tribal Enrollment," and encourages Indigenous nations to question their current enrollment practices and to develop culturally appropriate and intelligent criteria that will better serve Indigenous communities today. By calling into question the use of blood quantum as a determining factor in deciding who is Indigenous, Yellow Bird advocates instead for the creation of citizenship criteria that will build national loyalty, maintain fairness, ensure the survival of our cultures, and "foster a more honest, capable, and committed tribal citizenry." Following his discussion of tribal enrollment and citizenship, he provides a list of questions that may be used as a basis for implementing a thoughtful community discussion about how to decolonize tribal enrollment and implement a system that effectively addresses what it means to be a citizen of an Indigenous nation.

The last chapter in the collection addresses the issue of how historical trauma has impacted Indigenous communities. In "Relieving Our Suffering: Indigenous Decolonization and a United States Truth Commission," Waziyatawin argues that as Indigenous Peoples we can empower ourselves and initiate our own healing processes from historical or contemporary injustices by speaking the truth about those injustices. Based on her experience with the Dakota Commemorative March in Minnesota that retraced the route her ancestors were force-marched in 1862, Waziyatawin learned that the process of publicly telling long-suppressed stories about human injustices fostered individual and collective healing, in part because those stories directly challenged the colonial status quo and served as an empowering catalyst. Taking lessons from other truth commission efforts around the world, she offers a step-by-step process for communities and tribal nations to engage in truth commission work by carefully gathering testimony and other documentary evidence. This developing body of work by Indigenous nations throughout the country may be instrumental in the ongoing struggle for the restoration of Indigenous lands that is heavily reliant on a genuine sense of contrition and a desire for justice by mainstream Americans. Since the truth about injustices perpetrated against Indigenous Peoples has been largely denied in the United States, truth-telling becomes an important strategy for decolonization.

One commonality among all the chapters of this volume is that they illuminate the importance of understanding how colonization has taken root in our lives. Only by understanding how colonization works at subjugating our people can we begin to aggressively counteract its effects. When we can recognize it, we can work to actively disrupt the colonial system and take active steps toward our own decolonization. The book as a whole is designed to help us think about how we as individuals and collective entities can initiate discussions within our communities, employ whatever useful decolonization strategies are offered here, and create new ones based on our specific needs and objectives.

Above all, this handbook was created out of a sense of compassion. We were all motivated to create a workbook like this because we love our people. While we recognize the incredible strength and resiliency among our populations, we also recognize that there is incredible suffering. We watch as our people kill themselves slowly through chemical dependency, or more quickly through violence and suicide. We watch as diseases such as diabetes, heart disease, and cancer eat away at our people. And we watch as our populations continue to hurt one another, practicing the violence upon each other that we have learned from the colonizers. We believe there is another way for our people to exist, one that draws on the best of our traditions and through courageous acts of resistance, paves the way to our liberation. That way is through decolonization.

You have consciously joined the struggle. We're glad you're on this journey!

Tribal Critical Thinking Centers

Michael Yellow Bird

A. Introduction

Scenario 1: Your nation recently voted to open a casino for the purpose of economic development. The measure won by a narrow margin, with nearly half of the voters opposing it. Supporters believe that a casino will bring prosperity to the nation by generating new revenue that can be used to create jobs and build badly needed schools, health care facilities, and child care centers. This group is convinced that the extra money can be used to help the tribe to strengthen and protect its sovereignty by contributing to the political campaigns of mainstream politicians who will take the tribe's concerns to the appropriate state and federal levels. Supporters say, "Money talks." Those opposing the measure are convinced that a casino is another form of American colonization that will further erode your traditional culture, language, land base, and spirituality. This group believes that a casino will bring more crime, benefit only certain members of the tribe, cause people to become greedier, and create gambling addictions among the membership. Moreover, the group believes that the state government will take an unfair share of the profits.

Scenario 2: Following the September 11, 2001, attacks on the World Trade Center and the Pentagon, your tribal leaders immediately proclaimed their allegiance to the president's war on terrorism. They agreed with the president's statement that "the reason the United States was attacked was because terrorists are jealous of the freedoms enjoyed by people in the

United States and they hate democracy." Your tribal leaders now pledge that the young women and men from your community will "fight and destroy these cowards who attacked our country." They also support the recent movement by some members of the U.S. Congress to reinstate the draft to increase troop numbers to fight the president's war on terrorism, declaring, "We Indians have never been afraid to fight for this country and have always done our duty when it comes to serving in the U.S. military." They also privately say, "We are not really fighting for this government, but since we are the First Peoples of this nation, we are really fighting to protect these lands."

Most of the people from your community do not say whether they agree or disagree with your leaders. However, some community members cynically laugh when they hear what the president has said about why the United States was attacked, and become angry with your leaders for believing "this U.S. propaganda." They say, "While it is very tragic that all those innocent people died on September 11th, the reason this country was attacked is because the United States has been oppressing and killing Arab people in the Middle East for a long time and they have done this kind of thing to many other nations—especially nations of color—who cannot defend themselves against American imperialism. What goes around comes around." They ask you, "What would you do if some nation kept on attacking your country and killing your innocent women, children, babies, and elders? Wouldn't you fight back?" They also ask you, "Do think that a new draft would be fair? Do you think the children of the rich U.S. senators would be drafted and have to fight on the front lines alongside you poor Indian kids?" They end the conversation saying, "After you give your life for this country, do you think it will treat you—or us—any better, give us back our lands they stole, and live up to the treaties they made with us? It will be a cold day in hell when I let this country draft my kids so they can go and kill other people of color, so that this imperialist nation can continue to dominate the world and help the rich get richer."

In either scenario, how do you know which group is correct in any or all of their assumptions and beliefs? Did they use sound logic and facts to reach their conclusions? What is the evidence for what they are saying? What is "the truth"? Why would you, or how much can you, believe of what either group says? How can you, as objectively as possible, using all of the facts, discover what is most accurate about what has been said? Are there facts that the groups have ignored that must be included before conclusions are reached? Are there alternatives and positions that have not been considered? What are the advantages and disadvantages of the different opinions and positions presented? What are the consequences to you and your community if you support one group over the other? Can you use what the groups say and come up with different, more effective and creative conclusions, which will lead to well-reasoned solutions? How does what was said, in either scenario, support and honor the integrity of your tribal traditions and beliefs?

If you are willing to take the time to thoughtfully answer the above questions in a clear, concise, fair, rigorous, and honest manner, you are ready for critical thinking. Critical thinking requires us to be open to carefully considering and analyzing all possibilities that may be presented, ignored, trivialized, or censored in any argument, opinion, or what are considered to be "the facts."

B. Who Will—and Who Will Not—Benefit from This Chapter

Because critical thinking requires a mindful, dedicated, and honest process of inquiry that often requires us to question or reformulate our thinking and beliefs, to sometimes agree with those we do not like, and to admit to our limited viewpoint, the information contained in this chapter is not for everyone. While critical thinking can be a very liberating and empowering experience, it also can be too rigorous—and even threatening—to those of us who are not willing to push ourselves to constantly improve our thinking. Those that will have the most difficult time with critical thinking are:

- People who are intellectually lazy and avoid thinking deeply and purposefully about the ins and outs of an issue to find the best possible solution(s)
- People who do not like their authority challenged
- People who rely only on faith or single sources of knowledge
- People who have a strong desire for immediate answers
- People who have a low level of patience
- People who believe there are no solutions, only problems
- People who are willing to settle for mediocre explanations
- People who do not see the strengths in a person or situation, only the weaknesses
- People who do not believe that things can change
- People who make up their minds on an issue simply because of loyalty to others
- People who lack humility
- People who believe that "critical thinking is not something us Indians do; it's the white man's way."

I believe that most of us have a strong desire to be good, capable thinkers who can effectively and efficiently use our minds to solve any number of problems that we will encounter in our lives. I also believe that most of us do not want to turn over our thinking to others so they can do it for us. I am convinced that most us want to be good thinkers and are willing to work at it.

This chapter discusses the importance of developing a Tribal Critical Thinking Center in your community or organization to promote the development of the thinking skills and capacities needed to engage and evaluate the challenging situations that are brought about by "simple," everyday life challenges; by the continuing effects of colonialism; and by unforeseen events that may range from minor to catastrophic in nature. Throughout and at the end of the chapter, I provide a list of references, examples, exercises, readings, and materials essential to critical thinking. I begin this chapter discussing my introduction to critical thinking and next focus on the need for good critical thinking. I then discuss definitions of critical thinking, stages of critical thinking, barriers to critical thinking, and the phenomenon called "groupthink." I end with suggesting how to set up a Tribal Critical Thinking Center.

C. My Introduction to Critical Thinking

I was raised in a small community called White Shield on the Fort Berthold reservation in North Dakota from the late 1950s to the early 1970s. I come from a family of fifteen; ten brothers and four sisters, all born of the same mother and father. I attended a Bureau of Indian Affairs day school from kindergarten to tenth grade. Then, by personal choice, I transferred to a private Catholic boarding school for my last two years of high school because I was not learning much in the BIA school and it seemed to me that many of my teachers did not care about my academic success. Throughout my BIA school experience I learned very little about critical thinking and, instead, my classmates and I were forced to be compliant, not to question our teachers or what we were learning, not to bring attention to ourselves, and not to think beyond what we were told. Our earliest grades were filled with fear and a great dislike for school. It was typical for us to be shamed before our classmates, hit, slapped, beaten with rulers and long wooden blackboard pointers and yardsticks, yelled at, and forced into a closet all day without food whenever we made mistakes or did not pay attention in class. It is no wonder that, following high school, few of our people have ever attempted to go college and even fewer have ever graduated from college.

The transfer to my new school off the rez during my junior year in high school was an excellent decision. Many of my teachers encouraged me to think independently and critically about the world around me and about the academic courses I was enrolled in; the exception was religion class, where we were discouraged from debating any questionable aspects of this topic. Instead, we were expected to memorize what we were told and were rewarded or punished accordingly. During my summers in high school I was fortunate to be able to attend the Upward Bound program at the University of North Dakota, which enabled me to further develop and refine my thinking skills. Many of the staff, teachers, counselors, and directors of the program were interested in, and committed to, the academic and personal success of the program participants. On numerous occasions we were strongly encouraged to engage in critical thinking about what we were learning, the state of the world, our relationships with one another, and our plans for our future. I strongly believe that the Upward Bound program was very instrumental in preparing me for college.

In 1979 and 1980, respectively, I received my Bachelor and Master degrees in Social Work. While I learned a great deal in my undergraduate and graduate studies, I was not required to take a formal class in critical thinking or reasoning as part of my coursework, which became problematic in my professional career for several reasons. First, I did not have a well-thought-out method to critically assess the helping approaches I was taught to use and, therefore, had no clear way of knowing whether what I was doing was effective, oppressive, or appropriate for the people I was being trained to help. To make matters worse, the courses I took offered little direction on how I could effectively work with my own Indigenous communities and people.

Second, many of the helping strategies I learned did not include using or understanding the importance of the strengths of the individual, family, community, or culture. Instead, I learned to pay attention to the deficits and problems of each and to focus on solving them, which often reinforced the belief that the clients were incapable of solving their own issues. In fact, some approaches encouraged social workers to believe that the reason some individuals, families, and groups had high levels of social and behavioral problems and could not solve them was because they were lazy, weak, manipulative, of low intelligence, and culturally disadvantaged (justice-oriented critical thinkers have referred to these social incriminations as "blaming the victim").

From 1981 to 1986 I worked for my tribe as the Administrator of Human Resources. My position was challenging and I loved my work. My duties consisted of supervising and collaborating with the program directors and staff of all our health, social services, and education programs, and I reported directly to the Tribal Program Manager and the tribal council. In my position I had the opportunity to practice critical

thinking, although I did not call it that back then. I now realize that I used critical thinking during tribal "strategic planning" sessions and when I formulated my best arguments with my colleagues to get my priorities accomplished. However, there were many instances when I felt, whether it was real or imagined, that I had to censor or surrender my opinion, argument, or critical thinking to some of our elders out of respect for their vastly different views of the world. Although I was uncomfortable surrendering my critical views to these individuals, I almost always handled this situation by deferring to, and validating, their beliefs and concerns, and then, worked to gracefully integrate my ideas and positions into their frameworks of thinking. This formula was a very successful approach and I have used it in many different contexts. On the other hand, I always could find elders in our tribes that were excellent thinkers, open to the processes of critical thinking, and very capable of integrating and using new ideas.

I left my tribal position in 1986 and began working on a Ph.D. in Social Welfare at the University of Wisconsin, Madison. This particular doctoral program had an outstanding reputation that was earned through its emphasis on quantitative methods of research, which taught students to resolve critical social, political, and economic problems by using sophisticated statistical research designs. The program was challenging but very stimulating and rewarding because it attracted excellent faculty and students who were exceptional critical thinkers. My professors, who were very academically demanding and had the highest standards and expectations, persistently pushed me to rigorously argue, defend, and critique everything I read, said, and wrote, which helped to develop my skills of critical thinking more than I ever had.

I graduated in 1992, and took my first faculty position in the School of Social Work at the University of British Columbia, Vancouver. The interactions I had with university colleagues and First Nations communities were among the most enlightening and intellectually satisfying of my academic career. The development of my critical thinking shifted from quantitative research to developing critical consciousness, where I begin to recognize and take action against the many oppressive contradictions that existed in the social, political, and economic realities of Indigenous Peoples. This term (which I think of as a state of intelligent, active-informed awareness that one achieves through the practice of good critical thinking) was popularized by Paulo Freire (1921–1997), the author of *Pedagogy of the Oppressed*, who was a brilliant progressive educator whose writings have become classic works for critical thinking, social change, and education.

Several of my non–First Nations and First Nations colleagues and many of my students already knew Freire's work quite well and were using it in classes, in everyday conversations, and in their communities, which I found exciting and inspiring. Reading his work led me to study the work of other non-mainstream intellectuals such as Frantz Fanon (1925–1961), Howard Adams (1926–2001), Hussein Abdilahi Bulhan, Albert Memmi, bell hooks, Augusto Boal, and Ngugi wa Thiong'o—all of whom were strong proponents of teaching disenfranchised peoples to develop critical thinking skills to address the issues of racism, oppression, colonization, liberation, and decolonization.

When I left the University of British Columbia in 1994 and accepted a faculty position at the University of Kansas, School of Social Welfare, I brought with me the decolonized analytical views that I had gained from this first academic teaching experience. Unlike their Canadian counterparts, I found that many of the social work students in the United States were not challenged to read literature or learn social work approaches that required them to become critically conscious, skilled, and/or proactive about resolving racism, colonialism, and oppression, especially as it related to Indigenous Peoples. To complicate matters, the formal critical thinking readings and skills that could be used to address the problems that students would encounter in the practice of social work were just beginning to be introduced into the national social work curriculum around this time. My experiences as a faculty member at the University of British Columbia taught me that in order to help my students decolonize their thinking

and professional social work practice, it was necessary for me to guide them toward becoming the best critical thinkers possible.

I worked on this goal by reading and collecting existing materials about critical thinking and developing my own exercises and resources. A book that was very helpful to me at this time was *Critical Thinking for Social Workers: Exercises for the Helping Professions*, written by Leonard Gibbs and Eileen Gambrill. The authors of this text provide several excellent exercises that helped my students build their critical thinking skills. I also used Imaginative, Justice-Oriented Theatre to help my students make the connection between critical thinking and critical consciousness. In my senior undergraduate social-work practice classes I required students to study how to use theatre to combat oppression. The most helpful readings came from the works of Augusto Boal, a Brazilian theatre director who developed the Theatre of the Oppressed (TO) during the 1950s and 1960s. At the end of the semester, different groups in the class would choose a topic they could create a theatre performance around. They wrote their own scripts, developed the characters and plot in the story, created unique staging apparatus, and invited several friends, faculty, and family members whom they wanted to educate about their topic. We referred to our performances as Social Justice Theatre, since all of our presentations were informational and encouraged support from the audience against injustice, including oppression, racism, and colonialism. One group (that was almost all non-Indigenous) did a performance that focused on many illegal acts committed by the U.S. government during the arrest, trial, conviction, and imprisonment of American Indian Movement (AIM) member, Leonard Peltier. Other groups performed plays that focused on the discrimination against gay men and lesbian women, the reality of racial profiling and white (people's) privilege, and hate crimes against various disempowered groups such as the homeless. Another group (again, almost all non-Native students) did a performance focusing on educating the non-Indigenous public about the threats of local and state Kansas governments that were attempting to build a highway through the tribal wetlands at Haskell Indian Nations University.

From the fall of 2000 to the end of 2003 I was a member of the faculty in the School of Social Work at Arizona State University and served on the advisory board of the American Indian Studies program. I was fortunate to have my critical thinking skills enhanced by many wonderful colleagues and students in both environments. I continued using critical thinking materials and readings with my undergraduate and graduate classes, helping the students to apply critical thinking skills to the problems of racism, poverty, colonialism, and the problems associated with globalization, such as sweatshops, child labor and slavery, hunger, capitalism, environmental pollution, genetically modified foods, and unfair trading practices (all of which disproportionately harm Indigenous Peoples around the world). A book that I used, which contains excellent readings and exercises, is *Rethinking Globalization: Teaching for Justice in an Unjust World*, edited by Bill Bigelow and Bob Peterson.

One of the most difficult events that short-circuited the critical thinking of my Arizona State students was 9-11. While a small group demonstrated a willingness to interrogate the different reasons why the attacks occurred, other students shut down their skills of critical inquiry, and instead, took their cues of how to interpret what happened from the scripts of those who they deemed in authority. In one classroom discussion a student broke into tears and began screaming, "Why are we discussing why this terrorist attack happened? The people that did this are evil and my minister said we have to go after these evil people and kill them all." The events of September 11th remain a great challenge to critical thinking in the United States.

I returned to the University of Kansas in January 2004 as the director of the Center for Indigenous Nations Studies and as associate professor of American Studies. I continue to use many of the critical thinking materials that I have collected over the years in my classes and with my students. In the fall of 2004, our faculty developed a seven-day intensive orientation for our incoming Indigenous Nations Studies students.

Several of those days were dedicated to teaching them how to read, write, and think critically. On the days that I presented, I used the several of the same materials that I share with you in this chapter. I hope that you will find them useful.

D. The Need for (Critical) Thinking

The need for clarity of thinking and making good, informed decisions always has been a high priority for human beings. For Indigenous Peoples, decolonization is dependent upon an exceptional literacy in critical thinking. As such, we can enhance our literacy through the study of scholars, such as Edward de Bono, a former Rhodes Scholar at Oxford University and one of the foremost experts of developing programs for the teaching of thinking. De Bono argues that the "future well-being of the world is going to require good thinking. Personal life has always required good thinking but in the future the increasing complexity of demands and opportunities will require even better thinking." He identifies two types of thinking behavior:

"You want to think."
"You have to think."

In the first circumstance, de Bono explains that "you have a way of doing something, there are no problems and you can carry on doing things in exactly the same way—but you want to see if there is a better way…you are making a decision or a choice…you are not stuck." In the second situation "there is a problem you cannot solve. There is a dilemma that makes it difficult to reach a decision. There is a conflict that is getting worse. There is a need for new ideas and you cannot get one. You need to find an opportunity but cannot do so…. In short you are stuck. You cannot move ahead. You have no choice. You have to think…. Ordinary thinking will not help you. You have to think hard."

In order to decolonize in the most effective and efficient manner, we have to think. It is important to create and cultivate, within our people, the willingness and skills to think and respond critically to the colonial and noncolonial circumstances—including poverty, tribal infighting, substance abuse, uncritical compliance to oppressive rules and policies, and our perceived sense of powerlessness—that challenge our well-being. Colonialism is a deceptive, oppressive, and powerful institution and process that requires intelligent, creative, calculated, effective, and courageous responses. In fact, many aspects of colonialism are difficult to detect, understand, and analyze, and may be best addressed by entire communities and nations, rather than those individuals we elevate (or who elevate themselves) to the status of expert or authority figures. Even under ideal circumstances, it is difficult to arrive at a point of agreement of what works best when addressing the challenges of our communities, and it is clear that the reality of colonialism in our everyday lives obstructs the resolutions of our problems, whether political, social, economic, spiritual, or intellectual. I believe that the critical thinking minds of many, rather than the biased minds of a few, will enable a greater use of the intellectual capital of the people to combat the continuing effects of colonialism.

E. Critical Thinking Defined

Critical thinking is a powerful, liberating force. It can be applied to numerous issues and situations facing tribal peoples and can systematically guide a community or organization through a rigorous, sound, and credible discovery process of the most effective approaches to almost every imaginable problem. Critical thinking creates well-informed, creative, capable thinkers and maximizes the analytical and problem-solving capacities of any group or individual. However, Dr. Edward de Bono cautions that "critical thinking is important and does have a valuable place in thinking. But it is only part of thinking." He maintains that critical thinking is often reactionary, and that thinking must also be proactive, creative, constructive, and generative.

The results of good critical thinking—the facts, logic, "truths," intelligent arguments, innovations, and solutions—come from various bodies of knowledge and "ways of knowing," which is referred to as epistemology. Good critical thinking utilizes evidence from several sources: cultural traditions and stories; scientific

research and studies; expert authorities; personal intuition, experiences, and dreams; experimentation; observation; memories; creative teachers and mentors; emerging technologies; and accumulated knowledge, to mention only a few. Some argue that there are hierarchies of knowledge and truth, where some forms of knowing and evidence are considered higher than others. For instance, some regard the Bible as the highest source of truth. Others feel that the highest source of truth is "scientific" evidence. Some even argue that the knowledge that comes from oral histories, spiritual experiences, and cultural traditions of certain groups, such as Indigenous Peoples, occupy the lower levels of knowledge and truth. Despite such claims, it is important to remember that great critical thinkers are those who are unwilling to limit their investigation and courageous enough to consider evidence from as many sources as possible before they reach their conclusions. The following figure illustrates how one might draw conclusions on an issue based upon particular truths, evidence, and ways of knowing:

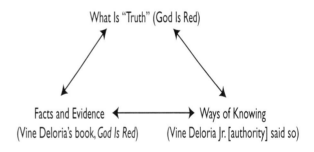

Figure 2.1: Connecting truth, epistemology, facts, and evidence. Vine Deloria Jr., a retired professor from the University of Colorado, Boulder, Lakota author/activist, and member of the Standing Rock Sioux Tribe of South Dakota published the book *God is Red* in 1972. A thirtieth-anniversary issue was published in 2002.

ACTIVITY:

Do you agree with the conclusions of this model? Have all the necessary facts, logic, and intelligent arguments been presented here? How could you improve the connections between truth, ways of knowing, facts, and evidence?

_____

_____

_____

_____

_____

_____

_____

Critical Thinking as an Intelligently Subversive Activity

Colonialism includes the empowerment and enrichment of the colonizers through the control and oppression of Indigenous Peoples and communities. The U.S. educational system has been one of the most hostile and oppressive aspects of colonialism. Historically, colonialism circulated in the form of boarding schools and, later, through the continued inferior education system that followed the boarding school era. Colonized-based educational systems contributed significantly to the destruction of self-esteem, the devaluation of cultural knowledge, and the imposition of the belief that Indigenous Peoples and their knowledge and ideas were—and remain—less than those of mainstream peoples. For instance, a Native student named Ralph Feather who attended Carlisle Indian boarding school in Carlisle, Pennsylvania, during the late 1800s, demonstrated this internalization of colonized beliefs when he wrote home, "I think of you all, but I don't like your Indian ways, because you don't know the good ways, also you don't know good many things."

Education and other racist policies and tactics have caused negative, oppressive effects on the critical thinking and responding capacities of the First Nations. The censorship and devaluation of Indigenous intelligence and philosophy throughout history, along with the imposition of colonized ideas and knowledge, were and continue to be the foremost activities of the colonization process. For this process to remain successful it relies immensely on the perpetuation of the ignorance of critical activity, for such ignorance is arguably one of the most powerful shackles of colonialism. People who are ignorant are easier to control, mislead, and oppress than those who are well informed, intellectually skilled, and constantly challenging themselves to discern the "truths" that make up and guide their existence.

Colonizers realize or intuit that an intelligent, critical thinking mind is subversive and dangerous to their enterprise of control and oppression, and they are quick to take action to prevent it. For instance, Frederick Douglass (1817–1895) is an outstanding example of why colonizers fear those who overcome ignorance through a process of systematic, critical education. Douglass, the son of a slave mother and a slave-owner father, was allowed to spend time in his (paternal) uncle's home. His aunt, Sophia, treated him like her own child. Since Frederick was intelligent and had a strong desire to learn to read, Sophia was happy to teach him. When she described to her husband how gifted Frederick was and that she was teaching him to read, he became incensed and forbade her to give him further lessons: "If you give a nigger an inch he will take an ell…learning will spoil the best nigger in the world." Douglass later escaped from slavery, continued to educate himself and others, and became one of the United States's greatest intellectuals and critical literacy activists.

Another example is Paulo Freire, who was mentioned earlier in this chapter. From the late 1950s to mid-1960s Freire developed literacy programs for the poor, outcast peoples of Brazil. The curriculum of these programs contained politically charged words and images and "generative themes," which inspired discussions that critically dissected topics such as exploitation, the meaning of culture, and the power of written language. Following a military coup in 1964, the new leaders arrested Freire, whose work was considered a threat to their hegemonic social order. While in prison, he began his first book, *Educacao como a Pratica da Liberdade* (*Education as the Practice of Freedom*), which popularized his teaching and critical pedagogy throughout the world.

Critical thinking has several definitions, characteristics, processes, and purposes. One definition is the application of "objective" logic to any process or content to reveal and assess accurate and inaccurate statements, beliefs, and generalizations. However, it is important to remember that what is objective or logical to one person may not be so for another. When practicing the skills of critical thinking, it is important to agree, as much as possible, upon the meaning of the words, concepts, and ideas that are used before one enters into a formal discussion and debate. This is called setting the parameters of the discussion.

Critical thinking also is regarded as "truth assessment," where the discovery of truth is accomplished by systematically using objective facts and reasoning to find out what may be "true" and "accurate," until another "truth" is revealed. Knowledge changes over the years, and what is true and accurate will often vary with people, according to their conceptions of "truth." I have found this to be true in my work as a university professor.

ACTIVITY:

In several of my classes, I have used this critical thinking exercise, which is helpful for assessing the "truth" about where humans come from. Students either love it or hate it, but always have fun.

1. Where are you from? Are you a product of a divine Creator or the result of the Big Bang theory and evolution?

_____

_____

_____

_____

2. What is the proof of your "truth"?

_____

_____

_____

_____

3. What do others think of your proof and "truth"?

_____

_____

_____

_____

_____

4. Does what others say make you change your mind or make you more confident that you know the "truth"?

_____

_____

_____

_____

_____

5. What did this exercise tell you about your critical thinking and that of others?

_____

_____

_____

_____

_____

_____

This exercise asks students to interrogate their core beliefs, which are often regarded as the "truth." Since critical thinking requires accuracy and objective facts to draw reasonable, well-rounded, and correct conclusions of even the most cherished beliefs, the intellectual disagreement that develops from this assignment can be interesting, intimidating, distressing, and challenging.

It is important to remember that the above exercise is _not_ about arguing with others and condemning them if they disagree with you. Rather, it is a formal invitation to test out and improve your critical thinking using facts that are "truthful."

Social work professors Leonard Gibbs and Eileen Gambrill write that "critical thinking involves the careful examination and evaluation of beliefs and actions. It requires close attention to the process of reasoning, not just the product...critical thinking involves the use of standards such as clarity, accuracy, relevance, and completeness." Include what Gibbs and Gambrill say about critical thinking to the above exercise you have completed. Do the processes they speak of and the standards they advocate change your conclusions? Why or why not?

_____

_____

_____

_____

_____

_____

1. Clarity of your "truth" (Is it clear to others where you are from and what is your proof?):

_____

_____

_____

2. Accuracy of your truth:

_____

_____

_____

3. Relevance of your truth to the questions:

_____

_____

_____

4. Completeness of your answers to the questions:

_____

_____

_____

Who the critical thinkers are, and how they examine their views vis-à-vis their assessments of other views, determines the quality of critical thinking. That is, critical thinking should not always be an act of solitude or performed in isolation from others. One definition of "critical thinker" that I use comes from "An Educator's Guide to Critical Thinking Terms and Concepts" (http://www.criticalthinking.org/resources/articles/glossary.shtml, 2004). This online publication refers to individuals with the highest level of critical thinking skills as "strong sense critical thinkers." A notable characteristic shared by these people is that they are not normally closed-minded to ideas in opposition to their own points of view. These people understand that they have their own views and they recognize the framework of assumptions and ideas upon which their own thinking is based. They also realize the importance of testing their assumptions and ideas against the strongest criticisms that can be brought against them. A strong sense critical thinker is characterized as having the following traits:

- An ability to question deeply one's own framework of thought
- An ability to reconstruct sympathetically and imaginatively the strongest versions of points of view and frameworks opposed to one's own (that is, to understand how others who are opposed to your thinking might have reached their conclusions and to be able to imagine how they did so)
- An ability to reason multilogically in such a way as to determine when one's own point of view is at its weakest and when an opposing point of view is at its strongest. *Multilogically* refers to the ability to think about an issue in a number of different ways, in order to find a solution.

ACTIVITY:

According to the above definition, do you consider yourself to be a strong sense critical thinker? Why or why not? How might you improve?

_____

_____

_____

_____

_____

_____

_____

_____

_____

_____

_____

F. Stages of Critical Thinking

Over the years I have had the opportunity to observe how students develop different levels of critical thinking. I have created the following stages to assist them in their understanding of where they may be in their development. There are many ways one could reconstruct my outline; I encourage you to create your own stages of critical thinking development that are appropriate for your community and/or organization.

Stage 1—Banking: This type of thinking reflects what Brazilian educator Paulo Freire termed the "banking approach." In this stage, the teacher is regarded by the student, and often by society as a whole, as the expert who must determine what is important to learn and how it should be interpreted and approached. The teacher "deposits" information, through predetermined lectures, into the student, who is taught to be a passive receptacle (or the "bank"). The student does not question the information and regurgitates it back to the teacher in the hopes of getting positive strokes and good grades. I also refer to this stage as the "Parrot Syndrome," since the skill the student most learns at this stage is the ability to recall and repeat what the teacher has said.

Stage 2—Analytical Independence: The student develops an independent ability to critique what is said, written, and done. The student detects themes and patterns of consistency and inconsistency (at times this detection is unplanned and occurs accidentally). During this stage, the student begins to apply their developing critique to some processes (for instance, what people do and say) and products (books, films, formal government policies, and research reports) to identify connections and disconnections between assumptions and conclusions.

Stage 3—Deconstruction: This is a form of critical scrutiny that carefully and minutely analyzes and uncovers the layers of a work or text, and its relationship(s) with other works or texts. During this stage the student demonstrates focused, purposeful analytical independence by challenging information using well-articulated alternative paradigms or worldviews and information that is reliable and valid (recall the "evidence from the several sources" that I discussed earlier in this chapter). The student now can demonstrate an ability to uncover what is being trivialized, ignored, and censored in what is said or unsaid or written and unwritten. However, one danger within this stage is that students often will engage in this type of critical thinking to out-argue others and to prove their perceived level of high intellectual standing. It is important to remember that the best and most confident critical thinkers are the most humble.

Stage 4—Conscientization: This is a concept that also is used to describe critical consciousness (see *Pedagogy of the Oppressed*, by Paulo Freire). During this stage the student:

• Listens, reads, and observes with a high level of critical consciousness

• Perceives and anticipates social, political, and economic contradictions that exist in society and understands how to take critical action against the existing oppressive situations

• Thinks, feels, and acts with independent purpose

• Is unafraid to engage with unfamiliar ideas, worldviews, theoretical perspectives, people, and cultural context

• Is willing to enter into dialogues and encounter ideas, knowledge, and experiences that challenge their preconceived notions of the world

• Understands that the world is not a static, closed system and that existing problems and challenges have multiple solutions

• Understands the principle of equifinality, which is the state of allowing, producing, or having the same effect or result from different events. For instance, if a northern-style grassdancer needed new moccasins for an upcoming powwow, he could pursue a variety of options. He might borrow a pair from a southern grassdance cousin, have his partner make him a pair, or he could purchase them on eBay.

ACTIVITY:

Refer to Stages of Critical Thinking. Which stage do you feel you are at? Using the characteristics of each stage, write down how you might advance your critical thinking skills.

Stage 1—Banking:

_____

_____

_____

Stage 2—Analytical Independence:

_____

_____

_____

Stage 3—Deconstruction:

_____

_____

_____

Stage 4—Conscientization:

_____

_____

_____

G. Barriers to Critical Thinking

There exist several barriers to critical thinking. First, most schools, communities, and cultures do not make it a priority to formally train people to think and respond critically to the challenges in their lives, especially if it questions or encourages paradigmatic leaps from the mainstream ideas, beliefs, and social order. While many people do possess the intellectual flexibili-ty and judiciousness to respond critically to different instances as a result of formally learned processes, others do not know how to do so consistently or competently. In fact, there are a good number of us who may use what we believe are critical thinking skills only when we are forced to defend our ideas and beliefs against challenges by those we deem equally or less capable or intelligent than us. However, this is what I refer to "constricted critical thinking," and is likely practiced only to reinforce our ego and system of beliefs and values, rather than to engage in an intelligent and thoughtful dialogue that enhances our critical thinking dexterity.

Second, critical thinking requires a thorough examination of, and often a challenge to, the ideas and beliefs of others, including those in positions of authority such as our teachers, elders, and religious and political leaders. Critical thinking might be vigorously rejected by those who, rather than embracing the gifts of this activity, fear that well-thought-out critical thinking will undermine their authority or power. Dr. Edward de Bono recognizes the social taboo against critical thinking when he writes, "For many people the idea of 'thinking' has come to mean challenge, protest, and argument. This is why many governments, education authorities and even parents are often against the idea of teaching thinking." Consequently, rather than learning how to engage in good thinking we are often discouraged from this practice.

For instance, when we articulate our disagreement with someone, offer contradictory evidence, or question and ask them to provide proof of their assumptions, beliefs, or values we are sometimes accused of creating disharmony, being impolite, or intellectually aggressive. If we feel that the respectful and right thing to do is to accept such accusations as true, many of us will shut down our request for further critical discussion and inquiry. And, because people are social beings who depend on one another, our desire for group harmony, especially with the groups we identify most closely with, can encourage the institutionalization of polite silence rather than active critical thinking. Our silence can foster groupthink.

H. Groupthink

If your relatives, church leaders, or tribal council members assert an opinion or belief that you disagree with (and in fact, you know that what they say or believe is inaccurate or unproven), but yet you do not make your disagreement known and instead go along with what they say, or remain silent, you are not thinking critically. Instead, you are participating in a process called groupthink, where you abandon your critical evaluation capacities to make certain that (1) the group remains harmonious, and (2) you are not rejected by the group because of your critical disagreement. Although practicing groupthink can keep you out of trouble with your group members by leading them to believe that you actually agree and support what they believe, your decision to think and respond this way can be dangerous and very costly.

The study of groupthink is very important for anyone who desires to become a strong sense critical thinker and wants to avoid acquiescing to group decisions or beliefs that can lead to disastrous consequences. Because my Social Work, American Studies, and Indigenous Nations Studies students will deal with situations that involve the safety and well-being of the people they work with, I require all of my classes to watch the video, *Groupthink*, which uses the 1986 space shuttle Challenger accident and other real-life examples, to explore the dangers of groupthink. Following the viewing and discussion of this film, students are offered an understanding of the eight symptoms of groupthink as well as strategies for avoiding it, which I discuss below.

Dr. Irving L. Janis says that groupthink is brought on by the group members' desire for "group unity." The positive feelings and acceptance that members obtain from inclusion in the group motivate them to keep performing whatever it takes to retain membership in the group; often this means abandoning critical thinking in order to maintain acceptance, peace, and friendship. A consequence of the desire for high group cohesiveness is the tendency to strive toward agreement despite flaws in the group's thinking, feelings, and reasoning. While there can be various factors that can predispose groups to engage in groupthink, Dr. Janis says four of the most important are:

- A highly insulated group with restrained access to outside ideas
- A stressful decision-making context
- Recent setbacks
- The lack of necessary resources.

Janis documented eight symptoms of groupthink (www.psysr.org/groupthink%20overview.htm):

1. Illusion of invulnerability—Creates excessive optimism that encourages taking extreme risks.
2. Collective rationalization—Members discount warnings and do not reconsider their assumptions.
3. Belief in inherent morality—Members believe in the rightness of their cause and therefore ignore the ethical or moral consequences of their decisions.
4. Stereotyped views of out-groups—Negative views of "enemy" make effective responses to conflict seem unnecessary.
5. Direct pressure on dissenters—Members are under pressure not to express arguments against any of the group's views.
6. Self-censorship—Doubts and deviations from the perceived group consensus are not expressed.
7. Illusion of unanimity—The majority view and judgments are assumed to be unanimous.
8. Self-appointed "mindguards"—Members protect the group and the leader from information that is problematic or contradictory to the group's cohesiveness, view, and/or decisions.

The more symptoms present, the more likely it is that groupthink has occurred and that any resulting decisions by the group will be unsuccessful, substandard, and possibly catastrophic. (I suggest that Tribal Critical Thinking Centers rent or buy a copy of the video *Groupthink* and, after viewing it, complete the exercise that I provide at the end of this section.) Groupthink can be identified in numerous situations where it is obvious that critical thinking has failed. For instance, it would be interesting for you to analyze how groupthink contributed to events as diverse as the torture of Iraqi prisoners by U.S. military personnel in the Abu Ghraib prison in Iraq in 2003, the September 11th attacks, the attack on Pearl Harbor in 1941, or Custer's Last Stand in 1876. You might even evaluate how groupthink led to "American Indians" participating in the U.S. invasion, war, and occupation of Iraq. I encourage you to consider how the principles of groupthink are related to any problems that you believe are the result of colonialism.

Janis says when any of the eight symptoms exist in a group that is trying to make a decision, there is a reasonable chance that groupthink will happen. When pressures for agreement seem overwhelming, members are less motivated to realistically appraise the alternative courses of action available to them. These group pressures lead to carelessness and irrational thinking, since groups experiencing groupthink fail to consider all alternatives and seek to maintain unanimity. Decisions shaped by groupthink have a low probability of achieving successful outcomes.

The video shares the following ways to avoid groupthink.

- Create an open climate for discussion and ideas.
- Avoid insulating the group from outside thinking. Make sure that all members of the group feel that they are welcome to have a role as a critical evaluator in the process.
- Make sure that group leaders avoid being directive and overly in control.

You can use the following activity to help you examine how groupthink may operate in your community, your personal life, and groups of which you are a part. Please use the above symptoms to describe how groupthink may function in each corresponding area.

ACTIVITY:

Groupthink Assessment Exercise

Groupthink Principle	Your Community	Personal Life
1. Illusion of invulnerability		
2. Collective rationalization		
3. Belief in inherent morality		
4. Stereotyped views of out-groups		
5. Direct pressure		
6. Self-censorship		
7. Illusion of unanimity		
8. Self-appointed "mindguards"		

When you have completed this exercise, determine how you might discourage the presence of groupthink in the above circumstances. Carefully write down the courses of action that may be taken and share them with the group you are working with.

_____

_____

_____

_____

_____

_____

_____

_____

_____

I. Setting Up a Tribal Critical Thinking Center

This section suggests how to establish a Tribal Critical Thinking Center in your community or organization. I suggest that the goal of your Tribal Critical Thinking Center be to serve as the central location where members of your community or group receive formal training to develop their critical thinking capabilities. I provide several critical thinking readings at the end of this section to help get you started. I encourage you to conduct your own research on this topic so you can develop resources and materials that are appropriate for your group. As individuals become more adept at critical thinking, the center can transition into a tribal "think tank," which can serve as a site for undertaking advanced research and analysis about important issues within or outside the tribal community (for example, government policies), provocative topics (for example, whether or not tribes are better than the mainstream in not contributing to global warming), or critical theories (for example, "how does power function in tribal communities?"). If you work toward continually avoiding groupthink and in intelligently using the principles and skills of critical thinking, you and your center will be able to offer well-thought-out, sophisticated, decolonized responses to the oppressive circumstances that now afflict your community.

Assemble the Members

• It is important to begin the development of your center by creating a strong organizational base of individuals who are interested in building the critical thinking capacities of the people in your community or organization. I suggest finding folks who are curious, well read, knowledgeable about various topics, patient, open to different kinds of knowledge and ways of knowing; enjoy debating but are not winner-take-all; enjoy learning from others; and like to "connect the dots," that is, find it rewarding to make the connections between their belief systems and lived experiences with new and different ideas.

Establish the Center

• There must first be a clear statement of why such a center is necessary. A good way to gain support for the center is to evaluate the critical thinking skills of individuals from your community and assess the results with all stakeholders. For instance, let people who do not own this book do the exercises in this section and then, with an open mind, discuss the results. Talk with others about how important critical thinking is and why it is important to have a Tribal Critical Thinking Center. It is important to create a name for the center that will reflect its character and support for its intent. To create the positive feelings and energy that are necessary to be associated with the center, a ceremony can be performed and memorialized through community songs, pictures, and writings of critical thinking of whatever you deem as appropriate and respectful. For instance, your tribe may have a traditional song or story that tells of how they had to think their way out of a situation. Or, maybe children from your community have drawn pictures and written stories about Indigenous leaders who were great critical thinkers, which can be posted on the walls of the center.

- It is important to decide whether the center will be associated and supported as a public nonprofit project, a tribal enterprise, or a university-sponsored program. The costs and benefits associated with each should be carefully examined.

Create the Mission Statement

- The mission statement should be created with input from all stakeholders who serve in an advisory capacity. It will help to examine the mission statements of various think tanks and policy centers to get ideas of how to craft one that feels appropriate. Something as simple as "the mission of our center is to increase the critical thinking capacities of our community in order to overcome the harmful effects of colonialism" may be appropriate.
- It is important to identify key values that are important to the community that can be incorporated into the mission of the center, for example, sovereignty, empowerment, family, cultural uniqueness, and strengths.

Formulate Basic Organizational Statements

- The center will require needs and values statements that are clear, concise, accurate, and appropriate.
- A major-activities statement is also necessary. For instance, recruitment of students, compilation of critical thinking materials, and course development are all key actions that can be pursued.

Draft a "Think Piece" or White Paper

A think piece or white paper (position paper) can be shared with members of the community focusing on the following topics.

- A short history of critical thinking, especially as it relates to your community
- Current status of, and need for, critical thinking in various settings in the community
- The need for critical thinking among Indigenous Peoples (for instance, the need can focus on issues such as those at the beginning of this chapter)

- Questions and issues you might tackle using critical thinking.

Design Basic Courses

- Research critical thinking courses currently being taught.
- Design courses that take into account your community's values, needs, and culture.
- Create syllabi and select critical thinking readings and develop appropriate exercises.

Weave a Web of Relationships

- Network with others in and out of your community to conduct a needs survey for critical thinking.
- Provide an invitation to all interested parties to participate in the center's activities for the purpose of forming an advisory group.
- Create a network of scholars and other successful critical thinking centers.
- Hold a biennial conference or summer institute on critical thinking for all stakeholders, for example, students, organizers, community members, scholars, and tribal leaders.
- Create a newsletter or website.
- Edit and publish a book of the conference or summer institute proceedings.

Create Useful Tools

- Design an overall Indigenous critical thinking model.
- Create critical thinking modules that focus on key issues, for example, sovereignty, tribal membership, and decolonization.
- Catalogue the outcomes of critical thinking and key issues; for example, after examining the issues using critical thinking skills, report the findings.
- Market your results and provide technical assistance to other tribal groups.
- Document successful community efforts using critical thinking, and do interviews of community members, talking about their use of critical thinking.

Acquire Resources

- It will be important to find grant funding to support the major activities of your tribal critical thinking center. Since this is such a new and unique idea the possibility of financial and/or in-kind support is very high. Possible sources of support include:

  Community

  Cooperative Extension Service

School/PTA/PTO
Tribal college
Foundations
Endowment funds
School board of education
Business
Federal Agencies
Department of Education
Bureau of Indian Affairs
National Science Foundation
State Agencies
Department of Education
Office of Indian Affairs
Local Agencies
Tribal business council
City/Town council
Education Institutions
Colleges/Universities
Cooperative Extension Service
Public policy institutes
Private/Nonprofit
4-H
Civic groups (Lions, Kiwanis, and so forth)
Parent-teacher associations
Industry
Banks
Corporate business philanthropy (see www.businessweek.com)
Chain stores (Target, Wal-Mart, and so forth)
Chambers of Commerce
National honor societies
Major Mainstream Political Groups
Democratic Party
Republican Party
Green Party
Global
United Nations Permanent Forum on Indigenous Issues, Department of
Economic and Social Affairs (www.un.org/issues/m-indg.asp)

J. References

General References

Howard Adams, *Tortured People: The Politics of Colonization* (Penticton, B.C.: Theytus Books, 1995).

Bill Bigelow and Bob Peterson, eds., *Rethinking Globalization: Teaching for Justice in an Unjust World* (Rethinking Schools, Ltd., 2002).

Hussein Abdilahi Bulhan, *Frantz Fanon and the Psychology of Oppression* (New York: Plenum Press, 1985).

Frederick Douglass, *Narrative of the Life of Frederick Douglass, an American Slave. Written by Himself* (1845).

Frantz Fanon, *The Wretched of the Earth* (New York: Grove Press, 1963).

Paulo Freire, *Pedagogy of the Oppressed* (New York: Continuum, 1970).

bell hooks, *Teaching to Transgress: Education as the Practice of Freedom* (New York: Routledge, 1994).

The Loss of Paulo Freire, 1921-1997, Rethinking Schools Online (http://www.rethinkingschools.org/archive/11_04/ edit.shtml, 2004).

Albert Memmi, *The Colonizer and the Colonized* (New York: Orien Press, 1965).

Books and Definitions

Augusto Boal, *Theatre of the Oppressed* (New York: Theatre Communications Group, 1990).

Edward de Bono, *Teach Your Child How to Think* (New York: Penguin Books, 1992).

John Chaffee, *Thinking Critically* (Boston, MA: Houghton Mifflin Co., 2003).

Francis Watnabe Dauer, *Critical Thinking: An Introduction to Reasoning* (Oxford, U.K.: Oxford University Press, 1989).

Leonard Gibbs and Eileen Gambrill, *Critical Thinking for Social Workers: Exercises for Helping Professions* (Thousand Oaks, CA: Pine Forge Press, 1998).

Irving L. Janis, *Groupthink* (Boston, MA: Houghton Mifflin Co., 1983).

Irving L. Janis, *Victims Of Groupthink* (Boston, MA: Houghton Mifflin Co., 1972).

"Paradigm" (www.google.com/search?hl=en&lr=oi=defmore&q= define: paradigm, 2005; www.worldtrans.org/whole/ wholedefs.html, 1995).

"SIGGS Education Systems Theory: Equifinality" (http://education.indiana.edu/~frick/equifina.html, 1995).

Wikipedia: The Free Encyclopedia (http://en.wikipedia.org/wiki/Main_Page, 2005).

Videos

Critical Thinking in Context (http://www.tlc.murdoch.edu.au/slearn/resource/Crit_Thinking_Order_form.pdf).

Critical Thinking Resources (www.northern.edu/ois/critbook.htm).

Groupthink, The DOES Institute, Inc. (www.does.org/index.html).

How to Teach Video Series, Socratic Questioning Video Series, Assessment Video Series, and *Current Educational Issues Video Series*, The Critical Thinking Community (www.criticalthinking.org).

Thinking Toward Decisions (http://college.hmco.com/english/chaffee/critical_thinking/2e/instructors/video/index.htl).

What I learned About U.S. Foreign Policy. The War Against the Third World. Covert Operations and U.S. Military Interventions Since WWII. What You Didn't Learn in School and Don't Hear on the Mainstream Media. A video compilation by Frank Dorrel (www.addictedtowar.com/video_Order.htm).

Websites

"A Commitment to Critical Thinking," The de Bono Group (http://debonogroup.com).

"Critical Thinking," Questia, The World's Largest Online Library (www.questia.com/Index.jsp?CRID=critical_thinking&OFFID=se1&KEY=critical_thinking).

"Critical Thinking Across the Curriculum Project," Longview Community College (www.kcmetro.cc.mo.us/longview/ctac/index.htm).

"Critical Thinking & Collaborative Learning," University of Kentucky (www.uky.edu/HES/NFS/foodservice/critical.htm). "The videos featured here are vignettes from the food service industry portraying employees and supervisors in typical situations that require supervisors to use their critical thinking skills to make decisions."

"The Critical Thinking Community," Foundation for Critical Thinking (www.criticalthinking.org).

"Critical Thinking Online Resources," Subject Links: Education: Critical Thinking Links (www.gwc.maricopa.edu/biblio/links/critthinklinks.html).

"Identifying the Argument of an Essay: A Tutorial in Critical Reasoning," Metropolitan Community College (http://commhum.mccneb.ed/argument/summary.htm).

K. Glossary

conscientization: a concept that is also used to describe critical consciousness

critical consciousness: to perceive social, political, and economic contradictions and take action against the oppressive elements of reality

critical thinking: the application of "objective" logic to any process or content to reveal and assess accurate and inaccurate statements, beliefs, and generalizations

equifinality: the state of allowing, producing, or having the same effect or result from different events

epistemology: ways of knowing

groupthink: a mode of thinking in which group members' premature striving for agreement overrides the members' ability to realistically appraise alternative courses of action when confronted with a problem

paradigm: a general agreement of belief of how the world works and establishes or defines boundaries and that tells you how to behave inside the boundaries in order to be successful

setting the parameters for discussion: agreeing, as much as possible, upon the meaning of the words, concepts, and ideas that are used before one enters into a formal discussion and debate as a practice of good critical thinking

truth assessment: the discovery of truth by systematically using objective facts and reasoning to find out what may be "true" and "accurate," until another "truth" is revealed. What is true and accurate, however, will often vary with people, according to their conceptions of "truth."

Author's Note

Special thanks to Julia GoodFox for her comments and suggestions.

Just Good Sports

The Impact of "Native" References in Sports on Native Youth and What Some Decolonizers Have Done About It

Suzan Shown Harjo

A. **Colonization and the Power of Naming**

B. **Evidence of Colonization in Popular Culture**

C. **Decolonizing Indigenous Imagery**

D. *Harjo et al v. Pro Football, Inc.*

E. **"I moved to Washington because I have business with the football team here"**

F. **Indian in the Bonfire in Oklahoma**

G. **Stereotypes of Native Peoples in Northern California**

H. **"Doctor Bitch" and Anti-Mascot Struggles in California**

I. **Native Warriors Cartooned in Colorado**

J. **"Fighting Sioux" in North Dakota**

K. **Honored?**

A. Colonization and the Power of Naming

When one country colonizes another, it disarms and controls the population, and changes the identity of the peoples, both nations and individuals, who are being colonized. This reidentification is done in several ways. First, the peoples being colonized are stripped of their names and called belittling ones, often in the language of the colonizer or another enemy of the colonized. Second, the traditional identifying names and icons of the peoples being colonized are used by the colonizer for undignified, demeaning purposes.

The theory behind these practices is that the way to break the spirit of peoples is to take away their symbols of freedom, independence, personhood, and nationhood, and to berate them, call them names, and denigrate all that they respect until they adopt the pejoratives as their own attributes. Why is it important to break the spirit of peoples? Because it is easier to take property and labor from broken peoples than from strong ones, and to force them to accept new religions, languages, national allegiances, and other systems through which they can be fully colonized and controlled.

Europeans came to this hemisphere and renamed almost all of the Native Peoples: "Sioux"—from an Anishinaabe word for "snake" or "enemy"—for the Lakota, Dakota, and Nakota Peoples; "Cheyenne"—a French version of a Lakota word meaning "talks funny"—for the Tsistsistas Nation; "Tonto"—a Spanish word for "stupid" or "silly"—for certain Apache Peoples; "Papago"—European adaptation of a term for "bean-eater"—for the Tohono O'odham Nation; "Creek"—from the English observation that the people of the Muscogee Nation lived around creeks. By contrast, the names of most Native Peoples in heritage languages mean "Our People" or "Human Beings" or "Us."

European colonizers also gave Native Peoples

ACTIVITY:

What is the traditional name of your Native People?

_____

_____

What does it mean?

_____

_____

_____

What is the name of your people today, if different, and what does it mean?

_____

_____

_____

_____

What are the implications for being known by someone else's term for you?

_____

_____

_____

_____

_____

group names. "Indian" was the first, of course, from Cristóbal Colón, the lost Italian seeking riches for Spain, who thought he washed up on the shores of India. The early colonizers also called Native Peoples "primitives" or "savages." Even though sovereignty was recognized in documents of the colonizers for the purpose of treaty-making and ceding land, Native Peoples usually were referred to as "tribes," "bands," or "groups," rather than as "nations," which would have been the correct term in the language of diplomacy and international relations. "Indians" and "tribes" were the misnomers that made it into the U.S. Constitution, while "savages" was the preferred reidentifier in the Declaration of Independence.

The most derogatory name for Native Peoples in the English language is "redskins." The term has its origins in the late 1600s, when Europeans introduced commercial bounty-hunting in North America. They first paid fur trappers and other mercenaries for the heads and whole bodies of Native men, women, and children. When that practice proved too cumbersome, bounty-payers accepted the bloody red skins and scalps as proof of "Indian kill." From that time and into the 1900s, "redskins" was the term that was used in newspapers and books when writers wanted to convey the worst impression of Native Peoples. In Hollywood westerns, the term was usually preceded by such adjectives as "dirty," "lazy," "no-good," and "thieving." The term is despised by most Native Peoples and is seldom used in polite society now, except as a "Native" sports reference.

B. Evidence of Colonization in Popular Culture

Today, the most apparent evidence of this colonization and reidentification process in popular culture is in the use of "Native" and "Native"-related references in American sports. The names, images, symbols, logos, mascots, and behaviors related to Native Peoples are used in every sport in both educational and professional athletic programs. The most common sports references are animals, birds of prey, and Native Peoples. No other living, viable peoples are so targeted in the sports world.

The use of "Native" references in sports is justified, some would argue, because there are teams called "Vikings" and "Celtics." While those peoples are ancestors of other people of this time, they no longer exist as themselves and now represent eras, while Native Peoples remain the same peoples, with the same languages, religions, and customs. Others point to the "Cowboys," "Pirates," and "Buccaneers" to justify "Native" references, but those are professions, and Native Peoples are human beings and nations, not a professional category. Some even put "Native" references in the category of "Titans" and "Giants," but those are ogres and mythical beings, not peoples.

Still others make the argument that the existence of the University of Notre Dame's "Fighting Irish" justifies the use of Native sports references. The "Fighting Irish" started when the team was comprised of Irish Catholic players. Its name is an example of self-description, rather than outside name-calling, and its corollary would be Native schools with all Native players on teams that use Native references. One common trait of the self-description teams is that they do not tend to mock, cartoon, or otherwise disrespect their own names and symbols. A common problem for them is that they play other teams whose fans do mock, lampoon, and disrespect them.

Professional and educational sports clubs appropriate Native Peoples' names and religious symbols, such as eagle feathers and ceremonial dances, for their recreational promotion and profit. Scores of schools call their teams "Cherokees" and "Mohawks," without bothering to ask permission of the Native Peoples who own those names. Not only did Florida State University fail until 2005 to ask the Seminole Nation to allow the use of "Seminole" for its team name, FSU actually trademarked the word "Seminole." FSU went even farther and stole the name and reputation of the great Seminole leader who resisted colonization and relocation—Osceola—for the FSU mascot.

A greater number of teams are called by the colonizing misnomers and pejoratives—"Redskins," "Indians," and "Red Raiders"—and are accompanied by stereotypical logos and other references. Some team names that are not necessarily offensive or Native-specific—"Braves," "Chiefs," "Warriors," and "Raiders" —are contextualized with stereotypes of Native Peoples and behaviors, such as the "tomahawk chop." The "chop" was started by fans of the Atlanta Braves and FSU, who mindlessly move their outstretched arms up and down at the elbow to represent hacking away at the opposing team. That practice, which is accompanied by fans groaning something they refer to as a "war chant," has spread to every venue where a team with a "Native" reference plays. The Kansas City Chiefs players dress up in "Indian" drag for publicity shots and call their end zone, "Sacred Ground."

ACTIVITY:

Does an athletic program near you use a "Native" or "Native"-related reference? If so, which ones and where are they located?

_____

_____

_____

_____

_____

Describe it/them and its/their origin.

_____

_____

_____

_____

_____

Do you know of any Native Peoples who have tried to get rid of this/these reference(s)? If not, explain why not. If so, describe the effort and result.

_____

_____

_____

_____

_____

_____

C. Decolonizing Indigenous Imagery

Sports teams that adopt "Native" references are portraying themselves as aggressive, mean killing machines. They do not intend these "Native" sports references to compliment or honor Native Peoples. These are societal messages that Native Peoples are the negative names and characteristics assigned by the colonizers. These messages lower the self-esteem and raise the negative self-image of many Native children, who often express themselves in the harshest possible terms of suicide attempts, suicides, violence, and other self-hating actions. For more than fifty years, the Native teenage suicide rate has been the highest nationwide, and many Native parents view "Native" sports references as a matter of life and death.

With the rise of Native suicides and other dysfunctions to the top of society's demographics in the 1960s, many Native Peoples began the decolonizing process of removing negative imaging, especially in sports, and engaging in cultural reclamation. As more Native Peoples reclaimed their traditional national names and personal names, Native pride grew and campaigns against Native references in sports increased. This chapter looks at the impact of "Native" sports references on Native youth and what some of these young decolonizers have done and are doing to make their schools and communities "Native" mascot–free zones. Some of their specific efforts are concluded and some are ongoing. All are successful, in that they have raised awareness about the problems and have presented reasoned arguments and solutions. This chapter leaves it to the reader to discover the common terms, themes, and impacts of Native stereotyping in sports in the voices of Native youth who have tried to remove stereotypes from their educa-tional and social environments. Each one of these campaigns and changes has been initiated by one student, teacher, or family, most often Native People, but sometimes by non-Native people. The road from identifying the problem to doing something about it is arduous, painful, and marginalizing, but empowering, which was addressed by each person interviewed for this chapter.

With the 1990 statement (below), the modern movement to end the use of Native references in sports was energized and given broad play in the American media. The 1992 Alliance and its organizational sponsor, The Morning Star Institute, seized the spotlight during the ramp-up period to the 1992 Columbus Quincentenary and led a nationwide campaign to increase awareness about stereotyping of Native Peoples. The target audiences were professional associations in the arts, education, journalism, and law, as well as the religious community and the media.

The modern anti-mascot movement began in the 1960s on college campuses nationwide. Native students started prominent campaigns to eliminate the "Indian" names, mascots, and behaviors from Dartmouth College in Hanover, New Hampshire, and Stanford University in Palo Alto, California; and "Little Red" from the University of Oklahoma in Norman. Initially, all the schools had team colors, not names, logos, or mascots. Oklahoma was "Big Red" and the mascot "Little Red" was portrayed by a series of prancing white students dressed in "Indian garb" performing "Indian war dances" at halftime. Stanford's team was and is "Cardinal" (the color, not the bird), which gave rise to the name and mascot "Indian." Dartmouth's color was "Big Green," which inexplicably morphed into "Indians."

> **"We call upon the entertainment and news industries, the sports and advertising worlds and all those with influence in shaping popular culture to forego the use of dehumanizing, stereotyping, cartooning images and information regarding our peoples, and to recognize their responsibility for the emotional violence their fields have perpetuated against our children."**
> —Statement of The 1992 Alliance and The Elders Circle, October 1990. The 1992 Alliance was established in 1990 to amplify Native voices on the occasion of the 500th anniversary of the 1492 Invasion.

"Little Red" was the first casualty, in 1970, followed shortly by dead mascots at Dartmouth and Stanford. The University of Syracuse in New York quickly dropped its "Saltine Warrior"—named after an Onondaga man, legend has it, who was taken from his grave to make way for a school building—and reverted to "Orange," the color, and soon moved on to "Orange," the fruit. At the same time, Seneca Nation clanmothers and a chief went to St. Bonaventure University in New York and quietly asked that the women's sports teams remove the name "Brown Squaw." The delegation explained that the word means "vagina" in certain Haudenosaunee and Algonquin languages, and that British and French trappers popularized it as a term for all Native women. The university dropped the term immediately and without fanfare, and eventually retired "Brown Indian" from all its athletic programs in favor of the "Bonnies."

After the first colleges eliminated their "Native" references, hundreds of high schools, middle schools, and elementary schools across the country did the same. Over the decades, St. John's University in New York City retired the "Redman" for the "Red Storm," and Marquette University in Milwaukee, Wisconsin, went from "Warriors" to "Golden Eagles." In the 1990s, the Miami Tribe in Oklahoma asked Miami University in Oxford, Ohio, to drop "Redskins," saying that "times change and sensibilities change." The university complied, with lightning speed, and its team is now named "Red Hawks."

There were more than 3,000 "Native" references in American sports when OU became the first school to drop its mascot "Little Red" in 1970. Today, fewer than 1,000 remain. The fact that two-thirds of the "Native" sports references have been removed during the past thirty-five years represents a monumental and rapid societal change, and gives reason for optimism about the removal of the last one-third.

"Native" sports references are eliminated on a team-by-team basis, and most conflicts follow a predictable trajectory. A hallmark of the conflicts is that most coaches, administrators, players, and fans claim that their team names and images honor Native Peoples and represent some longstanding institutional tradition. The dialogue usually runs along these lines: Native Peoples say, "We are offended by these references and behaviors." The Institution responds, "No, they are not offensive, they are traditional and honor you." Native Peoples insist, "No, we are not honored and yours is a tradition of racism." The Institution responds, "Shut up," and starts scouting for any self-proclaimed Native person who will say, "I'm a Native person (more commonly, "I'm part-Indian") and I like these sports names and mascots. Those other Native Peoples are troublemakers." The most contentious participants in conflicts over educational sports are school alumni. Native youth who object to Native references for their school sports teams are often shunned, bullied, threatened, and shut out of sports activities and other school events.

An early ally in the early 1990s' awareness campaign was the National Education Association, the largest organization of educators. The NEA supported an end to Native referencing in sports and circulated materials on the topic to teachers and school administrators. In July 1991, the NEA voted to "discourage the initiation and continued use of prejudicial and derogatory names and symbols of ethnic groups for schools, sporting teams and mascots." In June 1992, the NEA described its policy in a letter to the Kentucky Department of Education, which was considering eliminating (and eventually did eliminate) Native sports references in Louisville schools:

> ...the practice of using ethnic references to designate sports teams is demeaning to the particular group, promotes stereotypes and fosters misunderstanding and divisiveness among the various segments of the population. It has no place in a culturally diverse society. NEA recognizes that these names were not intended to cast aspersions or to belittle any ethnic group. However, our increased awareness of the sensitivities of individuals and groups makes it essential that we stop this practice, which can be hurtful and demoralizing.

Figure 3.1 Auth © 1992 *The Philadelphia Inquirer*. Reprinted with permission of UNIVERSAL PRESS SYNDICATE. All rights reserved.

D. *Harjo et al v. Pro Football, Inc.*

The 1990s' awareness campaign launched the seminal lawsuit on "Native" references in professional sports. *Harjo et al v. Pro Football, Inc.*, was filed in September 1992 before the U.S. Patent and Trademark Board by seven Native Americans, under the organizational sponsorship of The Morning Star Institute. I am the Harjo in the title of the lawsuit, as well as president of Morning Star. I am Cheyenne, on my mother's side, and Hodulgee Muscogee, on my father's side, from El Reno, Oklahoma. Harjo is the name of the Muscogee Warrior Society and means "Magic in Battle." I'm a writer, poet, curator, lecturer, and policy advocate, and have developed laws protecting religious freedom and sacred places; establishing museum, repatriation, arts, and cultural policies; and returning over one million acres of Native lands. I'm a columnist for *Indian Country Today* and have served as a School of American Research 2004 Native Artist Fellow and summer scholar, a founding trustee of the National Museum of the American Indian, past executive director of the National Congress of American Indians, and special assistant for legislation and liaison in the Carter Administration.

The other Native American parties to the lawsuit are prominent leaders with enormous accomplishments in their fields:

Raymond D. Apodaca (Ysleta del Sur Pueblo), former governor of Pueblo Ysleta del Sur; board member for the Indian Law Resource Center; and team leader of Native American Temporary Assistance for Needy Families, U.S. Department of Health and Human Resources

Manley A. Begay Jr., Ph.D. (Navajo), director of Native Nations Institute at the Udall Center for Studies in Public Policy and senior lecturer in American Indian Studies, University of Arizona; and co-director of Harvard Project on American Indian Economic Development, Kennedy School of Government, Harvard University

Vine Deloria Jr., Esq. (Standing Rock Sioux), author of 25 books, including the definitive work on federal Indian treaties; historian; professor of law at the University of Arizona; retired professor of Native American and Religious Studies at the University of Colorado; a founding trustee of the National Museum of the American Indian; and past executive director of the National Congress of American Indians

Norbert S. Hill Jr. (Oneida), director of the American Indian Graduate Center; former executive director of the American Indian Science and Engineering Society; and past chairman of the board of trustees of the National Museum of the American Indian

William A. Means Jr. (Oglala Lakota), executive director of the OIC State Council; board member and past president of the International Indian Treaty Council; and former executive director of the Heart of the Earth Survival School

Mateo Romero (Cochiti Pueblo), noted artist and arts educator whose paintings are in the most prestigious museums and collections nationwide; he was a School of American Research 2003 Native Artist Fellow, received his Master of Fine Arts degree from the University of New Mexico, and taught painting at his alma mater, the Institute of American Indian Arts.

I selected Mateo Romero as a co-petitioner because he was a young artist who had earned his undergraduate arts degree from Dartmouth College during the years when there was a sizable group advocating the return of "Indians" to the school. "It is time for the younger Indian people to join their elders in open opposition to racist names, images, and mascots," said Mateo in 1992. "[Native artists] cannot project our own positive images through the generations and layers of stereotypes and negative images projected on us."

Explaining that those of us who brought the lawsuit represent a broad cross section of Native culture and politics, Vine Deloria said, "This is not just a disenfranchised few calling for something only a handful would agree with. While American Indians, like other groups, are diverse in their views, most share a deep feeling of offense at terms like 'Redskins.' Enough is enough. We don't want future generations of Indian children to bear this burden of discrimination."

Senator Daniel K. Inouye, Democrat from Hawaii, also made a statement about the filing. "Today, Native American leaders have taken what could prove to be the first step in eliminating offensive names and images from the sports world. The Native American people who have talked to me over the years about this problem have characterized it as a continuing injury. This demeaning portrayal of American Indian people, their appearance, their traditional dress, their ceremonial dances serves as a constant reminder of the injustices they have suffered at the hands of the non-Indians throughout the past five centuries….It is time to leave this era behind with the symbolic and substantive evolutionary act of changing offensive names and negative images in sports."

Following almost seven years of litigation, a three-judge federal panel in April 1999 ruled unanimously that "Redskins" is disparaging and holds Native Americans up to contempt and ridicule. The Washington, D.C., football club was being sold at the time, for a record-breaking $800 million, and was changing owners, coaches, players, training camps, and uniforms. It was an ideal time to change the name, too. Instead, the new owner, Daniel M. Snyder, echoed the sentiments of his predecessors, saying that the name is traditional and not offensive, and would not be dropped.

Leaders of thirteen national Native organizations wrote to National Football League Commissioner Paul Tagliabue, urging him to let the decision stand and "to change the contemptible name to something that will not disparage Native Americans or any other segment of American society." The NFL is not a party to the lawsuit, but it is a merchandising partner with the team owners, taking 60 percent of the profits. The NFL has paid the litigation expenses for the Washington football club to fight our lawsuit.

"We, the undersigned, collectively represent and serve a majority of the diverse Native Peoples in the United States," continued the letter to the NFL. "Some of the undersigned organizations and individuals have worked for many decades to persuade past owners of the Washington team to change the name….The NFL and the team's owners have not accorded Native American representatives the fundamental courtesy of meeting on the subject of the team's name since the early 1970s. Responses of subsequent owners…became progressively contentious over time, prompting the 1992 filing of the lawsuit…which we enthusiastically support."

The NFL's and team's spokespersons maintain that the team's name honors Native Americans. After considering the voluminous evidentiary record, a federal panel of judges has disagreed with the Washington football organization's position, ruling on the Native American side of the case that the team's name is not now and never was an honorific.

Signatories to the letter were the American Indian

Movement Grand Council, Americans for Indian Opportunity, Atlatl-National Service Organization for Native American Arts, Indian Art Northwest, International Indian Treaty Council, The Morning Star Institute, National Coalition to End Racism in Sports and the Media, National Congress of American Indians, National Indian Education Association, Native American Artists Association, Native American Bar Association, Native American Journalists Association, and the Native American Rights Fund.

The NFL never responded to the letter. The new team owner appealed the Native victory to the federal district court for the District of Columbia, which decided against the Native parties in September 2003. The judge reversed the three trademark judges' ruling on summary judgment motions, without even holding a hearing on the issues. The judge opined that the Native parties are not offended and should have brought the case in 1967, when the Washington club first filed for trademark protection (and when only two of the seven Native parties were 21 years old, and one was even in diapers).

The case is now on appeal before the U.S. Court of Appeals for the District of Columbia Circuit. We are asking the appeals judges to reinstate the 1999 ruling of the trademark judges. The Native American Rights Fund and other lawyers asked the Appeals Court for permission to file an amicus curiae (friends of the court) brief in our case, so that the National Congress of American Indians, the National Indian Education Association, the National Indian Youth Council, and the Tulsa Indian Coalition Against Racism can make the judges aware of their views. The Washington club objected, calling the organizations biased. The appeals court disagreed and allowed the Native groups' brief. Once the brief was filed, the Washington club objected to the contents of the brief and asked the judges to disallow the brief itself. At the time of publication, this matter was unresolved. An oral argument hearing was held in April 2005 and an

> **"Liberation is a praxis: the action and reflection of men and women upon their world in order to transform it."**
> **—Paulo Freire**

interim decision was issued in July 2005, asking the district court to render advice about the passage of time barring disparaged Native Americans who were under age or unborn in 1967. In August 2005, the NCAA called for its teams not to display their "Native" references in championship games."

How did the "Redskins" get its start? Founder George Preston Marshall bought the sports franchise Boston "Braves" in 1932, renamed it "Redskins" the following year, and moved to Washington, D.C. "Redskins" grew out of the severe colonization period under the "Civilization Regulations," which were in place from 1880 to 1936 and outlawed traditional religions, medicine practices, travel off reservations, giveaway ceremonies for mourning or celebrating, any activities that were "anti-progressive in nature," and all dancing. They also mandated an English-only and Christian-only educational system, complete with corporal punishment for Native children. Violations by Native teenagers and adults resulted in imprisonment, starvation, and orders to the U.S. Army to capture or kill the "hostiles," "troublemakers," "ringleaders," or "fomenters of dissent." Native Peoples diminished to a population low of 237,196 in 1900 and were known as the "Vanishing American." Native and Native-related references proliferated in American sports, when the popular assumption was that Native Peoples were dead or dying.

"Redskins" founder Marshall was widely known as a bigot who refused to allow African Americans to play on the team. The Kennedy Administration forced desegregation of the team by threatening to deny renewal of the lease for the team's home stadium, which was on federal land. Washington was the last team in the NFL to be integrated, in 1962. Some 30 years later, former Senator Ben Nighthorse Campbell, then a Democrat from Colorado, who is Cheyenne, introduced legislation to disallow use of the same federal land and stadium for any event that focused on the physical characteristics of any persons. Then-owner

Cooke moved the team away from federal ⟨lan⟩ ⟨⟩t of the jurisdiction of Washington, D.C., in order to escape the reach of any new law along the lines of Campbell's bill. The new stadium, initially named for Cooke and renamed by Snyder as FedEx Field, is in Virginia. Technically, "Washington" should have been dropped already and the team should be known as "Virginia."

E. "I moved to Washington because I have business with the football team here"

Our lawsuit against the Washington football club has spurred activism nationwide. All of the leading Native rights and professional associations have specifically endorsed our lawsuit, which has raised awareness in every Native nation and community, and with myriad non-Native people. The case has been covered extensively in the media throughout the dozen years of litigation, and has focused attention on the hundreds of efforts to stop stereotyping of Native Peoples in sports. Since we began our awareness campaign in 1990, the issue of "Native" sports references has been the second most frequently covered Native-related issue, after Native gaming. The general issue was given another boost in 2001, when the U.S. Commission on Civil Rights called for "an end to the use of Native American images and team names by non-Native schools." The commission made all of the arguments for getting rid of "Native" references throughout the sports world, but ducked the most difficult area—professional sports—where team owners have banded together to combat Native Peoples and are financing selected educational institutions to hang on to their "Native" references.

One young Native filmmaker says, "I moved to Washington, D.C., because, like you, I have business with the football team here, and I won't be leaving until my business is finished." Monica Braine is Assiniboine from Montana. In 1988, her parents split up and she moved to her mother's hometown of Indiana, Pennsylvania. In 1991, when Monica was in the sixth grade, she wrote an article objecting to the "Lil Indian" mascot at Indiana Jr. High School.

Monica remembers that "the mascot was everywhere—big banners that said Scalp 'Em, and the cheerleaders wore face paint." When she was in the seventh grade, she responded to a newspaper survey on the mascot. "I wrote something about how the mascot was derogatory. They published the quote with my picture. The day the paper came out, I became the most unpopular person in my school."

Monica says she "left the issue alone for a year." As a ninth grader, she wrote to *Indian Country Today*, which "ended up publishing an article about my struggle on the front page. After that, I was on National Native News and in the local paper. It brought a lot of attention to the issue and I managed to get a few small things changed." The cheerleaders stopped using "war paint" and the word "scalp," but the mascot remains unchanged. In tenth grade, she went away to boarding school, where "it was a bit of a relief to stop with the activism and be a student."

Monica says that the "biggest thing I learned was that nothing was more important than getting the respect I deserved as a human being. I struggled with identity and recognition, but through the whole thing I knew I wasn't wrong about one thing, which is that you shouldn't use people as mascots." Reflecting on her early experiences, Monica says she "gained access to an inner voice that is stronger than any other voice I have. In no other place in my life have I been able to stand up for myself the way I do when it comes to this issue."

Monica has directed a 24-minute film, *If the Name Has to Go…*, which explores her own experiences, as well as anti-Native hate speech at the University of North Dakota and our lawsuit against the Washington team. Quiet Coyote Productions describes her 2004 film as a "personal documentary [that] examines Native sports mascots and the stereotypes from which they emerged…. The film poses the question, 'Are Indian mascots the next step in assimilating Native Americans?'"

Her "hardest lesson" came when she was on the front page of the newspaper and called her father to ask what he thought. She remembers his words with deep disappointment: "It's good, but you know no one out here [on the Fort Peck Reservation] gives a crap about this stuff." Ten years after that conversation, she told her father about someone in the UND audience at a showing of her documentary who asked her why she didn't "show the other side." "My father said, 'What other side—either you are racist or you're not.' So, of course, change is possible in many ways."

These experiences "laid a foundation for me to be a media activist for social change," says Monica.

"Horace Mann said, 'Be ashamed to die until you have won a great victory for humanity.' I think the great victories are in the small changes that happen each time someone says something—like maybe we shouldn't say 'scalp 'em' anymore." Monica Braine's current plan is to approach "the African American churches in D.C. to try to create a change in the fan attitude. In 2005, she sent her documentary to every school that uses an "Indian" mascot or logo.

Indian Psychologists: Retire Indian Personalities as Sports Symbols

In January 1999, the Society of Indian Psychologists of the Americas issued a statement that supported "retiring all Indian personalities as the official symbols and mascots of universities, colleges, or schools and athletic teams." The 300-member group expressed concern that:

"...the continued use of Indian symbols and mascots seriously compromises our ability to engage in ethical professional practice and service to the community. We believe that it establishes an unwelcome academic environment for Indian students, staff, and faculty and contributes to the miseducation of all members of the community regarding the cultural practices and traditions of an entire ethnic group. In our view, the use of an historically and culturally inaccurate, stereotypic image undermines the educational experience of all members of the community. It seems especially problematic for those who have had little or no contact with Indian people and their cultures.

"Stereotypical and historically inaccurate images of Indians in general interfere with learning about them by creating, supporting, and maintaining oversimplified and inaccurate views of indigenous peoples and their cultures. When stereotypical representations are taken as factual information, they contribute to the development of cultural biases and prejudices. In the same vein, we believe that continuation of the use of Indians as symbols and mascots is incongruous with the philosophy espoused by many Americans as promoting inclusivity and diversity.

"We understand that some affiliated with the institutions having a long history of use of these symbols may have a special attachment to them. We also understand and believe that this attachment may not have been formed out of maliciousness or negative intentions. To the extent, however, that tradition and/or economic issues are major obstacles to change, they should not usurp the principles of a society struggling to put an end to racism. What once may have been unifying symbols for the various bodies using these symbols has become a source of cross-cultural conflict. In light of all of these factors, we strongly support and encourage all such entities to develop a new symbol consistent with and contributing to the positive realization of national principles.

"...We applaud the current efforts across the nation to have this crucial issued raised and addressed in a responsible and productive way."

F. Indian in the Bonfire in Oklahoma

Nokose is a Muscogee (Creek) boy with a big name—Bear—in the Muscogee language. In 1999, when he was five years old, he saw an "Indian" being burned in effigy by a bunch of white teenagers in Oklahoma. His mother remembers him crying out in alarm, "Mama, what are they doing?" Nokose's Muscogee mother, Geri Wisner-Foley, says he was "concerned and confused and frightened."

It was fall, a few days before the state high school championship football game. The Union Redskins of Tulsa were playing the Trojans of Jenks, a town outside of Tulsa. Nokose, Geri, and Hugh Foley, Nokose's non-Indian father, stopped by the pep rally in Jenks. Like most Oklahomans, Geri and Hugh are football fans and wanted to show adult support for the high school team.

"The cheerleaders had a big fire going," Geri recalls. "They had a mannequin on a pole dressed up as a 'Plains Indian,' with feathers, buckskin, and a headband. They held it high, then lower, and started to burn it. That's when Nokose got scared. I told him that it wasn't a real Indian, that it was only pretend, but he was quite frightened and shaken up. Under the circumstances, we left immediately."

Geri is Itcho, Deer Clan of the Muscogee Nation. In 2000, she earned her bachelor's degree in political science from Oklahoma State University, where she was president of the Native American Students Association. An ex-Marine corporal and Gulf War veteran, she served in Saudi Arabia during Operation Desert Storm in 1991. Geri shows no emotion about her wartime experiences, but tears up at the memory of her son seeing the "Indian" on fire. "Just to see the look on his face was"—she searches for the right word—"awful."

Around the same time as the bonfire incident, an "Indian" dummy was hung from a basketball rim during half-time at another suburban Tulsa school and "fans took turns hitting it with baseball bats." In another situation, in an Oklahoma City public high school where she was recruiting for OSU, Geri noticed students wearing pregame ribbons with such rallying slogans as Crush the Indians and Kill the Indians.

In Stillwater, the OSU town where Geri and Hugh made their home for most of the 1990s, the Pioneers were gearing up for their game against the Redskins. "There was this big white football player sitting on top of an 'Indian' and pulling his braids," says Geri, steaming at the memory. "These are my tax dollars, too, even though most of the people around here don't think that Indians even pay taxes."

Growing up in Weleatka, Oklahoma, "I heard about these 'left-wing radicals' protesting mascots," says Geri, "and then I started learning what they were doing and understanding why." She was referring to the Indian students who had protested the University of Oklahoma's "Little Red" in the 1960s. Their demonstrations turned into a sit-in and takeover of the chancellor's office, gaining nationwide attention and considerable support on the campus in Norman, outside of Oklahoma City. In 1970, OU consigned "Little Red" to the pages of history and became the first institution of higher education in the United States to drop its "Native" sports reference.

"I started questioning how in the hell can we stop this abuse in the schools in this day and age," says Geri. "How can we protect Indian children from being exposed to these terrifying images and hateful messages?" She began researching Oklahoma tort law and found "something interesting" in the state's bill of rights, a guarantee of protection from bodily harm, personal insult, defamation, and injury to personal relations.

Prompted by the sight of Nokose's face at seeing the "burning Indian," Hugh Foley made a film of Native children's reactions to Native references in Oklahoma's athletic programs, and Geri Wisner-Foley entered law school at the University of Tulsa. What legal action Geri may take, either as a client or a lawyer, remains to be seen, but she is not likely to l et the matter rest. Her son is her most persistent reminder. "Every time Nokose sees any of that toma-

> "History is subversive because truth is!"
> —Ngugi wa Thiong'o

hawk arm-chopping on T.V. or a T-shirt with an 'Indian' stereotype and says, 'Mama, that's wrong,' my resolve is strengthened even more."

G. Stereotypes of Native Peoples in Northern California

Tayshu Bommelyn is Tolowa and Karuk. Tayshu means Fog Rain in the Tolowa language. At 20, she earned her degree in elementary education at Humboldt State University in Arcata, California. She was motivated to be a teacher by her family's experiences with "Native" sports references in Crescent City, her northern California hometown in Del Norte County, in original Tolowa territory. Tayshu's parents are Lena (Karuk) and Loren (Tolowa and Karuk) Bommelyn. Lena is an elementary school teaching assistant in Crescent City. A linguist, Loren teaches the Tolowa language and art at Del Norte High School, where he graduated from in 1974. Tayshu graduated from the same high school in 1997; Tayshu's brothers graduated from Del Norte after she did.

The only sour note for the Bommelyns at Del Norte is the sports team name and logo, "Warriors." As a student more than a quarter-century ago, Loren tried to get the school to drop "Warriors," to no avail. When Tayshu was a freshman, she picked up the cause, with her parents' support. "We never imagined that getting rid of that lousy mascot would be a generational fight," says Lena.

"In the '70s, Dad and other Native students tried to fight [the 'Warriors']," said Tayshu. "Then, it's the 2000s, and it's still there." Del Norte High School has approximately 1,300 students, mostly white, with a smattering of students of color. "Native students started out strong, about 40, in my freshman class," said Tayshu, "but only eight were in my graduating class." She says that the "mascot doesn't help the high dropout situation at all, and it's probably part of the problem."

Tayshu played the flute in the school band. "We had to play 'Scalp' at the games, a song that the band teacher's friend arranged in the '70s," she says. "I never liked that song. It's one of those *dum-dum-dum-dum* songs that's supposed to sound Native but doesn't. I

just quit playing 'Scalp' when I was a freshman," says Tayshu. "It was a typical stereotype, like that big head, big nose logo. I didn't want to be a part of carrying on a stereotype."

Tayshu has dealt with stereotypes for as long as she can remember. "I'm very involved in our culture. People would ask me if I lived in a tipi, and I would go, 'No, my people didn't have tipis, we had redwood plank houses.' And everyone seems to think that all Native people wear eagle feathers, like the mascot." She and her parents tried to explain to the school community that Native People in that territory wear woodpecker-feather head rolls, not the eagle feather headdress depicted by the sports symbol. "Then people started making fun of us, and we stopped telling them about things like the feather head rolls, because they really are sacred objects anyway."

Tayshu does not need to search her memory for the experience. Its impact is with her today. "We were out there, being sincere, and they just shot us down and stuck with the logo," she recalls. "I would try to tell them about our people who stood tall and survived a lot, but they couldn't see us, they couldn't see me. They just saw this thing, this logo. It really hurt. I told people how I felt. I really gave a lot of myself. It ripped me apart. It was very rough. Even now, it hurts a lot to think of friends since kindergarten who didn't hear anything we said. Our reasons were not good enough for them. The worst ones never took it back or apologized. Sometimes, I just hated school."

Tayshu also recalls a few positive reactions. The student council president, for example, "was so nice—she came up to me and said, 'I'm so sorry'—and that helped me to know that some people were educated, once they heard." She also commends "some of the teachers who encouraged discussion, openness, conversation."

When Tayshu was a senior in 1997, the school "finally agreed to drop the logo, but it wasn't done until my brother's graduation year in '99." The years were "hard on our family. People blamed my father and told him that he ruined the school, but he was just on the school committee trying to deal with it." She

Figure 3.2 Richard Crowson © *The Wichita Eagle*. Reprinted by permission.

said that "people would ask me and my brothers, 'Why didn't you say anything before it became the "Warriors"?' How old do they think we are? It became 'Warriors' in 1892."

The Del Norte High School did drop the offensive logo. "So now we're the 'W,' but still there's 'Scalp' and the tomahawk chop. It was hard for me to cheer for my brother and cousin in sports, with those things still going on." Tayshu says that "one of the worst things was a Native American kid there, who took 'Tonto' as his coach's name for the powder puff football game. 'Tonto'! He loves 'Scalp,' does the chop, and just became their token Indian. It's pretty sad."

H. "Doctor Bitch" and Anti-Mascot Struggles in California

"I've been called a bitch more than Lassie," says Amber Machamer (Coastal Band Chumash), who works with her parents to eliminate Native references in sports throughout California. Amber comes from a family of educators; her mother Sylvia Mata (Chumash) and father Milton (German) are teachers. Amber is the director of research and planning for a community college in the San Francisco Bay Area.

Amber received her Ph.D. in education in 2000 from the University of California at Los Angeles, where she also earned a bachelor's degree in history and a master's degree in education. Soon after being awarded her doctorate, she attended a meeting about changing a high school's "Native" sports name. "One alum called me a bitch," says Amber. "Education doesn't protect you, but it is empowering, and I was able to dismiss him in my mind by thinking, that's 'Doctor Bitch' to you, sir."

The Machamer Family won their first victory in the mid-1990s, when Fremont High School dropped "Indians." The Machamers were part of the successful coalition that convinced the Los Angeles County School District in the late 1990s to drop all "Native" names and symbols. That effort built on one begun in the early 1990s by Concerned Indian Parents, which initiated a process to rid all public schools in Minneapolis and St. Paul, Minnesota, of their "Native" names and imagery. The process was later extended throughout Minnesota and provided a model for various other cities, school districts (such as Dallas and Los Angeles), and states (including Michigan, Nebraska, Wisconsin, and others) to remove their "Native" sports stereotypes from whole groups of schools. The Machamers also organized the first national conference on the subject, "People, Not Mascots," in 1997 at the University of California at Santa Barbara.

"Because we're known for doing this," says Amber, "teachers and parents invite us to their schools to help." In 1999, a teacher at Sequoia High School asked the Machamers to join the effort to rid the Redwood City school of its team name and symbol, "Cherokees." "The school is 110 years old and was named for the tree, Sequoia, not for the Cherokee scholar, Sequoyah," said Amber. "They soon shifted from tree to man, they say, although the name is still spelled the same as the tree, not the man. 'Cherokees' came in because they were following Stanford's lead, but they forgot to follow Stanford 30 years ago in getting rid of the team name."

The Machamers' efforts resulted in a task force on the fate of "Cherokees," but Amber and Sylvia "were officially not allowed on campus," says Amber. Although displeased about being banned from the school grounds, Amber was "happy" about the task force. "That's just where we wanted things, in a task force, in a process that brings some order to the issue, where people aren't just screaming at anyone who wants a change." After the task force and other processes, Sequoia dropped "Cherokees" and its team is now called "The Raven."

While results have been positive, reactions to the Machamers have been "mostly negative," says Amber. She jokes about "wearing tennis shoes to school board meetings, just in case I need to make a fast getaway. At best, we are written off as a little 'off.' At worst, we get threats of violence." She thinks that "all people should ...walk around wearing an anti-mascot button, hat, or T-shirt. A few of my parents' non-Indian friends have done this and have been amazed at how badly they have been treated. They have been approached in line at the store or by a coworker and yelled at. People who think that racism is dead should try this."

Amber could not be clearer on the issue of "Native" references in sports: "I'm against 'em. No compromises." She is eloquent on the subject of the impact of "Native" sports referencing on Native youth. "It produces feelings of self-doubt and self-loathing. It isolates us. Images are extremely powerful and have lasting impacts."

When she was growing up in Cupertino, a suburb of San Jose, she was "always aware that it bothered me, but as the only Indian family—or minority for that matter—in my neighborhood, I didn't think I had the right to have an opinion that differed from the norm. Using Indians as mascots is and was so accepted that, although I knew it bothered me, I did not know it was wrong. I guess I did not feel I had a right to have such an opinion, let alone voice it. When you grow up in an all-white neighborhood, you quickly learn to keep your mouth shut or suffer the consequences. Social ostracization is pretty difficult for anybody, let alone a kid. Now that I think about it, that's really sad."

Even with the company of four siblings, Amber recalls her childhood in Cupertino as "very isolating." It "makes you think something is wrong with you [and] realize how different you are from everybody you know." In her late high school years, she was "more confident and less afraid." In college, "I really became an activist. I finally had peers that held the same beliefs. It was safer. It was good to know that I was not crazy."

Amber remembers that it was an ally in the anti-mascot effort, Eugene Herrod (Muscogee), who "first said something about Joe Camel." Eugene works on behalf of Advocates for American Indian Children in Garden Grove and initiated the complaint that resulted in California's ban in 2000 of personalized license plates sporting "Redskins" or any derivation. Eugene filed the complaint in California after Utah withdrew its approval of plates with the derogatory term in 1999. "Eugene said the federal government banned 'Joe Camel' and the 'Marlboro Man' because those images were so powerful that they were dangerous to children," says Amber. "Images are powerful. If a camel playing pool influences kids to smoke, then what does it do to the minds of kids to see a sign that reads 'Scalp the Indians'?"

"Native" references in sports makes us "cartoons," says Amber. "We are not real. We are not human. We are not at their level. You don't respect the rights of inhuman cartoons. This is the most fundamental issue facing Indian people. It affects how we are treated by governments, schools, and individual Americans. It does affect our lands, mineral, religious, and economic rights. It may not be the most urgent issue, but it is the most fundamental."

Amber Machamer, Eugene Herrod, and Native Peoples throughout California are leading a legislative effort to rid the state's public schools of "Redskins" as a team name or mascot. The broad-based coalition to pass the California Racial Mascots Act is organized by the Alliance Against Racial Mascots (ALLARM), which is supported by Native Peoples nationwide. An earlier version of the legislation, which would have banned all "Native" sports references in the public schools, failed after a state legislator who claimed to be "part Cherokee" opposed the bill, saying he was all for "Indian mascots." A subsequent measure passed in the legislature, but was vetoed by the governor. The bill has been reintroduced and is working its way through the legislative process again.

I. Native Warriors Cartooned in Colorado

Wanbli Williams was a middle-school student when he changed a big part of his world. He got his school to retire its "Warriors" logo. "It was a cartoony, big-nosed guy riding a pony," says Wanbli. "It was on the school building, at the center of the gym, here and there, and I got mad every time I saw it." The school is in Westlake Village, a subdivision of Broomfield, Colorado, and its team has been the "Warriors" since the early 1970s.

One October day in 1992, when he was an eighth grader, Wanbli "was coming in from lunch, saw that plaque, and couldn't take it." The 3- by 3-foot wooden plaque outside the entrance to the school featured the "Warriors" logo. "I threw a spit-wad at that plaque and got hauled into the principal's office," Wanbli recalls.

"So, how it all started was that I got in trouble. I was angry and really expressing my views. The principal was shocked that someone in junior high would have opinions—and those opinions— but he did a pretty good job of becoming culturally aware."

Wanbli's opinions were supported by his parents, Richard B. Williams (Lakota and Cheyenne) and Sally Carufel-Williams (Ojibwe and Dakota), who are long-time residents of Colorado and advocates for Native rights and education. Sally is with the Native American Fish and Wildlife Society, and Rick directs the American Indian College Fund, both in Denver. Wanbli was "really surprised" by the initial reactions of the handful of Native students at the school. "They said what their parents said, that it was just a team, just a cartoon, not offensive, so I just tried to make them more aware. Being suburban Indians, not being raised in a more traditional manner, they weren't culturally or politically aware. I don't know if I changed their minds, but they became aware of my views."

"My own awareness had a context," he says, "just being aware of cultural and historical priorities and how important it is not to be trading stereotypes or handing them over to children." From the time he was in Centennial Elementary School, where the team was the "Miners," Wanbli was aware of many efforts

> **"Get rid of the belief, I mean really get rid of it, that we are somehow inferior."**
> **—Manulani Aluli Meyer**

nationwide to change stereotypical images and names in sports. "My creative process to change the logo began when I started seventh grade and thought about it and researched it and developed my personal views about it."

Wanbli talked "to a lot of others about changing the logo, getting rid of that cartoon." He took his concerns to the administration, faculty members, and other students. A process began with a faculty poll, which favored a change, and culminated in a student vote on drawings for a new logo. A depiction of a lake won and is the school logo today. By the end of the school year in 1993, "that Indian joke logo was gone."

Wanbli is Oglala Lakota, Santee Dakota, Northern Cheyenne, and Ojibwe. His name means Eagle in the Lakota language. Now in his twenties, he is the father of a daughter, Teresa Eclipse, whose mother is Ojibwe. Wanbli attended high school on the Standing Rock Reservation in Fort Yates, North Dakota, and graduated in 1997 from the Chemawa Indian School near Keizer and Salem, Oregon. He went on to Haskell Indian Nations University in Lawrence, Kansas, and the Lac Courte Oreilles Ojibwe Tribal College in Lac Courte Oreilles, Wisconsin. "The best thing that ever happened to me," says Wanbli, "was to go to schools with lots of other Indians, especially at Chemawa and Haskell, where there were Indians from all over the country, and we made lifelong friends." Together with friends from Haskell, he formed a contest-winning drum group, The Tribe, which was lead drum at Stanford University's Pow-Wow 2000, and recorded their second album (T2K) for Canyon Records.

Reflecting on his experience about changing the Westlake logo, Wanbli says he "went from feeling the insult to anger—not too much sorrowness or hurt. I felt like a real loner, being the only real Indian there, or the only Indian with a real Indian perspective. Afterward, it made me feel unique. I had actually done something, accomplished a thing, even this one little thing. It was an enjoyment, a fulfillment. Just me, I had shown them cultural diversity that was in their face all along. I felt good."

On his way to retiring the logo, Wanbli wrote a guest editorial for the school paper, the *Westlake Warcry*:

I feel it is necessary for me to offer my opinion regarding the issue of Indian mascots. This issue means far more to me than anyone else at this school. Every day when I enter this school, I see this ridiculous caricature of an Indian warrior. This parody does little to help with my self-identity, self-concept, or my self-esteem. I am fully aware of the 500 years of oppression that my people faced. And yet every day, I am faced with that continuing oppression. Using Indians as mascots is just another manifestation of the oppression....You cannot continue to oppress me by creating a distorted image of my ancestors and calling it a mascot. We are not your Indian anymore....You cannot continue to distort the history of your oppression and justify demeaning us by calling us your mascots....The next 500 years must be different. We will not continue to participate in our own oppression by ignoring these oppressive issues. You see this means a lot more to me than it does to you.

You say you want to honor my people by using mascots....Why not HONOR our treaties? Why not support the return of the sacred Black Hills to my people? Why not honor Tribal Sovereignty? Why not support a viable economic program to revitalize our Tribal economies to allow us to become self-sufficient? You can honor us in this way. You see it does mean more to me.

We are not your Indian anymore. It is time to unlearn the stereotypes. We must learn to consider each other's feelings and stop doing this to one another simply because that is the way we have always done it. Please no more racism, because it hurts me more than it will ever hurt you. We need a positive change for the good of everyone, especially in OUR school.

ACTIVITY:

Have you ever written a letter of protest or concern about anything? If so, did you receive a response? Was the issue resolved? If so, how?

_____

_____

_____

_____

_____

_____

_____

_____

Write a letter of protest or concern about a "Native" reference in sports, including a concise description of the issue, a brief summary of who you are and how the issue affects you, and your three strongest arguments or points advocating your position.

ACTIVITY:

Start a campaign by encouraging friends and family members to write their own letters, asking them for copies for your file, and even offering to copy and mail their letters for them. (Avoid petitions. They usually are ignored by people who make policy and business decisions.)

J. "Fighting Sioux" in North Dakota

Alvin White (Arikara/Winnebago) is a library aide at the Little Priest Tribal College in Winnebago, Nebraska. He earned a degree in computer science from the University of North Dakota in Grand Forks, where UND's team name, "Fighting Sioux," earned Alvin's lasting enmity. He worked to change the name as a member of BRIDGES, a student organization at UND that objects to "Fighting Sioux" and the behavior it engenders from both fans and foes. They are not alone in their fight. The Campus Committee for Human Rights (CCHR), a faculty and staff organization founded in early 2000 by some fifty-five members, also is devoted to changing the team's name and associated references.

Alvin's position against "Fighting Sioux" was influenced by what he observed as its "negative impact on the children of Natives who attend school there. The children don't understand at the games that it is not they who are being referred to when the crowd starts chanting, 'Sioux Sux! Sioux Sux!' Such turmoil must be going on in a mind so young and I can see where it will affect them for the rest of their lives in a negative way."

The university's team was called the "Flicker Tails" until 1930, when a student wrote to the school newspaper advocating for a change to "Sioux" or "Fighting Sioux." Either name, he reasoned, would strike fear in UND's sports rival, the North Dakota State University "Bison." The letter sparked debate in the paper's pages, according to a historical overview of the name prepared by UND alumnus Michael Saunders. Some students supported the change because of the "savage, warlike spirit" of the Sioux. Others opposed it because Indians were lazy and "had never contributed anything to the history of the State or the school."

"Fighting Sioux" became the team's new name in the fall of 1930 and, as reported in the Saunders chronology, there "was never a mention of honoring Native Americans with the change, but again a reference to the [NDSU] Bison." He chronicles anti-Indian bigotry and protests by Native students at UND, as well as some progress in the 1990s, including the retirement of the "Sammie Sioux" logo and the Chicago hockey team's "Indian Head" symbol. The Saunders account concludes that "as long as the name continues, there will be an atmosphere of harassment toward the Native student population."

In February 2000, UND President Charles Kupchella appointed sixteen commissioners to study the "Fighting Sioux" issue. His choice of appointees drew immediate fire from the Campus Committee for Human Rights, which pointed out that two former state governors are on the panel, but no tribal leaders were appointed. CCHR also noted that, while UND alumni and athletic interests are well represented, the commission does not include Native or multicultural studies educators. In their next meeting, the UND commissioners focused on donations that might be lost to the school if it changed the team's name and

alienated alumni, according to the *Grand Forks Herald* (June 6, 2000). "Without substantial contributions from alumni, UND will have difficulty maintaining itself as a credible higher education institution," said Allen Olson, a commissioner and former North Dakota Governor, as quoted in the *Herald* article.

The main donation the commissioners were concerned about was that of former "Fighting Sioux" hockey player Ralph Engelstad, who threatened to stop construction on the $100 million UND hockey arena he was buying if UND dropped the team name. The commissioners elbowed each other out of the way in order to be the first to vote against changing "Fighting Sioux." A collector of Nazi memorabilia, Engelstad was found too crass for Las Vegas, where he made his fortune in gambling operations. Nevada's gaming commission once fined him $1.5 million for throwing two parties at his casino to celebrate Adolph Hitler's birthday. Engelstad had allies in some UND students, who made posters against the Native students who wanted to get rid of the team name. The "Fighting Sioux" boosters wrote, "Go back to the res, or work @ the Casion, Prarie Nigga [sic]."

Jesse Taken Alive, former chairman and tribal council member of the nearby Standing Rock Sioux Tribe, appealed to the UND commissioners to change the name, saying that name-calling only leads to more name-calling. He showed the commissioners a copy of an obscene sign from a UND–NDSU football game that depicted a "Native" person engaged in a sex act with a bison. "Sioux Sux" was the sign's caption. "What can be done to stop this kind of thing?" asked Taken Alive. "This is what is so dehumanizing."

"My own belief is that committees are often smokescreens that are ineffectual," says Alvin White, "and that pressure should be put upon the president from many state and national groups to ensure that change is accomplished." Alvin first perceived anti-Indian racism when he was four years old in Denver, Colorado, and witnessed "Native men being beaten by police with billy clubs." At age sixteen, in Sioux City, Iowa, Alvin, his brother, and his brother's wife went to a Burger King. "We are both dark and his wife is light skinned [and] the young white lady behind the counter turns to my brother's wife and asks, 'What would you like?' She replied, 'Why don't you ask them? They were here first.' I'm glad she was thinking on her feet and the cashier had no recourse but to ask what we wanted. It still amazed me that that attitude exists in the service industry of a franchise. That wouldn't happen in Denver, but it did in Iowa."

And in North Dakota? Alvin says that "it was difficult to judge the opinions of my classmates in reference to the 'Fighting Sioux' issue. Since many students on the UND campus are noncommunicative anyway—no smiles and few Hi's when walking on campus. It often makes me feel isolated or as perceived as a troublemaker." Despite Alvin's best efforts as a student, UND clings to "Fighting Sioux." The school's hockey arena named for Engelstad opened shortly after its benefactor's death in late 2000, and the new UND basketball and volleyball center named after Engelstad's wife opened in 2004.

ACTIVITY:

Write slogans and design buttons, stickers, or T-shirts for campaigns to retire "Native" references in sports.

Here is a design of a sticker used in campaigns nationwide to eliminate "Redskins" as team names.

RESPECT NATIVE PEOPLES

REDSKINS

CHANGE THE NAME

Other campaigns are using buttons and stickers with the slogan People, Not Mascots.

Your ideas for slogans and designs:

_____

_____

_____

_____

_____

_____

_____

_____

_____

Suggested slogans:

WE ARE NOT "REDSKINS" / WE ARE NATIVE PEOPLES

WE ARE NOT MASCOTS / WE ARE INDIGENOUS PEOPLES

Sample slogans, using Native languages:

In Cheyenne: **NA-SAA-MAE'HO'EEVE / NA-TSIS-TA**

In English: **I AM NOT A "REDSKIN" / I AM CHEYENNE**

In Mohawk: **IAN'ITEOSSERONNIRONNO / I'IONKWEHONWE NONE**

In English: **I AM NOT EUROPEAN / I AM A REAL HUMAN BEING**

Does your language have a word for "mascot"? In the Cheyenne language, there is no concept for a human mascot, so "pet" would be the nearest word:

In Cheyenne: **NA-SAA-MA-HTOTSE / NA-XAMAA-VO'ESTANE-HEVE**

In English: **I AM NOT YOUR PET / I AM A NATIVE HUMAN BEING**

Your ideas for slogans using your heritage language or other Native languages:

_____

_____

_____

_____

_____

_____

_____

_____

K. Honored?

In concluding this report, the final word is given to Adriane Shown Harjo, who is a performance poet and visual artist, also known as ASH. She is Cheyenne and Hodulgee Muscogee, lives in Washington, D.C., and is the daughter of this writer. Adriane wrote the following poem "about ten years ago, but I really started on it when I was a teenager." Her poem "honored?" premiered in the 1999 DC Arts Center's production of *fire & ash*, which also was performed in Portland, Oregon, at Indian Art Northwest 1999 and at Freak Planet 2000.

honored?

navajo, cherokee, dodge dakota, chevy, cheyenne
winnebago chieftain rv?
where is the zulu pick-up truck
hasidic honda, semite sedan, cholo camper, la raza?
where are they? 'cause here i am, still alive
in case you've forgotten & i know that you have

cleveland indians, washington redskins
atlanta braves
chop, chop, chop, whoo, whoo, whoo
should i feel honored? funny, i don't
not with a stadium full of whites
smeared in grease paints
crowned with primary colored turkey feathers
new jersey jew boys, detroit dagos
cincinnati spics, nebraska niggers
no? well where are they?
it's a case of mistaken identity
i'm not a sag card bearing hollywood Indian
but that's me up on the screen
bent at the waist, dancing around with bugs bunny
i'm the fat bellied moron in something near a g-string
stern arms crossed over chest
limp, frayed feather hanging
from headband over eyes
loosely woven braids over ears
papoose strapped over humped back
aren't you over it yet?
frito bandito finally heard the alarm & woke up
little sambo finally got pants & got to grow up
while we are still pictured sitting cross-legged
in parking lots full of bigoted cars
drinking fire water
crazy horse malt liquor, thunderbird fortified wine

should i feel honored? dare i find offense?
eh, senor speedy mouse?
i ask you, ms. jemima. got any clue, buckwheat?
cartooned caricatures
tell me chief, degraded? honest in'jun, dehumanized?
now why should a little squaw like me
feel anything but honored?
along with scores of other indian women
raped & mutilated, at least enslaved
hair scalped off, vaginas carved out
slipped over the saddle horns
of those riding off into the sunset
yippie-ki-yea-away
away from the living, breathing, writhing, dying
their great-grand-daughters barely alive
though survived
but it isn't really what you'd call living, now is it?

impoverished broken treaty reservation lands
it's not thousands or even hundreds of miles away
among others, it's pine ridge, bad lands of north &
    south dakota
lakota, nakota, sioux
it's not ethiopia, bangladesh or the outskirts of korea
it's bi-coastal & renamed plains
it's what used to be my own backyard
& what now remains, not yours, now yours
do you think sally struthers will campaign for & save me?
answer my prayers with rice & meal & medical supplies?
turn my life around with a mere tax deductible
forty-five cents a day?
cure poverty? diabetes?
give me a lack of lactose tolerable diet
without white rice, white flour, white sugar or
cow's milk? moo, moo, moo, where's the cure
'cause here i am

oh, great spirit, am i still alive?
history books barely mention so
saturday afternoon cartoons don't say it's so
car manufacturers just won't believe
& neither will dear walt disney
& i'm starting to wonder if the authors may be right
where are they?
'cause here i am
still alive
even if you have forgotten
& i've finally come to the understanding
that you have

—Adriane Shown Harjo, *fire & ash* (1999)

Decolonizing NAGPRA

James Riding In

A. Repatriation Is Unfinished Business

Decolonizing the Native American Graves Protection and Repatriation Act (NAGPRA) of 1990 is vital for bringing closure to one of the most gruesome, horrific, and divisive chapters in the history of Indians–United States relations. Before NAGPRA, the U.S. government gave the scientific community, along with other grave robbers, virtually complete authority to loot and plunder our graves without fear of punishment under the law. Native Americans, defined by NAGPRA as American Indians and Native Hawaiians, never approved of these acts nor surrendered our dead. The perpetrators disregarded our views, beliefs, and rights because colonialism instills the colonizer with a notion of absolute entitlement—a notion that denies the colonized the respect and rights afforded to other humans. An industry composed of museums, the disciplines of anthropology and archaeology, professional organizations, and individual scholars, sprouted and flourished from the sacrilege and desecration. The offenders placed the human remains, funerary objects, and other items in federally funded institutions, of which the Smithsonian Institution is perhaps the most notable example.

Recently, museum attitudes have changed somewhat, because of our resistance to the abusive treatment of our dead and because of our calls for justice. It was during the late 1960s that U.S. society took notice of Indigenous voices of protest regarding the immoral, sacrilegious, and rampant abuses committed against our dead. Our movement conveys a simple message rooted in the language of spiritual outrage: We want our ancestors returned, or repatriated. Our activism challenges the privileged status that archaeologists, physical anthropologists, museum curators, and others had enjoyed through racism and discriminatory laws. Put another way, our movement is imbued with a decolonization philosophy. Slowly, our efforts changed public attitudes and consciousness, paving the way for national reform. Congress responded to our pleas for justice, burial rights, religious freedom, and repatriation when it enacted the National Museum of the American Indian Act (NMAIA) in 1989 and NAGPRA the following year.

Both NMAIA, which applies to the Smithsonian Institution, and NAGPRA, which pertains to other museums and agencies that receive federal funding, represent major accomplishments in the Indigenous struggle against contemporary colonialism and oppression. Those laws establish a legal avenue for Native Americans to repatriate, or regain legal control over, stolen bodies and funerary objects, and to protect sacred burial sites from non-Indian incursions. The laws also criminalize the selling of human remains. Although Native Americans have repatriated more than twenty-seven thousand sets of human remains, tens of thousands of other ancestral remains still sit on museum shelves out of reach for repatriation because institutions have not assigned them a culturally affiliated status. What this scheme of labeling declares is that human remains from old, isolated, or disappeared peoples have no cultural ties with present-day Indians, and so are not bound by the same ethical and legal standards that govern the treatment of human remains from federally acknowledged tribes. This way of thinking, sponsored by the scientific establishment, encroaches dangerously on Native concepts of kinship and ancestry. Although a few museums have adopted policies that enable Native Americans to repatriate all human remains in their collections, the war clearly is not over.

NAGPRA also enables Native Americans to repatriate some types of cultural objects. This chapter, however, only discusses human remains and funerary objects, not other cultural objects.

B. Vision and Purpose

This chapter has three purposes. First, it focuses on the relationships of Indigenous Peoples with U.S. law and policy, archaeologists, and museum curators, and how this interaction has affected our burial and religious rights. Second, it examines problems we face vis-à-vis the imperialist assumptions and practices of archaeology when trying to repatriate ancestral human remains classified as "culturally unidentifiable." These are human remains that supposedly lack a cultural relationship with present-day Indian nations and people. We repatriation activists do not accept this argument because it is our belief that Indians of the present are descendents of those who came before us on this continent. The phrase *imperial archaeology* used in this chapter denotes the intimate links between federal law and policy and those fields of science (that is, archaeology and physical anthropology) that have engaged in repeated acts of grave looting and pillaging. Finally, it offers solutions for resolving the controversies surrounding the disposition of human remains still in museums.

Addressing the shortcomings of NAGPRA in a forceful and culturally sensitive manner is an important mission of the decolonization mission of us Indigenous Peoples. If we accept the notion of scientists that the remains of our ancestors are specimens for study and that we evolved from apes, we will have moved a giant step closer towards assimilation. If the scientists want to argue that they came from apes, I will accept their position without question. When it comes to the treatment of our deceased relatives, many of them have acted in an apish manner. However, all of our nations and Native Hawaiians have stories about our origins and burial traditions that we must honor and respect.

This chapter is primarily about my experiences in and knowledge of the repatriation struggle. You should be aware that grave looting has affected all Indigenous nations throughout the world. This means that there are many accounts and many different views about how this problem should be resolved.

C. The Repatriation Struggle

My involvement in the repatriation struggle stems from my Pawnee citizenship, including the commitment I have for my people's welfare, my spirituality, and the environment of protest that challenged this country's racism and oppressive practices during my adolescent years. The reburial and graves protection movement that began during the 1960s had as its core principle the decolonization of laws and policies that sanctioned grave looting. This goal continues to guide our efforts. The philosophical underpinnings of the Indian movement, often called the Red Power Movement, that surfaced during the late 1960s and continues to this day, not only shaped my activist outlook toward life, but it has also influenced my cultural and intellectual development. The movement called for Indians to marry Indians; to reclaim our cultures; to defend our spirituality, lands, cultures, treaties, and sovereignty; and to confront anti-Indianism in all of its racist forms. I have attempted to do these things in my personal and professional life.

These experiences have provided me an outlook that has served me well in the dirty business of decolonizing imperial archaeology and NAGPRA. My involvement with the repatriation movement began during the late 1980s, before the enactment of federal repatriation laws. Before then, I had obtained some knowledge of the grave looting and plundering operations of archaeologists. While in the service in 1970 during the Vietnam War, I visited the Smithsonian and looked in utter dismay and disgust at its public display of Indian crania. That image sticks with me to this day. As a graduate student at the University of California at Los Angeles during the 1980s, I helped organize campus protests by Indian students and our supporters that called attention to the holding of human remains there. Although few in number, we boldly confronted archaeologists, physical anthropologists, and their supporters at forums convened to convince us that the study of human remains held important information for revealing secrets about the Indian past. We defiantly maintained that oral traditions provided our understanding of our place in the universe, that their immoral and unethical research must cease, and that they should develop a plan for returning the physical remains to the next of kin for proper burial. However, there was no legal mandate in place then that required universities to repatriate human remains. Nothing was done, but we set a tone at UCLA for what was to follow.

ACTIVITY:

What is the origin story of your people?

_____

_____

_____

_____

_____

_____

_____

_____

_____

_____

In your culture, what are the proper and improper ways to treat deceased relatives? Can these matters be discussed?

_____

_____

_____

_____

_____

How would you feel if someone disrupted the grave of one of your relatives?

_____

_____

_____

What would you do if you found out that someone had looted the grave of one of your relatives?

_____

_____

_____

_____

At about the same time, UCLA administrators developed a plan to move the American Indian Studies Center from the third floor of Campbell Hall, a historic place where student protests during the late 1960s gave rise to the formation of American Indian, Asian American, Chicano, and African American studies, to the basement of Haines Hall, a dreary site where Native human remains had been stored. Native students, faculty, and staff successfully resisted the planned move using the cultural argument that Haines Hall contained spirits that could harm the living.

As the battles against archaeological desecration and administrative fiat raged at UCLA, the Pawnee Nation had begun to question the Nebraska State Historical Society and Smithsonian Institution regarding Pawnee remains in their collections. My work as a repatriation researcher began when the Native American Rights Fund asked me, on behalf of the Pawnee Nation, to investigate the identity of six human crania at the Smithsonian listed by accession records as Pawnee.

When the Pawnee leadership requested information about those remains, a Smithsonian official denied that the skulls were Pawnees, saying that many Indian raiders had been killed in Kansas and it would be impossible to positively identify the skulls in question as Pawnees. My research acquainted me with the dark, secretive history of white America's treatment of our dead. By examining documentation held at the Smithsonian and the federal archives, my research determined that those remains belonged to six Pawnees, just discharged from the U.S. Army, who had been killed in 1869 by U.S. soldiers and settlers near Mulberry Creek in Kansas. Following a lengthy search for the bodies, a Fort Harker surgeon had the heads severed and sent to the Army Medical Museum for craniometric study. This study was published with other documents and the testimony that contributed to the enactment of NMAIA.

Those experiences at UCLA and the Smithsonian not only revealed the arrogance of imperial archaeology, but they also gave me direction that has influenced my professional endeavors. Through recurring dreams during this time came a clear, resounding message that I should dedicate my life to the Indigenous struggle against scientific inquiry with Indian remains. While at the Smithsonian in 1989, gut-wrenching feelings of anguish, pain, and oppression had overwhelmed me as I walked through an area where thousands of human remains were stored in drawers. At that point, I began to think of my work as "liberation research." Liberation research is a methodical investigation into historical and oral sources for the purposes of decolonizing the law and freeing the incarcerated souls of Native Peoples trapped in an unburied state. Since then, I became a committed activist scholar. Working on behalf of my people, I compiled information about Pawnee objects of cultural patrimony and sacred objects at Chicago's Field Museum, the Denver Art Museum, and the Colorado Historical Society. I have written various studies and given numerous presentations across the nation about NAGPRA and repatriation issues.

D. Participants in the Controversy

NAGPRA leaves unresolved the fate of "culturally unidentifiable" human remains now in museums and federal repositories. Representing perhaps as many as two hundred thousand individuals, these human remains are an ongoing source of friction between the repatriation advocates and our pro-science adversaries. We do not know the exact number of remains still in museums, because many of those institutions with human-remains collections have not completed inventories. Without those lists, furthermore, it is difficult for repatriation initiatives to proceed.

Museums, supported by the scientific community, often claim that present-day Indians are not related to those remains because they want to keep large collections for the purpose of study. That claim, however, is false. Indigenous cultures did not simply live in isolation and vanish. Since the beginning of time, peoples of those cultures intermingled with one another through trading, kinship, marital, war, and social ties. Through these connections, members of those so-called culturally unidentifiable cultures passed their genes and cultures on to us.

At center stage in this controversy is the NAGPRA Review Committee, which was established "to monitor and review the implementation of the inventory and identification process and repatriation activities." The secretary of the Interior appoints Review Committee members from nominations by Indian tribes, Native Hawaiian organizations, traditional Native American religious leaders, national museum organizations, and scientific organizations. From 1996 to 2001, the Review Committee considered four sets of recommendations drafted by the National Park Service (NPS) without endorsing any of them. In June 2002, NPS presented another set of proposed regulations to the Review Committee that prompted new protest from the reburial advocates. If adopted, these regulations would empower individual institutions, without Native consultation, to make the final determination regarding the disposition of all human remains in question in their collections.

ACTIVITY:

How do your cultural values and beliefs shape how you view the issue of culturally unidentified remains?

_____

_____

_____

_____

_____

Based on your cultural beliefs and values, do you think it is more important that Indigenous remains are reburied by some Indigenous group, or do you think they should only be reburied by the nation able to prove a direct ancestral line to the remains in question? In other words, would you rather have culturally unidentifiable remains kept in institutions waiting for a time when cultural affiliation might be proven, or have them be reburied earlier by some Indigenous nation?

_____

_____

Should the United States demand the repatriation of U.S. service personnel who were killed in Vietnam, Korea, and other places around the world? Why do you feel this way?

_____

_____

_____

_____

_____

Fearing that this proposal undermines our ability to repatriate and rebury our ancestors by raising the interests of science above those of Native Americans, we protested vigorously, giving testimony at the NAG-PRA Review Committee hearings, writing to the secretary of the Interior, and presenting the matter to the National Congress of American Indians, which responded with a resolution opposing the recommendations. The latest set of proposed regulations now stipulates that the institutions must offer to repatriate human remains in their collections. Although this proposal is more acceptable than the previous one, there are complex interests and players still involved in the controversy.

E. Three Basic Schools of Thought

Three basic schools of thought come to bear on discussions over the disposition of culturally unidentified human remains. Representatives of each of them present testimony before the NAGPRA Review Committee and produce scholarship to promote their perspectives. The first camp, to which I belong, takes the position that all human remains and funerary objects in museums and federal agencies must be returned to the next of kin, or to a coalition of Native Americans, for proper reburial. Composed of traditional spiritual leaders, grassroots activists, scholars, and others, we draw our guidance from spiritual beliefs, Native concepts of justice, and a deep awareness of the historical relationship between Indian nations and the federal government. Arising from a 2001 meeting of American Indians at the Arizona State University's College of Law, the Committee for the Disposition of the Culturally Unidentified Human Remains (consisting of Suzan Shown Harjo, Walter Echo-Hawk, Pete Jimerson, Rebecca Tsosie, Mervin Wright, Kunani Nihipali, and Ho'oipo Kalaena'auao Pa, myself, and a few others) has become a key player in the battle. We emphasize that NAGPRA is Indian law, and that scientific grave looting is immoral, unethical, and illegal, as well as a desecration and a sacrilege. We assert that there is no such thing as culturally unaffiliated human remains and that museums and federal agencies acquired them by acts of theft. The National Congress of American Indians, tribal leaders, and others support our position and efforts.

Members of the second school, which I would call the scientific establishment, argue that human remains and funerary objects are so valuable to scientific study that the repatriation and reburial of those collections would destroy data necessary for unraveling mysteries of the past. These archaeologists, physical anthropologists, museum curators, and professional organizations often characterize us as irrational religious fundamentalists who hold antiscience perspectives. To them, the taking of human remains occurred legally under preexisting policies and laws, and their scientific interest in them trumps any ethical or legal claims made by Native Americans.

They argue that when enacting NAGPRA, Congress sought to strike a balance between the interests of science and Native Americans. That compromise, they assert, provides only for the repatriation of human remains culturally connected to present-day Native Americans by lineal descent and cultural affiliation. To them, those human remains from older cultures that cannot be linked to modern Native Americans belong to science.

Not only do they reject our positions, but they belittle, mock, and ridicule us as well. During the 1980s, for example, a member of the opposition used the term URPies (Universal Repatriation Proponents) to slander us. During that same decade, the president of the Society of American Archaeology (SAA), in a tasteless rehashing of the old Indian-killer quip, remarked that the only good Indian is an unrepatriated one. Others attack colleagues who "sell out," or hold a sympathetic (that is, an unscientific) attitude to arguments about universal repatriation. In an August 26, 1999, letter to the NAGPRA Review Committee, G. A. Clark, head of the archaeology division of the American Anthropological Association, blusters:

> I have no patience with, nor sympathy for, NAGPRA and the political correctness that underlies it. Moreover, I am deeply embarrassed for, and ashamed of, American archaeology and physical anthropology. One might've thought the various professional societies would've done a better job contesting this lunacy when it was possible to do so. Academics are not very politically adept, however, and when erstwhile Smithsonian Secretary Robert Adams agreed to repatriate the Smithsonian's skeletal collections, it knocked the pins out from under any efforts the SAA and AAPA [American Association of Physical Anthropologists] might've undertaken to prevent it. This is what happens when politics is allowed to take precedence over rational and disinterested evaluation of the credibility of knowledge claims about the human past.

Clark had no fear of articulating his feelings, but others take a more subtle approach.

The 1986 policy statement of the Society of American Archaeology declares: "Whatever their ultimate disposition, all human remains should receive appropriate scientific study, should be responsibly and carefully conserved, and should be accessible only for legitimate scientific or educational purposes." This position unquestionably favors a policy that would result in the retention of thousands of human remains in museums, leaving the older ones especially vulnerable. Another organization, the American Association of Physical Anthropologists, asserts that "when a clear relationship of shared group identity cannot be traced …then those remains should be considered part of the biological and cultural heritage of all people."

The third school advocates a compromise between Indians and science. These academics, museum officials, and federal agencies hold that culturally unidentified human remains should be subjected to scientific study before they are reburied. Like their counterparts in group two, they often accept the Western worldview of the origins of life and of human migrations into the Americas. They want Indigenous Peoples to accept their views as well. It could be argued that those with this attitude who work in museums with collections of human remains stand for holding our ancestors hostage until we comply with their wishes.

The mainstream media, along with documentary production companies, tends to fluctuate between favoring the views of the second and third groups, while tribal newspapers and the Indian press, especially *Indian Country Today*, often support the view of the first school.

ACTIVITY:

Do you feel that those scientists who oppose Indian views on the matter of repatriation understand Native American cultures and beliefs? Do they care about Indian cultures and beliefs the same way that you do? Explain.

_____

_____

_____

_____

_____

The scientists who opposed repatriation and who favor studying human remains before repatriation occurs have a colonizer's mindset. Do you agree or disagree with this statement? Why?

_____

_____

_____

_____

_____

F. Ways to Decolonize NAGPRA

As Indians, the most basic aspect of decolonization calls for us to accept individual and group responsibility for the fate of our ancestors. Failure to do so suggests that we have either been assimilated by accepting non-Indian intellectual, moral, and legal authority or that we have not acted in an appropriate manner towards ancestors. We will have succumbed to the power of imperial archaeology at the expense of our burial rights and spirituality. We will have become intellectually and religiously colonized. We cannot assume that others, including Indians who work in tribal and institutional settings, will act in a culturally appropriate manner in repatriation matters. In fact, some of our relatives who work in public and private institutions collaborate with the forces of colonialism and imperial archaeology. They, along with their mentors, use a "missionary" approach that encourages Native Americans to pursue educational studies and careers in archaeology and physical anthropology, thereby giving these disciplines a kind of surface Indigenousness and legitimacy in Indian matters.

We must empower ourselves in this struggle by expressing our traditional knowledge and beliefs. We can never forget that when those who came before us buried their loved ones, our ancestors, they did so with the intent that the bodies would remain forever within the sanctity of the grave. We must reject the use of such terms of imperial archaeology as "archaeological populations" and "archaeological sites." These expressions imply that our relatives lived for the benefit of future archaeologists, and that our cemeteries are merely rich fields of potential knowledge.

I propose that to decolonize NAGPRA, we must:

- Accept individual and collective responsibility for the fate and disposition of our ancestors' remains that are in museums, federal agencies, and still in the womb of Mother Earth
- Understand traditional knowledge and customs regarding the proper treatment of our dead
- Comprehend the history of scientific grave looting and its relationship to other aspects of colonialism
- Reject those scientific methodologies and principles that violate our burial rights, values, and beliefs
- Challenge imperial archaeology and colonialism through collective resistance
- Understand NAGPRA and repatriation processes so that this statute will indeed be Indian legislation
- Work cooperatively with our nations and organizations in repatriation initiatives
- Join coalitions whose purpose is to reclaim and rebury our ancestral remains
- Launch protests to attract public attention to the problem if the other methods fail.

There is a way to make NAGPRA work in its current form in terms of repatriating the so-called culturally unidentifiable human remains. This method involves coalitions composed of official representatives of Native nations coming together and making "shared group identity" claims to remains, based on oral history, migration patterns, and geography. In 1998, amid a bitter controversy surrounded by allegations of mistreatment and the destruction of human remains at the University of Nebraska, Lincoln, university officials invited Pemina Yellow Bird, a committed Sahnish (Arikara) repatriation activist, and me to serve as NAGPRA consultants on behalf of the university. In this capacity, we attended a meeting with representatives of fourteen Indian nations with a historical connection to Nebraska, and UNL officials. During a lunch break, with Pemina taking the lead, several of us drafted an agreement calling for the UNL to repatriate all of the human remains and funerary objects in its collections to the Indian nations in attendance by virtue of a shared group identity relationship with those remains. The agreement also called for UNL to cover the cost of research so that Indian nations could determine if they had a cultural affiliation with any of the remains. It stipulated that a monument be erected near the site where UNL staff had incinerated Indian human remains several decades earlier. Finally, it asked UNL to pay the cost of reburying the remains. When UNL officials, seeking to end the public relations nightmare surrounding the situation, accepted the terms of the agreement, tribal people in attendance cheered loudly while others sang a Lakota song.

ACTIVITY:

What is your Indigenous nation's tradition regarding contact and/or relationship with the dead?

_____

_____

_____

_____

In October 2002, with many Indians and non-Indians in attendance, the monument was dedicated. Its inscription reads:

> This memorial honors an unknown number of Native Americans whose remains had been taken from their graves for the inclusion in the University of Nebraska's archeological collections. In the mid-1960s, these remains were incinerated in a facility located near this site, in a manner totally inconsistent with the beliefs and practices of the tribes of the Great Plains. In 1998, UNL Chancellor James Moeser and tribal representatives agreed to set aside this site as a memorial to honor these Native Americans and to remind future generations of this cultural injustice. Memory of these events must be more than symbolic, for people who forget the past are bound to repeat its mistakes. May we learn from this and treat all persons with honor and respect.

Several years later, in northern Nebraska, we reburied more than eight hundred sets of human remains and funerary objects on a beautiful bluff overlooking the Missouri and Niobrara Rivers. It was a sad and beautiful spring day.

In 2001 in Denver, the Colorado Historical Society (CHS) sponsored a meeting that brought together scholars and tribal leaders, including repatriation officers, to discuss ways in which research could establish a cultural affiliation between the representatives of Indian nations in attendance and more than three hundred sets of human remains, classified as culturally unidentifiable, in the CHS collections. The non-Indians dominated the discussion, so the Indian participants asked them to leave the room. When the non-Indians were invited to return several hours later, tribal representatives presented them with a repatriation accord based on a shared group identity claim they had drafted following the basic model of the UNL agreement. CHS officials accepted the agreement, which stipulated that CHS would cover the cost of the reburial, and a reburial took place several months later.

Despite these successful efforts, the truth is that under NAGPRA, museums and federal agencies have the last word in matters pertaining to the disposition of Native remains. Not surprisingly, repatriation opponents, whether in federal, state, or private organizations, have negated reburial initiatives. In Nevada, the Northern Paiutes claimed the remains of a ten-thousand-year-old mummified body called Spirit Cave Man, who was found in the 1940s. After hearing the Paiutes present historical, ethnographic, and archaeological testimony, the NAGPRA Review Committee recognized the cultural affiliation of the Spirit Cave Man with the claimants. However, the Bureau of Reclamation, a federal agency under the Department of the Interior responsible for managing millions of acres of federal lands in twelve western states, rejects this determination. As a result, Spirit Cave Man remains unburied in an Idaho repository.

Kennewick Man is another controversy involving a shared group identity claim that has gained widespread media attention. In 1996 near Kennewick, Washington, two men stumbled on a very old set of human remains on lands controlled by the Army Corps of Engineers (COE). The 9,300-year-old bones quickly became the center of an intense legal battle between scientists, who want to study the remains, and the federal government, which had ruled that the physical remains belong to Northwest tribes who claim the remains as an ancient ancestor and want to bury them. When a physical anthropologist declared that the remains had "Caucasoid" features, a media frenzy ensued, including declarations that the man was of European origin and that Indians were not the first Americans. Rejecting this view, the Colville, Nez Perce, Umatilla, Yakama, and Wanapum governments claimed the Ancient One, as they came to call him, on the basis of a shared-group-identity cultural affiliation. Their oral traditions indicate that they had originated in the area where they now live, had always been there, and had once looked different than they do now. Scientists want to study the physical remains to see if it represents some unknown source of migration to North America apart from the dominant scientific theory of a land bridge migration from Asia to North America.

When a few scientists filed a legal suit to stop the repatriation, a federal judge referred the matter to the Department of the Interior (DOI) for resolution. On September 21, 2000, after reviewing the evidence and congressional intent, Secretary of the Interior Bruce Babbitt held that "Section 12 of NAGPRA recognizes the unique legal relationship between the United States and Indian tribes. Given its purpose and this recognition, DOI construes the statute as Indian legislation. Therefore, any ambiguities in the language of the statute must be resolved liberally in favor of Indian interests."

Babbitt upheld the COE's decision, but the scientists, supported by the SAA, AAPA, and others, blocked the repatriation of the Ancient One by filing another lawsuit. Among other legal arguments, they claimed that Babbitt and the COE had violated their First Amendment right because the Constitution allows them the right to study the remains. In *Bonnichsen v. United States*, issued on August 30, 2002, Judge Jelderk launched a scathing attack that denounced the actions of Babbitt and the COE. "Allowing study is fully consistent with applicable statutes and regulations, which clearly intended to make archaeological study information available to the public through scientific research," he declared. Jelderk insisted that the COE had made a "hasty decision" to recognize the tribal claim to the Ancient One. Evading the intent of Congress, he dismissed the shared-group-identity relations of the claimant tribes with the Ancient One and ordered the federal government to allow scientists to study the remains. Essentially, Jelderk elevated the rights of science beyond the claimant Indian nations in this case, undermining the intent of Congress by refusing to apply the rules of construction to laws involving Indians. In doing so, he staked out a position that has the potential to undermine NAGPRA's promise to rebury all human remains.

The claimant Indian nations appealed Jelderk's decision to the Ninth Circuit Court of Appeals, but lost again. The decision prevents five Indian nations who claim the Ancient One as their ancestor from reburying him. Given the conservative makeup of the U.S. Supreme Court, it would be unwise to seek justice there in this matter. Since the 1970s, the Supreme

Court has handed down a series of anti-Indian decisions that have undermined tribal sovereignty and endangered our religious freedom. Others feel that Congress, which is friendlier to Indians, should amend NAGPRA so that Indian nations can rebury older remains.

ACTIVITY:

In your opinion, who made the correct decision, Babbitt or Jelderk? Why?

_____

_____

_____

_____

_____

_____

_____

G. Conclusion

NAGPRA creates a legal avenue for American Indians and Native Hawaiians to reclaim our lost human rights. Museums still hold tens of thousands of Indigenous human remains, along with funerary objects, classified by them as culturally unidentifiable. Through the decolonization of NAGPRA, we demand the right to repatriate the remains and funerary objects of all of our disinterred ancestors held in a state of spiritual imprisonment.

We hold firmly that ancestral remains taken for scientific study is an infringement on our spirituality and burial rights. Some of us feel that the spirit of a deceased individual is associated with the physical remains, and that disinterment disrupts their spiritual journey. Traditionally, relatives and friends often place items considered necessary in the afterlife alongside the body of our deceased loved ones. Realizing that the dead possess a sacredness that encompasses our values and beliefs, our cultures have acceptable ways of acting while in cemeteries and in the presence of the deceased. Our burial places are sacred sites, and tampering with

the dead is considered an act of desecration and sacrilege, if not outright witchcraft. Many of us stress that what affects the dead also impacts the living. We reject the contention that the investigations of scientists using the remains of our ancestors is Indian research, because these studies are rooted in values of Western science that ignore, belittle, and trivialize our traditions and spirituality by placing our history in the context of an evolutionist paradigm.

At the December 2001 meeting at Arizona State University's law school, the Native American participants drafted an affirmative declaration, filled with the decolonized principles of group and individual responsibility, and addressing the issue of our ancestors still to be returned to the womb of Mother Earth, spirituality, and justice. The preamble to these recommendations contains a declaration of Indian and Native Hawaiian ownership of the contested human remains. The recommendations state:

1. Culturally unidentifiable Native American human remains are culturally affiliated with contemporary Native peoples, including federally recognized tribes,

non-federally recognized tribes, Native Alaskan peoples, and Native Hawaiian people.

2. All Native American human remains and associated funerary objects, including those deemed "culturally unidentifiable," shall be under the ownership and control of contemporary Native peoples.

3. All "culturally unidentifiable" Native American human remains shall be speedily repatriated to Native peoples in accordance with procedures to be determined by contemporary Native American groups.

4. All scientific study of "culturally unidentifia[ble] American human remains shall immediately [cease].

5. The federal government shall be responsible fo[r] the costs of this repatriation.

What we ask for is a simple matter of justice. In order for us to decolonize ourselves, it is essential that we learn, uphold, and defend our values, beliefs, and sovereignty.

ACTIVITY:

How would you resolve the conflict over the so-called culturally unidentified human remains?

_____

_____

_____

_____

_____

_____

What have you learned about the Native American repatriation struggle?

_____

_____

_____

_____

_____

_____

How might this be applied to your own nation's struggle with repatriation?

_____

_____

_____

_____

_____

_____

H. Suggested Resources

The following websites may be helpful in finding out more information about the status of your tribal nation's remains.

http://www.arrowheads.com/burials.htm: Update of Compilation of State Repatriation, Reburial and Grave Protection Laws (July 1997)

http://web.cast.uark.edu/other/nps/nacd/: National NAGPRA online database

http://www.cr.nps.gov/nagpra/: National NAGPRA website

http://www.pbs.org/wotp/nagpra/: "Who Owns the Past? The American Indian Struggle for Control of their Ancestral Remains"

I. Suggested Readings

C. Roger Echo-Hawk and Walter R. Echo-Hawk, *Battlefields and Burial Grounds: The Indian Struggle to Protect Ancestral Graves in the United States* (Minneapolis, MN: Lerner Publications, 1994).

Kenn Harper, *Give Me My Father's Body: The Life of Minik, the New York Eskimo* (South Royalton, VT: Steerforth Press, 2000).

Devon Mihesuah, ed., *Repatriation Reader: Who Owns American Indian Remains?* (Lincoln: University of Nebraska Press, 2000).

James Riding In, "Our Dead Are Never Forgotten: American Indian Struggles for Burial Rights." In *"They Made Us Many Promises": The American Indian Experience, 1524 to the Present*, edited by Philip Weeks (Wheeling, IL: Harland Davidson, 2002).

James Riding In, "Six Pawnee Crania: The Historical and Contemporary Significance of the Massacre and Decapitation of Pawnee Indians in 1869." *American Indian Culture and Research Journal* 16, no. 2 (1992):101–17.

J. Glossary

anti-Indianism: hostile feelings and actions by others towards Indigenous Peoples

archaeology: the scientific study of the life and culture of the past through the examination of dwellings, graves, tools, and other items, usually dug up from the ground

canons of construction: interpreting laws in ways that favor Indians

Caucasoid: having characteristics of Europeans

craniometric studies: studies conducted in the name of science designed to prove the superiority of white people by measuring the size of skulls

culture: beliefs, customs, practices, and social behavior of a particular people or nation

culturally unidentifiable remains: human remains that supposedly lack a cultural relationship with present-day Indian nations and people

cultural patrimony: a term in NAGPRA that refers to cultural objects that are central to a people's identity and culture

desecration: the act of damaging something sacred or do something that is offensive to the religious nature of something

disinter: to dig up or take a dead body from a grave

funerary objects: items placed in a grave for spiritual purposes

imperial archaeology: intimate links between federal law and policy and those fields of science (that is, archaeology and physical anthropology) that have engaged in repeated acts of grave looting and pillaging

missionary: somebody who attempts to persuade others to join their belief, cause, or movement

museum curator: the head of a museum, exhibit, or collection

Native American Rights Fund: a legal organization that defends the rights of Indigenous Peoples in the United States, including Hawaii

physical anthropology: a division of anthropology that studies the development over time of human physical characteristics and the differences in appearances of people in the world

sacred objects: in NAGPRA, cultural objects that are needed for ongoing religious ceremonies or ceremonies that might be revived in the future

sacrilege: the disrespectful treatment, theft, or destruction of something considered holy or sacred

sovereignty: the exercise of political authority by a particular people or nation

treaties: agreements between sovereign nations

values: accepted principles or standards of a group or an individual

Decolonizing Indigenous Diets

Waziyatawin

A. How Is Our Health Today and How Was It in the Past?

As we examine the health status of our people today, it is clear that our overall health has deteriorated as a consequence of our colonization. Our colonizers taught us to think just the opposite. Our colonizers taught us to believe that our health has improved because of Western medicine, Western foods, and Western technology. In a society that values progress, our colonizers taught us that conditions in the world are perpetually improving, that with each new technological advancement, each new discovery, each new way to utilize resources, each new way to alter the environment, that the world is getting better, that it is advancing. These are all lies. The world, especially environmentally, has dramatically deteriorated to the point where we as human beings are heading on a path toward our own extinction. Microwave ovens and satellite televisions are poor compensation for the extinction of life-forms and a toxic earth.

Prior to the destruction of Indigenous ways of life, our diets were filled with both nutritious and delicious foods that allowed us a better quality of life than we now enjoy. For example, in an article that appeared in the *American Economic Review* in 2001, Richard Steckel and Joseph Prince reported that Plains Indians were the tallest humans in the world in the late 1800s. Because height is a strong indication of nutritional health, by these standards Indigenous Peoples on the plains were some of the healthiest people on the planet. That is until we were ravaged by invasion and

67

colonization. While Plains populations who relied heavily on hunting and gathering were indeed healthy, Indigenous populations throughout the Americas also maintained their health and nutrition by cultivating more than three hundred food crops (many with dozens of varieties or strains). These foods comprise about three-fifths of the food crops now under cultivation in the world. Our rich and varied diets included such basics as numerous varieties of corn, beans, squash, and three thousand varieties of potatoes, planted and harvested by numerous Indigenous Peoples covering a broad geographical sweep in the Western hemisphere, as well as more regional foods such as blueberries, cranberries, wild rice, and black walnuts. As Indigenous foods from the Americas spread across the oceans, they radically transformed the rest of the world through improved nutrition and allowed for tremendous population growth. Populations adopted our Indigenous foods and their diets were dramatically altered; the cuisine of the Italians was transformed by the tomato; that of the Irish, Russians, Germans, and Poles by the potato; the Koreans, Chinese, East Indians, and Hungarians by hot chili peppers; and for millions of people around the world, sweet potatoes, cassava, and amaranth have become dietary mainstays. Other foods widely used today include peanuts, pineapple, sunflowers, vanilla, and of course, chocolate.

In spite of these tremendous food gifts to the world from our lands and peoples, the destruction of our lands and peoples did not cease. Instead, Europeans and Euro-Americans maintained their sense of superiority and forcefully imposed their ways, including their comparatively unhealthy diets, upon us. This has only served to deteriorate the health of our people. Now our people have some of the shortest life spans and highest rates of diseases on the planet. Diseases such as diabetes and heart disease are killing our people. Our bodies clearly have not benefited from colonization.

Modern medicine is also often said to be continuously improving our quality of life. This idea must be critically examined. Indigenous knowledge regarding medicine and healing was extremely sophisticated prior to colonization, and in some cases still is. Because Indigenous Peoples were intimately familiar with their environments, and the foods that were eaten were from the environment, nearly every illness also had an Indigenous remedy. The vast pharmacopoeia developed by Indigenous Peoples included such medicines as aspirin-related tree bark extracts, laxatives, painkillers, antibacterial medicines, petroleum jelly, and quinine. In fact, it is estimated that about 25 percent of the world's medicines today came from knowledge held by Indigenous Peoples. In addition, because nutritional health was far superior in past centuries and people physically exerted themselves every day, our ancestors were in much better shape and able to fend off sickness far better than we are today.

This chapter is designed to provide possible strategies for decolonizing contemporary Indigenous diets. It is important to understand, however, that this does not simply mean eating healthy and exercising more. It is not intended as a recipe for a new fad diet that will create your dream body in six weeks. It is not promoting a South Beach, Atkins, or Butter Busters diet. Instead this is about promoting a lifestyle centered on traditional Indigenous foods—a lifestyle that will promote good nutritional health, physical activity, spiritual and cultural strengthening, and a revitalized relationship with the land and its beings. It is about undoing the negative effects of colonization on our health and diet and restoring a sense of well-being to ourselves, our families, and our communities. But first we have to understand how invasion and colonization impacted our health.

B. So What Happened?

The first attacks on Indigenous health came through foreign disease introduced by the invaders to our lands. Completely unexposed to illnesses such as smallpox, measles, bubonic plague, cholera, typhoid, diphtheria, mumps, and pleurisy, Indigenous populations were devastated when the diseases swept through the continent. Even sicknesses such as influenza and colds were nonexistent in the Americas prior to invasion. Scholar Henry Dobyns has estimated that a total of 93 *serious* epidemics and pandemics (meaning the epidemic spread across the whole continent) of foreign diseases spread among Indigenous populations from the early sixteenth century to the beginning of the twentieth century. Indigenous weakness to these foreign germs was compounded by the violent acts accompanying invasion. As populations were weakened by disease, our ancestor's food sources, homes, and medicinal supplies were also destroyed; the people were frequently enslaved, slaughtered, or forcibly removed and our populations had little ability to ever physically recover. The violence and disease worked together to kill at least 90 percent (and that is a conservative estimate) of all Indigenous populations and to eradicate some populations entirely.

At the same time that Indigenous populations were dying through disease and violence, attacks were made on Indigenous food sources. For example, in the nineteenth century, it is estimated that 50 million bison on the plains of North America were exterminated. When that lean, high-protein source was eliminated, the people starved, further weakening them and making them more susceptible to disease. In addition, with invasion came dramatic changes to the environment. Indigenous plants and animals were often eliminated as farmlands and grazing lands were created for foreign animals such as cattle and sheep. These acts of invasion and colonization meant a total disruption of Indigenous ways of life and a tremendous loss of life.

The attacks on Indigenous life did not stop after the invasion phase, however. The colonization process required that Indigenous ways of life be eradicated completely so there would be no distinct population to object to or resist the continuing theft of Indigenous lands and resources. As it affected all aspects of Indigenous life, the health of Indigenous Peoples was no exception. Once Indigenous Peoples had been largely subdued and confined to reservations or reserves, so

> **"Come, then, comrades; it would be as well to decide at once to change our ways. We must shake off the heavy darkness in which we were plunged, and leave it behind. The new day which is already at hand must find us firm, prudent, and resolute."**
> **—Frantz Fanon**

began the process of attacking Indigenous ways of life through the children. In federally mandated boarding or residential schools, the children were fed starchy and fatty diets. While the children did eat fresh produce often grown by their own hands, they were also fed a lot of dairy products and meats from the livestock they raised as child laborers at the schools. They were also introduced to sweets, which would have been a rare treat in most Indigenous diets. To compound the detrimental effects of the poor diets, many Indigenous children were fed these same foods in very small rations, leaving them hungry and undernourished.

Ironically, the dairy products only served to exacerbate health problems as an extremely high percentage of Indigenous people are lactose intolerant. In fact, adults in general are not built to consume dairy products. At birth, humans have an enzyme called lactase that allows them to break down the lactose in human breast milk so that it can be absorbed and utilized by the body. As humans mature, lactase decreases to very low levels, making it difficult or impossible for adults to effectively break down lactose. That is why 80 percent of the world's adult population is lactose intolerant. Our bodies simply cannot efficiently process dairy products.

Treaty annuities and the government commodities program additionally served to wreak havoc on Indigenous diet and health. Instead of eating hand-grown and -harvested fruits, nuts, and vegetables, the lean meat of wild game, and fish loaded with essential fats, Indigenous Peoples instead consumed highly processed canned, salted, and sugared foods, canned fatty meats, and high quantities of refined sugar and bleached white flour. Once these foods entered Indigenous diets, they became firmly entrenched in spite of their ill effects on our bodies. For example, fry bread has become an Indigenous staple, but it only serves to worsen the health of our people. As Suzan Harjo aptly describes, "Fry bread was a gift of Western civilization from the days when Native people were removed from buffalo, elk, deer, salmon, turkey, corn, beans, squash, acorns, fruit, wild rice and other real food." Many of us have acquired a taste for it, but when we give some serious thought to the ingredients, we have to wonder why. Harjo further questions, "Fry bread is bad for you? Well, let's see. It's made with white flour, salt, sugar and lard. The bonus ingredient is dried cow's milk for the large population of Native people who are both glucose and lactose intolerant." We are not helping ourselves by continuing to eat it. While most Indigenous societies had some kind of bread prior to invasion and colonization (frequently made from such nutritious bases as corn, beans, or nuts), fried foods generally were not a part of the Indigenous diet. Because hard-earned oils from animal fats were precious commodities, they were not used for the wasteful practice of deep-frying other foods. In fact, they were sometimes not consumed at all, but instead used for such things as fuel or as moisturizing and softening agents. We might then consider the adoption of such food practices as deep-frying as a colonized adaptation, one that has not served the health interests of Indigenous Peoples, but instead serves the colonizers' interests because it leads to the deterioration of our health and survival.

However, in today's society, much of our population is affected by the same health struggles affecting the colonizing society because we have not only become avid eaters of highly processed and refined foods, we have also become participators in the fast-food frenzy. It is estimated that Americans now eat on average three hamburgers and four orders of french fries every week. As Eric Schlosser, author of *Fast Food Nation*, remarks, "What we [Americans] eat has changed more in the last forty years than in the previous forty thousand." As a consequence, Americans are facing an epidemic-like rise in obesity rates, with obesity now being the second highest cause of mortality in the United States (smoking is the first). This American disaster is now spreading throughout the world as American fast-food chains and lifestyles infiltrate other countries, creating an eruption of what are being dubbed "Western diseases." The major culprit, obesity, is linked to a variety of debilitating and deadly conditions such as heart disease, type 2 diabetes, various forms of cancer, arthritis, high blood pressure, infertility, and strokes. Indigenous populations have been equally impacted by the American diet, but the consequences appear to be affecting our people more severely. Indigenous populations in the United States, for example, suffer the highest percentages of diabetes in the country. Many Indigenous communities now require full-time diabetes treatment and prevention personnel to address this overwhelming problem killing our people.

ACTIVITY:

What is your typical weekly diet? For the next week, keep a record of what kinds of food you consume, note whether they are processed (P), fatty (F), sugary (S), fresh raw (FR), fresh cooked (FC), or whole unprocessed (WUP) foods. (Whole foods are unrefined grains, beans, nuts, fruits, and vegetables. These are foods that have not been refined, bleached, fried, or filled with preservatives, additives, artificial sweeteners, or colorings.)

Sunday

Breakfast:

Lunch:

Dinner:

Snacks:

Beverages:

Monday

Breakfast:

Lunch:

Dinner:

Snacks:

Beverages:

Tuesday

Breakfast:

Lunch:

Dinner:

Snacks:

Beverages:

Wednesday

Breakfast:

Lunch:

Dinner:

Snacks:

Beverages:

Thursday

Breakfast:

Lunch:

Dinner:

Snacks:

Beverages:

Friday

Breakfast:

Lunch:

Dinner:

Snacks:

Beverages:

Saturday

Breakfast:

Lunch:

Dinner:

Snacks:

Beverages:

Is your diet in line with that of the average American? If yes, how so?

_____

_____

_____

_____

_____

Now let's tally how many healthier fresh or whole unprocessed foods you ate compared to processed, fatty, or sugary foods:

Number of processed food items: _____

Number of fatty food items: _____

Number of sugary food items: _____

Number of fresh raw foods: _____

Number of fresh cooked foods: _____

Number of whole unprocessed foods: _____

Can you make some generalizations about the quality of your current diet? Would you benefit from a return to a traditional diet?

_____

_____

_____

_____

Most of us know if we are overweight and if our bodies are suffering because of our weight problem. We do not necessarily need a doctor to tell us that we should go on a diet. However, we do know that many of our people who are currently suffering the effects of diabetes may not yet know that they are diabetic. If you are overweight and have not been tested for dia-betes in the last year, it is important to get the proper testing and consult with a doctor or tribal health prac-titioner. We cannot tell you whether you have diabetes in this chapter, but we can help you determine for yourself how overweight you might be and whether or not you have crossed into the category of obesity, which places your health and life at risk.

ACTIVITY:

Determining Your Body Mass Index

The most accurate method for determining how overweight you are is by calculating your Body Mass Index (BMI). This is a ratio figured by dividing your weight by your height squared (height multiplied by height).

Weight (kilograms) _____ = BMI

Height x Height (meters)

If you do not know the metric measurements to plug into the formula above, you must first convert your measurements from pounds to kilograms and from inches to meters. To calculate from pounds to kilograms, multiply your weight in pounds by 0.4536.

(weight in pounds) x 0.4536 = (weight in kilograms)

To calculate from inches to meters, multiply your height in inches by 0.0254.

(height in inches) x 0.0254 = (height in meters)

Then plug these numbers into the formula above. For example, a 71-inch man (5 foot, 11 inches) weighing 200 pounds would be calculated as follows:

200 pounds x 0.4536 = 90.720 kilograms

71 inches x 0.0254 = 1.803 meters

$$\frac{90.720}{1.803 \times 1.803} = 27.905 \text{ BMI}$$

Men should ideally keep their BMI between 20 and 26. Women should ideally keep their BMI between 19 and 25. Overweight is considered to be a BMI between 26 and 29 for men, and 25 and 29 for women. Obesity is defined as a BMI over 29, and at this level, your health is in danger.

ACTIVITY:

Has your family and community been impacted by obesity? If yes, how so?

_____

_____

_____

_____

The spiritual, cultural, and psychological effects of this dramatic change in diet are just as important to consider as well. The plant and animal food sources described thus far have only been addressed in terms of their nutritional value. They are far more important, however, than the nutrients they provide. As Indigenous Peoples, our relationship to the land and to all of its beings is not merely physical, it is also spiritual. We believe that part of our spiritual responsibility as human beings is to maintain respectful relationships with all of creation. For some of us this might mean singing to the corn, offering prayers to plant and animal beings, or harvesting in a sacred manner. These culturally and spiritually significant actions nurtured us as well as the spiritual beings we encountered. The resulting foods then fed our bodies and our spirits. When our environments were destroyed or altered, it was not just our physical health that was placed in jeopardy.

C. What Do We Do Now?

As Indigenous Peoples who have been detrimentally affected by the changes in our diet as a result of colonization, it makes sense that some kind of decolonization of the diet would help reverse those effects. But how do we go about that? The first step may be developing a firm grasp of what your nation's diet consisted of prior to colonization.

ACTIVITY:

Describe your nation's precolonization diet below. If you do not have this knowledge currently, conduct research on this topic by asking elders or reading published accounts.

Protein sources (meat, beans, legumes):

_____

_____

_____

Harvested (wild) vegetable sources:

_____

_____

Planted vegetable sources:

_____

_____

_____

_____

Fruit sources:

_____

_____

_____

_____

Nut sources:

_____

_____

_____

For most of us today, there is a glaring difference between what our diets look like today and what our ancestors' diets looked like prior to colonization. When our traditional diets are examined ("traditional" in this context referring to the ways we harvested, hunted, and prepared the plant and animal food sources native to our homelands prior to invasion), it is clear that they were not only extraordinarily healthier than our diets today, they were also quite diverse.

In regards to our nutrition, the challenge for us in the twenty-first century is to recover the diets of our past, but this is no easy task for a variety of reasons. In some cases, food supplies may have been exterminated or greatly diminished (such as the buffalo on the plains or the salmon of the Columbia River). In other cases, animal and plant life may have become toxic as a consequence of contamination from corporate chemical runoff, exposure to radioactivity, or farm pesticides (such as the PCB-contaminated fish in the waters used by the Akwesasne Mohawks). Disrupted and altered landscapes may also mean that Indigenous food sources are no longer present (such as waterfowl that may have fled converted wetlands, or wild turnips gone because of prairie conversion to farmland). In other instances, Indigenous Peoples may not have access to any foods from their homelands because of confinement to reservation lands or forced removals. The recovery of Indigenous diets, then, is linked to broader Indigenous struggles such as land rights, environmental protection, and ecological restoration. It becomes overwhelming to imagine tackling all these issues at once, so it is important to determine your current access to traditional foods and prioritize your attempts to recover various foods.

ACTIVITY:

Based on your previous activity listing your nation's food sources prior to colonization, now assess to what extent those foods are currently accessible to you and your community and under what conditions. (An example is provided below.)

Food	Accessibility
Yellow lotus dug from the bottom of swampy areas with the feet	We don't have any swamps on our reservation and now there are only a few people who remember how to locate them—perhaps we could consult with those elders to determine which swamps were favorites off-reservation and attempt access to those.

For those of us who work hard to decolonize our diets and recover our traditional foods, there is very encouraging evidence to suggest we could not only prevent future instances of obesity and its accompanying problems among our populations, but also that we could actually reverse the ill effects for those already suffering from this damage. In a recent essay, Michael Milburn highlights the work of other scholars who had recorded the effects of diet changes among a group of Aborigines from the West Kimberly region of Australia. At the beginning of the project, many of the participants were already suffering from high blood pressure and diabetes and had poor cardiovascular risk profiles. Relying on elders who retained knowledge about how to survive entirely off the land, this group followed that Indigenous lifestyle for a two-month period. Individuals lost fifteen pounds on average, their insulin metabolism improved, blood sugar levels dropped, and blood pressure, cholesterol, and triglyceride levels improved. They actually reversed the effects of Western diseases within a very short time period.

While many Indigenous People are not interested in abandoning everything from the modern world and attempting to live the way our ancestors did even if it were a possibility for all of us, this project illuminates the important link between traditional food and lifestyle. Relying heavily or exclusively on Indigenous foods for most Indigenous Peoples would require a return to an extremely active lifestyle. Even relying on a partial recovery of Indigenous food sources would require more activity than many of us engage in today. Food and lifestyle are interconnected and if we seek out our traditional foods, our lifestyle will become more active and we will experience the resulting positive benefits.

Furthermore, restoration of food practices will also restore a sense of well-being and interconnectedness with the rest of creation. It has now been proven, for example, that gardening reduces stress, refreshes our mental outlook, and increases feelings of self-worth. When people have the opportunity to nurture plant life, they are touched on a deep emotional level. Indigenous Peoples have understood the importance of this connection and have created, or were divinely given, ways to further nurture the spirits of our plant relatives as well as ourselves. For example, in my own family I was taught that the planting of corn is an important part of Dakota life. Every time I plant my grandmother's corn, I feel a sense of connection to her and the long line of grandmothers who planted the same strain of corn before me. Every cycle of planting and harvesting renews a commitment to and love for the corn plants and the land and soil on which they grow. It reaffirms that connection to mitakuyapi owas'in (all my relations). Then, as I process the corn in preparation for winter storage and later for eating, every smell and sound reminds me that I am my grandmother's granddaughter, that I am Dakota. This experience is never reproduced in a grocery store.

D. Committing Ourselves to the Decolonization of Our Diets

How can we commit ourselves, our families, and our communities to work toward the decolonization of our diets? The first step is deciding that a change is necessary. Many communities have acknowledged that obesity and diabetes are a problem and have dedicated personnel to addressing it. For example, your community may have a diabetes prevention or treatment coordinator, a dietician, a fitness coordinator, a cook, or a nurse or nurse practitioner to help those who already suffer from these debilitating conditions. However, even when this recognition is present, rarely does it spread to community action. Fry bread and fatty, sugary, and processed foods often still grace the tables at community functions rather than more wholesome traditional foods. And, rather than viewing our contemporary diets as a consequence of colonization, we have increasingly and uncritically accepted this change in diet, even incorporating many unhealthy foods into what we deem "traditional."

ACTIVITY:

Who benefits from Indigenous Peoples becoming increasingly more obese and diabetic? How?

1. _____ benefit(s) because _____

_____

2. _____ benefit(s) because _____

_____

3. _____ benefit(s) because _____

_____

4. _____ benefit(s) because _____

_____

Who would benefit from Indigenous Peoples becoming increasingly healthy? How?

1. _____ benefit(s) because _____

_____

2. _____ benefit(s) because _____

_____

3. _____ benefit(s) because _____

_____

4. _____ benefit(s) because _____

_____

What kind of pattern do you see? _____

_____

Who do you want to benefit from the status of your health?

_____

Because heart disease and diabetes are byproducts of colonization, as individuals and communities, we can consciously reject those and decide that we will no longer participate in this continuing aspect of our colonization. If we can learn to consciously correlate our eating habits with our participation in our colonization, the experience becomes less enjoyable. If we keep this idea at the forefront of our minds, every piece of fry bread and every order of french fries becomes less and less desirable. On the other hand, if we view our traditional foods as a means of making our populations strong and independent, eating those foods will become increasingly more enjoyable because we will equate them with our own well-being and good health.

As individuals, and then as communities, we can commit ourselves to rejecting that which makes us weak and ill, and striving toward that which makes us strong and healthy.

E. Strategies for Change

After understanding which traditional foods you can currently access and how you might work to access others, strategies can be developed to acquire those foods, disperse them to your families and communities, and enjoy them. This will have a far more profound impact than a simple reduction in your waistline.

ACTIVITY:

Using the list you developed in the previous activity on traditional foods and their accessibility, now go through that list to determine whether you can try to acquire those foods as an individual, in a small organized group, or if it requires the help of your governing body or tribal council. (Some examples are provided.)

Food?	Who Can Access It?
Yellow lotus	Tribal Council may help us gain access to lands off-reservation where we can harvest it.
Piñon nuts	My family can organize a day-trip this season to harvest the nuts.
Venison	I can sharpen my hunting skills and make time for hunting this year.

In determining who can access foods, we can recognize how we can impact our diets as individuals, as families or small groups, and as entire communities. Keeping the list of traditional foods in mind, some healthy steps may be taken immediately. For example, as individuals we could decide that we will no longer buy processed foods. If we decide that we will eat foods we prepared from fresh or whole ingredients, our diets would immediately become healthier. Other small steps might be taken as well. If maple sugar is a traditional food, perhaps you can access it immediately by purchasing it from others if you have not gone sugar-bushing yourself, and completely replace your use of white refined sugar or chemical sweeteners with the maple sugar. As a small, organized group, perhaps you could decide to organize a community garden where you could grow a host of your traditional foods, or even attempt to obtain seeds for plants that were typically harvested and not cultivated ("wild" turnips,

potatoes, or beans, for example) to revitalize them on your lands. For further information about obtaining Indigenous seeds, contact Native Seeds/SEARCH in Tucson, Arizona, at (520) 622-5561 or visit www.nativeseeds.org. Or if acorns were a traditional food but you have not harvested and processed them in recent years, perhaps you could organize a small group to collect and process them together. Activities may also be conducted on a community-wide scale at the governmental level. For example, perhaps the tribal government could decide to help restore the buffalo population and eventually help provide buffalo meat to the reservation families. Or perhaps a tribal government could decide not to participate in the further colonization of the Indigenous diet by not permitting any fast-food establishments on reservation lands or by deciding to serve healthy traditional foods for meals provided to the community.

ACTIVITY:

Now that you have a greater understanding of how your diet has been impacted by colonization as well as what your traditional diet looked like, take the time to prepare this information for dispersal in your community. Ask elders and other knowledgeable community members for information on the variety of ways these traditional foods were prepared and collect these for community dissemination. Perhaps your traditional diet handbook can be included in your tribal newsletter or newspaper, or tribal monies can be used to professionally print copies for every household in your community. The important thing is to share your ideas about how your community can decolonize its diet through the recovery of your precolonization diet and accompanying lifestyle.

In decolonizing our diet, it is also important for us to be mindful of when and how we can coordinate this with other decolonization activities. For example, among many of our societies, rites of passage often use food in ritualized ways that are physically, culturally, and spiritually nourishing. Many of our societies that depended on successful hunting practices trained boys

as early as possible in hunting techniques and celebrated each boy's first kill. Among some Plains tribes, that first kill would be distributed to other members of the community so that people could celebrate the boy's success and acknowledge his contribution to the society. This gave him a sense of accomplishment while also providing nutritious food to the people. Or for larger kills, such as elk, deer, or buffalo, the various parts of the animal would be divided up and distributed widely. In today's communities, this would greatly help single mothers and the elderly in particular. If these practices were revitalized, it would serve some important community functions that far exceed nutritional health. The growing boy would feel a sense of pride in being a contributing member to society; he would be encouraged to continue to provide food to the community with the positive support; and, he would gain confidence and skill in hunting techniques. When many of us come from communities in which our teenage men have extraordinarily high rates of suicide, the implications of revitalizing such practices cannot be overestimated. It may, in fact, be the difference between life and death.

Similarly, many cultures require a mastery of food preparation during young women's rites of passage. For example, in some of the Southwestern tribes such as the Hopi and the Apache, grinding corn is an important part of community recognition of a young woman's passage into womanhood. By maintaining such practices, traditional preparation of food is also maintained and the way is paved for a lifetime of more healthful eating.

ACTIVITY:

What is the role of food in your nation's rites of passage for your young men and women? How might revitalizing these practices influence both your diet and other aspects of your community life?

Passage into manhood: _____
_____
_____

Influence on diet and community life: _____
_____
_____

Passage into womanhood: _____
_____
_____

Influence on diet and community life: _____
_____
_____

ACTIVITY:

In considering how Indigenous Peoples will be affected culturally and spiritually by the recovery of Indigenous food practices, it is important also to take into account the ceremonies, songs, and prayers that accompany the nurturing of other life-forms as well as those that accompany the death of other life-forms. Which ceremonies, songs, and prayers traditionally accompanied the harvesting or hunting practices among your nation?

_____

_____

_____

_____

_____

_____

How would the revitalization of these spiritual practices impact your community?

_____

_____

_____

_____

A revitalization of group hunting or fishing techniques may also be a way to provide leaner or healthier meats to your community. However, hunting has diminished among many Indigenous populations for a variety of reasons. It may be that some of these practices diminished because of government and missionary "Christianizing" and "civilizing" campaigns, in which tremendous pressure was placed on Indigenous People to abandon hunting or fishing practices in favor of full-time farming. Or, it may be that with the invasion of Indigenous lands, the animal population was depleted to such an extent that people could no longer survive from those practices. If the case of the former fits your community and you decide you want to decolonize your diet, the recovery of these practices becomes a means of countering the forces of colonialism as well as a way to restore health and well-being to your population. If the latter case fits your community, recovering traditional hunting and fishing practices might require extensive and purposeful efforts toward ecological restoration.

ACTIVITY:

Which group hunting and fishing techniques were used among your nation?

_____

_____

_____

_____

Is it possible to revive those practices now? If not, what prevents you from revitalizing those practices?

_____

_____

_____

_____

Wild game is typically much leaner and more nutritious than the meats from domesticated animals, such as cattle, pigs, and sheep. Undomesticated game tends to be higher in protein and minerals such as thiamine and niacin, while also being lower in fat and calories and without the chemicals commonly given to domesticated animals. Similarly, the more we eat fruit and vegetable foods that we plant and harvest ourselves or that are native to the lands we live on, the more nutritious that food will be. When we can harvest the food when it is ripe, it will be at its peak nutritionally. As fruits and vegetables ripen on the vine, phytochemicals are produced in the plants and these help to prevent cancers and other diseases. If fruits and vegetables are picked before they ripen and shipped to distant locations, their nutritional value and health benefits have been weakened. This is true of the 60 percent of commercially grown fruits, vegetables, and greens in the United States that are picked before they are ripe so they can be transported to stores in a wide geographic area. Furthermore, when we engage in planting and harvesting our own foods, we can ensure they are free of chemicals such as pesticides or herbi-

cides. This is not true of most of what is available in American supermarkets.

Returning to Indigenous foods also means a more active lifestyle. Going to the grocery store or to a restaurant of any kind requires little physical activity. Even preparing food in the kitchen requires relatively little energy. Since this is how many of us now come by our food, it is no wonder that our obesity rates have increased. This changes when we contemplate acquiring Indigenous foods. If foods are hunted, major physical activity is required. Hiking through the hills, across the plains, or through the forests, often for miles, in search of game will get any hunter in shape quickly. Setting traps and walking trap lines also requires physical exertion as does fishing, especially if one is working with large nets or is spearfishing. Similarly, engaging in agricultural labor is no easy task and usually requires daily physical activity in the plowing, planting, weeding, and harvesting cycle. Anyone who has spent summers working under the hot sun in a garden or agricultural field can attest to this. The same thing is true in the harvesting of Indigenous plants, roots, nuts, and berries. Every hour spent engaging physically in these activities will make our bodies stronger and healthier. Recovery of Indigenous diets is thus not solely about what we eat, it is also about a change to a more active lifestyle.

These changes also require a reworking of our contemporary relationship with the environment. Our well-being is connected to the well-being of the land and all of its inhabitants. When we devote our time and energy to understanding those rhythms and cycles, we are closer to truly understanding who we are as Indigenous Peoples. The decolonization of our diets is thus linked to other forms of decolonization that will help us physically, culturally, psychologically, and spiritually. We have nothing to lose by decolonizing our diets and so much to gain. Let us all work on healing and helping ourselves through the recovery of our traditional foods and lifestyles.

F. Suggested Readings

Nelson Foster and Linda S. Cordell, eds., *Chilies to Chocolate: Food the Americas Gave the World* (Tucson: University of Arizona Press, 1996).

Suzan Harjo, "My New Year's Resolution: No More Fat 'Indian' Food," *Indian Country Today*, January 20, 2005.

Devon A. Mihesuah, "Decolonizing Our Diets By Recovering Our Ancestors' Gardens," *American Indian Quarterly* 27, no. 3 (2003).

Michael Milburn, "Indigenous Nutrition: Using Traditional Food Knowledge to Solve Contemporary Health Problems," *American Indian Quarterly* 28, no. 3 (2004).

Eric Schlosser, *Fast Food Nation* (New York: Perennial, 2002).

Jack Weatherford, *Indian Givers: How the Indians of the Americas Transformed the World* (New York: Crown Publishers, 1988).

The Decolonization of Indigenous Governance

Robert Odawi Porter

A. What Is the Purpose of this Chapter?

This chapter provides the justification and a strategy for allowing Indigenous Peoples to regain greater control over their own lives. Indigenous Peoples in the Americas have little control over their own lives because of colonization. A basic definition of colonization is that it is the exercise of power and control over one people by another. In the Americas, this is a story of how Europeans came to this continent and took control over the lives and lands of the Indigenous Peoples who lived here. This power and control continues to be exercised over Indigenous nations and Peoples to the present day.

Most people do not give much thought to the way that power flows within their society. When we talk about power, we are inevitably talking about government and the way in which government functions. Most often, people view government as being intertwined with "politics." While the concepts are related, there is an important difference. When we speak of government, we are talking about the rules and procedures that have been developed by a people to allow them to take collective action as a society. When we speak of politics, we are talking about the activities that individuals engage in to obtain and use the power of government.

A strong, functioning government is important because if a people do not work together to get things done, then their society cannot survive. Almost always, individuals must cooperate to accomplish the basic tasks necessary for their survival. They need to find ways to provide enough food for everyone to eat, to make sure children learn what they need to take care of themselves and others, and to protect themselves from the harms presented by other peoples and nature. If a people cannot work together, they cannot survive. Yes, it is possible for a select few to thrive. But in a society where individuals are left to fend for themselves, most will suffer.

A society without a functioning government is a society in chaos, in which the strong get stronger and the weak get weaker. Some people may find this way of life attractive. Most, however, do not because of the unfairness and misery that it generates. As a result, people must know how government works, and work to develop a good, strong government so that they can survive and thrive. This has been true for all peoples, whether they be Indigenous or colonizing.

The rules and procedures relating to the conduct of government are reflected in a special kind of law called "governing law." Before the arrival of the Europeans to this land, all Native societies had some kind of governing law. Some societies were quite large and had a very complex governing law designed to order the affairs of thousands of people. Others societies were not so large and had more basic governing law suited to their way of life. The Europeans usually did not understand these laws, and so they said that the Indians were "savage" and "lawless" wild peoples without government or law. Of course, this was not true. Indigenous Peoples did have government and law; they simply did not write down their laws like the Europeans did. Because the Europeans wanted to justify their colonizing behavior, they made it appear that the Indigenous Peoples were stupid and "uncivilized." They thus created and perpetuated the myth that the "Indians have no law."

The Europeans who arrived in the Americas intended to take control over all of the lands that they "discovered" in what they called the "New World." The biggest obstacle to accomplishing this task, of course,

was the existence of the Indigenous Peoples and nations. The Europeans knew that destroying Indian governments was the key to controlling Indigenous Peoples. And so, in almost every Indigenous nation that has survived colonization thus far, the colonists have taken control—sometimes complete control—over the operation of Indigenous governments. As you might guess, these changes were designed to serve the colonists, not the Indigenous Peoples. This chapter discusses how this transformation occurred and how the damage inflicted by colonization might be repaired.

B. Why Is Decolonization Important?

Freedom is essential to the survival of all peoples. If a people are not free to determine their own future, then they cannot expect to survive as a distinct society. Decolonizing Indigenous government is thus essential to achieving the freedom necessary for Indigenous Peoples to survive.

Time and time again, human history reveals that freedom is the essential characteristic necessary for human survival. If one is controlled by another, then one's life force will soon be extinguished. When we think of individual people without freedom, we imagine prisoners or slaves. When we think of entire peoples without freedom, we must think of peoples who have been colonized by other peoples. This experience, unfortunately, is part of human history. While the tendency may be to believe that colonialism is an inherently European characteristic, it is not. Many peoples, including some Indigenous Peoples, have engaged in colonialism and have subjugated other peoples in furtherance of their own purposes.

Because colonialism has been so prevalent throughout human history, and because it is so damaging to the basic human rights of the colonized peoples, international law today forbids colonialism and supports the right of all peoples to be free. The International Covenant on Civil and Political Rights reflects this aspiration: "All peoples have the right of self-determination. By virtue of that right they freely determine their political status and freely pursue their economic, social and cultural development."

It is easy to think of colonialism as simply an exercise of military power. It is not. When one thinks deeply about what is required to take over another people and their land, it is easy to see how difficult, expensive, and time consuming the process is. First, one must raise an army and conduct a military campaign to subdue the target population. This phase of colonization is the most dramatic, because it takes place over a short span of time amidst much violence. But after the military conflict is over, the most significant changes in the lives of the colonized people begin to occur.

This second phase of colonization reflects the colonizer's efforts to gain control over the target population and to change their society, and the people themselves, to suit the colonizer's needs. Most often, what this means is that the culture of the colonized people is affirmatively changed to be more closely aligned with the culture of the colonizing people.

Cultural change at this level could be called "acculturation" or "assimilation," but the more accurate term is "social engineering." At first, the colonizer uses violence to force the colonized people to change who they are as people. This occurs through the application of new laws and punishments that outlaw traditional behaviors, such as religious practices, dancing, and certain family and marital relations. The next phase is equally as violent, but takes the less overtly threatening form of taking children away from their parents and raising them in the colonizer's educational institutions. This "educational" process, often referred to as "promoting civilization," involves beatings, hard labor, and psychological abuse. The "benefit" associated with this is that the seeds of the colonizer's culture are planted deeply in Indigenous Peoples at a very early age. Eventually, this "reeducation" takes place devoid of any overt violence. Today, it is simply called "going to school."

In 1492, the colonization of our lands by Europeans began. Millions of our people were killed by European diseases and, thus weakened, were ripe to be militarily neutralized. In some cases where the Native People survived, peace was established with the colonists by treaty. But ever since the formal "peace" was established between our nations and the colonists, the colonists have violated these agreements and have continued to assert control over our lives and lands and to change us as peoples. These actions have included forcing us to change our religious beliefs, our educational practices, our economic systems, and our political beliefs. While the colonizers justified their efforts on the grounds that they were giving us a "better life," the reality is that promoting "civilization" was only a cover for their effort to assert control over our peoples and lands.

Since the establishment of the United States as the dominant colonial influence in North America, the most direct control over our nations has been exercised by the U.S. government through its Bureau of Indian Affairs (BIA). The head of the BIA is authorized by American law to "have the management of all Indian affairs and of all matters arising out of Indian relations." Based upon these laws, the American courts have ruled that the BIA has absolute power over Indian affairs. In relation to Indigenous governance, this power has been exercised to overthrow traditional governments, to recruit and employ Indigenous government officials to establish "friendly" puppet governments, to define what an "Indian" is, to establish tribal membership rolls, and even to create new tribes. That is why today some Indian nations today have governments that cannot take any lawful action without the permission of the secretary of the Interior.

What all of this means today is that hundreds of Indian nations in the United States are subject to the direct controlling authority of the U.S. government. Being under the control of a foreign sovereign is, by definition, a violation of the inherent right of self-determination of the occupied people. To some Native People today, this may not be a problem to them. After all, what is wrong with being colonized and under control of the wealthiest and most prosperous nation in the world? The problem is that the loss of freedom associated with living under the authority of another people strips away our ability to survive as distinct Indigenous societies.

Decolonization is the process of ending colonization and restoring the path of self-determination for a colonized people. Decolonization is important for Indigenous Peoples because it creates the possibility that we can regain our inherent right of self-determination, and thus ensure our survival.

C. What Is My Experience with Decolonization?

I am a Seneca (*Onodowaga* in our language, meaning "the People of the Great Hill") and was raised on the Allegany Territory of the Seneca Nation within western New York State. The Allegany Territory, for unique historical reasons, has a lot of white people living there, outnumbering us by about five to one. The reservation and the surrounding area is very rural and, as a result, mostly poor. The public schools are located on the territory, and so everyone goes to school together. The school curriculum is set by the New York government and so, like public schools everywhere, is designed to produce hard-working, self-sufficient American citizens. Because of this objective, very little is taught about the unique history of the Seneca Nation and its people and how the United States and the state have influenced us. This is rather amazing, since the entire city where I grew up is located on lands owned by the Seneca Nation!

Outside of school, thankfully, I was able to learn more about my own nation, which greatly helped shape my future development. My mother was the Seneca Nation's first education director, and my grandfather was a tribal council member for forty years. In fact, most of my mother's extended family are involved in the nation's politics and government. As a result, much of my Seneca identity was shaped through the lens of Seneca political life.

What was missing from my youth, unfortunately, was a strong connection to traditional Seneca cultural life. Like many Indian families, mine was dramatically altered by Christian missionaries. From the time she was a little girl, my Seneca grandmother attended the Quaker boarding school that was located in our territory. At this school, they taught her to speak English by beating her if she spoke Seneca, to reject the Longhouse religion and become a Christian, and to abandon her own culture in favor of Euro-American culture. She was also taught to instruct her own children someday that they should leave the reservation, get a college education, and marry a white person so that they could have a good life.

Needless to say, this kind of upbringing had an impact on my mother, and later, on me. My mother did leave the reservation and was one of the few Senecas to go to college. There, she met my father, whom she married. But, it seems, not all of the destructive Quaker teachings took hold of her. (I later found out that she alone among her siblings had insisted on being given an Indian name.) She left my father and returned to the reservation. She married and divorced again, went back to college to get both her bachelor's and master's degrees, and went about the hard work of raising four children as a single parent.

I share this story because I believe it explains why I was ignorant for so long about the way in which my family had been transformed by the colonizers. I call this "colonization amnesia" and it occurs when Indians have little or no knowledge of how their lives have been shaped by the colonists. This lack of knowledge occurs because the truth of how this change occurred—through the horrors of boarding schools and missionary influence—is too painful for the survivors to pass on to their children and grandchildren.

Without a doubt, the fact that I pursued higher education and the life that I did when I was younger, was the direct result of the Quaker influence on my grandmother. My mother insisted that I go to college and, ever so subtly, encouraged me to not come back to the reservation. After a rough start, I eventually graduated from Syracuse University and Harvard Law

> "The colonial condition cannot be adjusted to; like an iron collar, it can only be broken."
> —Albert Memmi

School, became a lawyer, practiced business law in Washington, D.C., and married a white woman.

Knowing that this was not the life for me, I felt the urge to return to the Seneca homeland to do what I could to help our people. I convinced our council to create the position of attorney general and to appoint me to that position. I remember well the resistance from my mother and grandfather about my plan to come home. They thought I was crazy for wanting to leave my corporate law firm to come back and work for the nation. Thankfully my mother never passed on to me some of the hateful things about Senecas that she had learned from her own mother. Indeed, my family's lifelong example of serving our people conveyed just the opposite message, that those of us with special skills should use them to help whenever we can. I know now that this is why I wanted to find a way to serve my nation.

My tenure as attorney general was a time of tremendous growth and personal awakening. I was involved in some important legal projects, like amending our nation's constitution. But most importantly, I experienced a few tremendous moments that changed my life.

Perhaps the most significant positive influence was in 1992, when hundreds of Senecas blocked the interstate highways running through our territories, to fight back against the state's efforts to tax the cigarettes and gasoline trade that is the foundation of our economy. I was involved in representing the nation in discussions with state officials and we ultimately succeeded, driving back more than a thousand heavily armed state troopers who had surrounded us. It was a great moment for Seneca sovereignty and a moment that changed me forever.

The most significant negative influence occurred during the winter of 1994–95, when our nation was ravaged by civil war. Three of our people were killed. It was a sad, sad thing that happened, and all of our lives were changed by it.

When I was working with our people, my life changed in ways that have taken me years to understand. My first marriage ended when I was home, but the Creator blessed me with the opportunity to fall in love with a Seneca woman to whom I remain married. My appreciation for our language and culture grew, and I began to realize the importance of our cultural identity more than ever before. A few years ago, as a symbol of this journey, I received a Seneca clan name, *Odawi*, which means "given something." I truly believe that I have been "given something," and it is very special indeed.

I didn't become fully aware of what it meant to be a colonized Indian, though, until I started my teaching career at the University of Kansas. There was much conflict among our people when I served the Seneca Nation as attorney general. My new position gave me the opportunity to spend time to think, read, and write about those experiences. The big question, to me, was why did our people fight each other, to the point that people were killed?

It was then that I began to dig deeply into America's history of subjugating Indigenous Peoples. And since the gruesome details were all pretty much new to me, I was shocked. Perhaps I too had been influenced by the myth of conquest, that America just happened to win the war against our nations because of its superior power. What I learned, however, was that America really didn't win anything, that it was the fact that our ancestors just couldn't survive the filthy diseases that these invaders brought with them from Europe. I was also overwhelmed by the systematic efforts to forcefully assimilate our ancestors through policies that supported boarding schools, missionaries, and land confiscation. This knowledge made me realize that what happened to my grandmother was not an accident. It was an evil experiment in mass social engineering, designed to destroy our unique Indigenous cultures and assimilate us into American society whether we liked it or not.

Since coming to that realization, I have tried to focus both my professional and personal life on promoting the decolonization of Indian life and the restoration of true self-determination, a process I call "indigenization." In my professional life, I have tried to pursue the truth about the history of European colonization and how it has affected Indigenous societies, especially my own. From that foundation, I have tried to develop solutions to solve some of the more acute problems that arise from colonization that now afflict our nations. These areas of my work include dispute resolution, political identity, as well as the topic of this chapter, governance and the decolonization of the colonists' Indian control laws.

In my personal life, I have tried to take a similar course. I am ever mindful of the ways in which I am shaped, and have been shaped, by colonial society. I have also sought to reconnect my own life path with the traditional foundations of my people, through the Longhouse and our time-honored ceremonies. On both the personal and professional fronts, the task of decolonization has been extremely difficult. Nonetheless, this journey has been its own reward—participating in the preservation of a distinct Seneca identity for me, and a distinct Seneca society for all of us.

Because of the specific nature of this chapter, I think it is important to see how these general experiences in decolonization have played out in relation to tribal governance. Most of these direct experiences arise during my time serving as the Seneca Nation's attorney general. In 1992, my first major project was to work on proposed constitutional amendments to change my nation's court system. The amendments were eventually approved by our people in a referendum, and I learned much about the process of how long-term change can occur. I also learned how easy it is to aim low when engaging in constitutional reform. Looking back, while I think the changes were an improvement over the old system, they did little to address some of my nation's more fundamental governance problems.

I was also involved in a yearlong effort to restructure the administrative operations of the Seneca government. The project was ambitious, and was designed to give our people a greater voice in the government, to empower the council, to redefine and strengthen the leadership role of our president, and to otherwise develop a systematic method for ensuring accountability among the eight-hundred-member tribal workforce. Eventually, the restructuring occurred. Unfortunately, it was implemented less than a year

before the general election, and it became a political issue. After the election, the laws implementing the changes were nullified.

What this experience taught me is that many of the most important changes that must be made within Indian nations are outside of the government's power. The administrative reform effort I was involved in tried to do too much in too short of a time frame. Many of our deepest governmental problems should have been taken directly to the people and effectuated through constitutional change, not simply through council actions. Simply put, the merits of proposed changes mean little if the process by which they come about is not accepted. With time, I am confident that all people can learn these lessons without simply having to rely on their own method of trial and error. When we do so, we will have gone a long way toward unleashing the power of our peoples, and we will have thus prepared ourselves to effectively address the challenges to our sovereignty that might arise in the future.

From these lessons, I offer the following guidance for other Native Peoples who wish to gain greater power over their lives by decolonizing their government.

D. A Process for Decolonizing Indigenous Governance

The process of decolonizing Indigenous government is difficult and time consuming. In many situations where the United States has taken control of a tribal government, it has been decades—and maybe more than a century—since the people themselves had control of their own government. As a result, the concept of being truly free may be foreign to them. It may even frighten them. Thus, it may take years before any meaningful change can be made. To aid in this process, it is important to approach the decolonization effort systematically and with great patience.

1. What kind of tribal government do you currently have?

To begin, it is first necessary to understand the different kinds of tribal governments that exist and to identify the kind of tribal government that you now have. There are three basic types of tribal government. First, there are the traditional governments, which retain an unwritten form that has been in place since before the arrival of the colonists. Second, there are the autonomous constitutional governments, which are written forms of government established by the people themselves through a democratic process. Lastly, there are the dependent constitutional or corporate governments, which are established through the direct influence of the United States. As you might imagine, most governments do not fall cleanly into one of these categories. Instead, most Native governments today reflect a combination of these different governmental types.

ACTIVITY:

On the basis of the above-described categories, identify the type of government that exists within your own nation. Research its origins. Who created your tribal government and under what conditions?

_____
_____
_____
_____
_____
_____

Where did the model for your form of tribal government come from?

_____
_____
_____
_____

How has the form of your government changed, if at all, since it was created?

_____
_____
_____
_____
_____
_____
_____

2. How well does your tribal government currently function?

Each of the various forms of Indigenous government naturally has its own strengths and weaknesses. Traditional governments, very few of which remain, generally have a more deliberative process that ensures that decisions affecting the people are well thought out. Constitutional governments based upon elected representatives tend to be more effective at taking rapid action on pressing issues. Regardless of the form, a "good" government can be said to exist when the people are able to work together to satisfy their basic needs and achieve their common goals. In short, "good" government exists when the people perceive its actions to be legitimate.

All governments, however, have weaknesses. Some of the most prominent weaknesses that afflict tribal governments are poor administration of tribal resources, too much dependence on outsiders, and ineffectiveness. Worst of all, some tribal governments are perceived by tribal members as completely illegitimate.

When viewed at the surface, one might conclude that these problems have simple origins. Increasingly, Indigenous Peoples are engaging in fierce competition for economic opportunities and political power. Historically, this has occurred in nations afflicted with tremendous poverty, in which there are too few resources to benefit everyone. But recently, this has also begun to occur in Indian nations that have a lot of money and resources. While one might think that having more money is the solution to governmental infighting and dysfunction, this is not the case. Instead, even wealthy Indians are engaged in the worst kind of infighting, resulting in violence, banishment, and disenrollment.

ACTIVITY:

Identify the problems that exist within your current tribal government.

_____
_____
_____
_____
_____
_____

What do you think are the causes of these problems?

_____
_____
_____
_____
_____
_____
_____
_____

3. What are the sources of conflict within your nation?

It is not easy to identify all of the distinct factors associated with modern tribal government dysfunction. One might be tempted to attribute simple reasons for the conflict, such as "poverty," "jealousy," or "selfishness." However, invariably the cause of most tribal government dysfunction is much deeper than that.

One possible cause of this infighting relates to the changes that have been taking place within Indigenous societies in recent years. For example, because of the surge in gaming activities on reservations, Indigenous Peoples who have lived away from their nations for some time have decided to move back to their homelands. When this happens, they bring back with them attitudes and beliefs learned from living in American society, which are often self-serving and at odds with the communal beliefs of the reservation people. They also bring with them an ignorance of how things "work" within the nation. At the same time, however, some of these returning Indigenous People often bring the positive benefit of being able to think critically about some time-honored but possibly corrupt and self-serving tribal traditions. Overall, this clash of values, beliefs, knowledge, and education is a deep source of conflict among Native Peoples.

Though there may be many reasons for tribal infighting, I believe that there are two underlying causes: the social and cultural changes associated with the colonization of the Indigenous nations by the United States, and the assimilation of Native Peoples into American society. The shift from traditional subsistence lifestyles to the profit-seeking capitalistic lifestyles has created economic problems. Our transition from pure democracies, where people have equal power, to republics and autocracies, results in a situation where people have less of a voice. The influence of the U.S. legal system has skewed the goals of our laws from peacemaking to litigation. Our culture has suffered from the change from Native-language-speaking communal people to English-language-speaking individual people. At every turn, I believe, the factors associated with tribal government dysfunction have everything to do with the colonization-induced transformation that has been occurring within our nations for a long, long time.

ACTIVITY:

Identify the conflicts that exist within your nation.

_____

_____

_____

_____

_____

Which conflicts are caused by money (either too little or too much)?

_____

_____

_____

_____

_____

What are the other sources of conflict?

_____

_____

_____

_____

_____

_____

Have the kinds of conflicts changed over time?

_____

_____

_____

_____

_____

4. How has colonization changed Indigenous governments?

By definition, traditional tribal governments are those that have been least changed by the influence of American colonization. Unfortunately, colonization has destroyed most traditional governments. And even for the few that exist, it is likely that the people of those nations do not share the same identity and values as a community that they once did. From this cultural discord arise the seeds of acrimony and dysfunction. As a result, colonization has created governance problems for traditional nations not because the form of government has changed, but because the character of the Indians being governed has changed.

As opposed to the more traditional tribal governments, American colonization has had a greater effect on the formation of the autonomous constitutional governments. Even though autonomous constitutional governments were not adopted without the direct involvement of the United States, they were modified under the heavy influence of American governance traditions. For example, even though these govern-

ments are of autonomous origin, they invariably take on a written constitutional form. They may also include such American notions of governance as courts and bills of rights. While there might be some evidence that traditional governing practices were preserved in written form, these adapted constitutions are mostly derived from the U.S. Constitution. It is in this way that American influence can be seen.

The most dramatic effect of American colonization on Indigenous governance has occurred in those nations that have dependent constitutional or corporate tribal governments. Approximately half of all tribal governments in the United States have been established pursuant to U.S. law. To highlight the manner in which this occurred, it is necessary to focus on the two U.S. statutes that have had the most significant effect on transforming native governments: the Indian Reorganization Act and the Alaska Native Claims Settlement Act.

In 1934, the U.S. Congress passed the Indian Reorganization Act (IRA) to end the destructive legacy of the General Allotment Act of 1887 and to provide a mechanism for the revitalization of tribal government. Allotment destroyed the tribal land base in many Indian nations, and resulted in the transfer of about two-thirds of all Indian lands in the United States at the time to the control of non-Indians. It also had the effect of destroying traditional Indigenous life. Based upon the notion that tribalism was an evil behavior of uncivilized people, allotment was designed to transform the basis of Indian identity from the community to the individual. The ultimate failure of allotment as a policy and the abandonment of its fundamental premise—that traditional tribal life should be destroyed —precipitated the move toward supporting Native self-government and the adoption of the IRA.

Proponents of IRA believed that by adopting a written form of government with defined powers, Indian nations would be able to pull themselves out of the mess that the United States admitted it had put them in. Thus, the IRA provided that any Indian nation could reorganize its governmental affairs by establishing a constitutional government in accordance with IRA's provisions. In addition, the IRA also provided a mechanism for an Indian nation to adopt a corporate charter for purposes of conducting economic activity. In doing so, the IRA was intended to eliminate much of the administrative control over tribal governance that had previously been exercised by the Bureau of Indian Affairs (BIA).

As a general matter, the IRA constitutions were simple and of a similar "boilerplate" design. They were form documents that provided for the election by the people of a single branch of government called a "council." The council was to have only a few members, usually five, and was responsible for all legislative affairs. Executive functions were handled by a chairperson, vice-chairperson, treasurer, and secretary, who were all selected by the council from the council membership. The constitutional form set forth the various powers of the council, but perhaps most significantly, required that the secretary of the Interior approve all tribal laws before they could become effective.

One of the significant effects of the IRA constitutions was the further erosion of traditional tribal governing traditions. For example, establishing constitutional governments under the IRA resulted in the concentration of power in the hands of a few people, a situation that had not previously existed. To the extent that traditional governance was characterized by decentralized power structures, elders, women, warriors, and often children had roles to play in the decision making and ordering of the traditional society. The chiefs were not the dictators that the American invaders assumed they were. They were leaders, but they possessed only with the power to persuade, not to coerce. Against this backdrop, the establishment of a form of government that vested all official authority in the hands of as few as five people was a radical departure from traditional practice.

Unfortunately, the concentration of tribal political power greatly served American colonial interests. Under traditional government, it was always difficult for American officials and speculators to know who exactly within Indian societies had legal authority to bind the tribe. Familiar only with a system where power was vested in one person (a president) and laws generated by a legislature (the Congress), American negotiators were frequently frustrated in their efforts to secure rights-of-way, land cessions, and peace treaties. Thus, the establishment of council-type governments, with only a handful of officials, greatly increased the ability of the United States to control the Indian nations.

However, the IRA governments had an even broader purpose than just easing control over the tribe. Ultimately, the extension of written constitutional and corporate governments to the Indian nations under the IRA was consistent with the colonizing society's philosophy of revitalizing Indian societies in its own mirror image. It was believed that forcing changes in government would eventually aid in the assimilation of Indian People into American society.

The process of gaining control over Indians through government manipulation was not limited to the nineteenth and early twentieth centuries. In 1972, the United States acted to safeguard its valuable oil interests in Alaska when it passed the Alaska Native

Claims Settlement Act. ANCSA had a dramatic effect of transforming traditional Native governance, primarily by establishing corporations as holders of the land and as a tool for economic development. And most recently, the United States is considering legislation that would recognize the Indigenous People of Hawaii, the Kanaka Maoli, through a process in which the United States will establish and control a unified government for them.

While the precise degree to which colonization has influenced Indigenous governance is hard to measure, it is a safe assumption that all tribal governments have been affected by it. What these changes mean for the future of tribal governance is critical and lies at the heart of the tribal governance problem. Government is the mechanism by which a people seek to channel their energies, virtues, and vices in such a way so as to allow for the pursuit of their common interests. Whether a government is successful at achieving those interests is dependent, in large part, upon the degree of public support for that government. If there is strong or widespread public support, government can function and the public interest can be served. If there is weak or divided public support, government cannot function and the public interest will be frustrated by private interests.

Colonization has had a disruptive effect on the otherwise natural development process of tribal governance. In the absence of colonization, of course, tribal governments would have evolved, subject to the influences of other Indigenous societies. Given the relatively decentralized nature of these Indigenous societies, it seems unlikely that any one Indigenous society would have been able to exert influence upon all of the others. While the Great Lakota Nation might have maintained its original form, or there might have ended up being thirty nations of the Haudenosaunee rather than six, it seems highly unlikely that any one Indigenous society would have been able to colonize the entire continent.

ACTIVITY:

How has colonization changed your nation's government?

_____

_____

_____

_____

_____

What was the traditional form of government of your people?

_____

_____

_____

_____

_____

_____

How might it still operate in the same manner?

_____

_____

_____

_____

Can you identify other Indian nations with a history of governance like your own?

_____

_____

_____

_____

5. How has colonization affected your people?

American colonization was aggressive, forced, violent, and widespread. It attacked the territorial, cultural, spiritual, social, and political aspects of our societies. Given the numbers of our people who died and the number of cultures and peoples that have already become extinct as a result of it, it was a truly a holocaust.

The effect of colonization on tribal governance, at least as I see it, is one that has induced deep division within our nations solely by virtue of its transformative effect on the character and identity of our people. Some of us may possess the defining characteristics of our people, as if we had not been colonized. Perhaps we have a relatively "pure" Indigenous ancestral background, a highly distinct cultural foundation, and an uncompromised political loyalty to our Native nation. On the other hand, others of us may be culturally and philosophically indistinct from members of the colonizing American society. Most of us, no doubt, are somewhere in the middle.

Thus, it is my central working theory that it is the colonization-induced diversity of our tribal communities that is precipitating many of the problems in Indigenous government and Indigenous society in general. Perhaps at no other time in our collective histories are our nations comprised of so many different kinds of people, different cultural foundations, and different political philosophies. Allotment, boarding schools, Christianity, intermarriage, and the American rights revolution are just a few of the factors that have had the effect of contributing to this transformation. While it is obvious that not all nations have undergone the exact same degree of change, all have been affected in some way.

A crude barometer for gauging the degree of this diversity is to assess the "culture gap" that exists between the so-called traditional people and the so-called progressive people within any particular Indian community. For those familiar with Native communities, it seems that most political problems that arise in Indian country can be broken down into conflict between these two groups. As a technical matter, of course, these conflicts are wholly internal because they all involve "card-carrying" tribal members. As a practical matter, however, these conflicts take place between very different groups of people. Quite literally, if a tribal community is comprised of people who were raised in the traditional way, speak the Native language, and practice the traditional religion, then the tribal members who were educated in the missionary school, know little of the traditional culture, and live an assimilated lifestyle might as well be from another planet. It is hard to imagine a greater chasm of identity existing between people who all profess to be the same.

ACTIVITY:

How has colonization changed your people?

_____

_____

_____

_____

Do these changes make it easier or more difficult to "get along" and get things accomplished?

_____

_____

_____

_____

6. How has colonization affected your sovereignty?

Sovereignty is the power of a people to control their own destiny. The extent of sovereignty is dependent upon three things: (1) the degree to which the people believe in the right to define their own future; (2) the degree to which the people have the ability to carry out those beliefs; and (3) the degree to which sovereign acts are recognized both within the nation and by the outside world. Colonization has disrupted Indigenous governments and made them weaker than they should be, because it has influenced each of these three factors.

Tribal governments must function against the backdrop of colonization. The mechanism set in place to channel the passion and power of our increasingly diverse communities—our governments—is wholly inadequate to meet the challenges of our modern tribal nations. Autocratic systems imposed by the U.S. government cannot possibly be expected to address our traditional faith in pure democracy. Moreover, traditional systems that carried on for hundreds of years cannot possibly be expected to address the cultural pluralism characteristic of many tribal communities.

Where this schism exists, there is conflict; where there is conflict, there can be no governance; and where there is no governance, there can be no ability to influence the future.

It is likely that no tribal governing structure is immune from this syndrome. The dysfunction may be most easily identifiable in the dependent constitutional or corporate tribal governments. For nations with these types of governments, the "official" government has been established by the United States with no formal role for the participation of the traditional leadership. In most instances when this has occurred, the traditional leadership simply did not magically disappear. It remained intact and was thus simply bypassed by those tribal members selected to serve as the "official" tribal council. There seems little doubt that the establishment of constitutional governments within those Indian nations where viable traditional governments remained, served to institutionalize division among the people.

Even traditional governments have also been disrupted by colonization-induced diversity. Aside from any structural changes that may have occurred over time, it is the case that the tribal membership itself has gotten more diverse. In this way, disruption in traditional governance has occurred primarily because the people, not the government, have changed. Conflict exists because of the inability of the traditional leadership and the traditional system to keep pace with the needs of an increasingly assimilated tribal membership who simply do not accept its authority.

It is not likely that the culturally induced divisions that exist within our nations can be eliminated in the near future. A long-term goal is to reunify Indigenous People within a nation based upon updated traditional teachings and ways of life. Achieving the maximum measure of self-government requires that divisiveness and cultural diversity at this level be redressed. Given how many generations it has taken to create the problem, and the fact that global forces promote rather than inhibit diversity, it is hard to imagine that a simple or short-term solution can be developed. This means that for the near future, Indian nations are "stuck" with a tribal citizenry that will likely become even more diverse in political, economic, cultural, and spiritual ways. Thus, to the extent that this diversity is the prime factor contributing to internal acrimony and conflict, Indian nations will be "stuck" with that, too.

The challenge, then, is to find a mechanism that can somehow contain and better manage the boiling cauldron of modern Indigenous life. As I see it, this requires a transformation of tribal governance. While there may be a few Indian nations where all or most tribal members agree as to the form of government, in the many places that do not, I believe that serious and concerted effort must be given to governmental reform in order to avoid the further disintegration of our tribal existence.

In many respects, what I am suggesting is the governmental equivalent of getting a new boat rather than simply trying to patch the leaks in the old one. Piecemeal tinkering with governing structure or administrative operation is the practical equivalent of putting a new coat of paint on the *Titanic*. No matter how good things might look when you are done, your efforts will undoubtedly have little long-term meaningful effect.

ACTIVITY:

Do you think that your government must be changed to reflect the needs and desires of your people? Why or why not?

_____

_____

_____

_____

Is sovereignty important for improving the lives of your people? Why or why not?

_____

_____

_____

_____

_____

_____

7. Suggested Steps for Achieving Governmental Decolonization

The process for decolonizing and reforming an Indigenous government is a unique process tied to the uniqueness of the people involved. Because of this, it is impossible to know with certainty what is the "right" path towards governmental decolonization or even what should be the "right" outcome of such a process. At best, one can only recommend a set of general guidelines that can maximize the likelihood of success. What follows are my suggestions.

Step 1—Form a working group. Reforming government is a process that affects everyone within a particular Indian nation. Regardless of how the existing government functions (or doesn't function), making even minor change is a process that requires the participation of many, many people. The problem, however, is that it is almost impossible to address complex problems like governance with hundreds of people directly involved. The mix of ideas, personalities, and politics makes it impossible to come together on even the smallest issues.

The best approach for moving forward with constitutional reform is to form a working group of between ten and twenty people. If the reform movement is conducted through the authority of the existing government, the council or executive officer could appoint the working group. If it is a community reform movement, individuals could volunteer for the working group. It is important that the participants selected be very dedicated and willing to meet repeatedly to get the job done. They must also be committed to working on the reform effort for *years*.

Ideally, the working group should reflect a diversity of political views from within the community. Because reform affects so many people, it is better to address competing political perspectives early on in the process rather than later. If a working group is mistakenly comprised of all like-minded people, then it

> **"Trusting the people is the indispensable precondition for revolutionary change."**
>
> **—Paulo Freire**

might be easier for them to come to an agreement on a reform proposal. Of course, it is also quite possible that such a working group could be quite wrong in its thinking about what the people want from the reform process. In such a case, a lot of time and effort could be wasted developing proposals that are soundly rejected by the community.

The working group should also have some degree of administrative support. The most important resource need is the ability to copy and distribute proposed reforms to the citizens of the nation. Since it is the citizens who must make the decision (assuming a democratic government), it is vital that they be given the information necessary to make an informed decision. The working group, in effect, merely serves as a development forum. The ultimate decision must be made by the people themselves based upon the proposals developed by the working group.

Some nations may feel the need to be more formal in the creation of the working group. They might want to call it a "government reform commission" or a "constitutional review board" or even a "constitutional convention." Regardless of the terminology, the critical component for success is to ensure that the working group has *legitimacy* in the eyes of the people. Ordinarily, legitimacy is tied to involving individuals in the working group who represent different political interests within the nation.

Step 2—Redefine the role of tribal government. The initial task of the working group is to formulate ideas about what should be the central purpose of tribal governmental authority in their lives. This should be an idealistic process, one driven by notions of what the ideal government could do to help people's lives, not what the old government could do to make things even worse. This is likely to provoke a wide range of responses, but it is necessary to include as many definitions of government function as possible. Once these differing ideas are brought out and shared, the working group should then engage in a consensus-building process. The end of this process may result in a mission statement or preamble. Once this visionary framework for action is established, it is then possible to develop the more specific provisions necessary to bring the vision to life.

Step 3—Research the historical political behavior and the historic function of tribal government. The next important function for the working group is to examine the history of the nation's government. If a constitutional government is in place, it is important to find out how that government came into being and what kind of government it replaced. From this experience, much knowledge can be gained about the values and beliefs of the people. For example, if it is discovered that long ago women selected certain men to serve as leaders in the nation, then it might follow that the nation has a long history of respecting the power of women and gender equality. The values and beliefs that are discovered are the most important factors in decolonizing tribal government.

When engaging in a government reform effort, however, it is instinctive to want to examine what other peoples have done to reform their government. Depending on the people chosen for study, this can be disastrous. Unfortunately, colonization has impressed upon too many Indigenous People the governing traditions of the United States and not their own nation. If one anchors to American governing traditions, then it is possible to engage in what I call *auto-colonization,* or the process of reaffirming colonial policies under the guise of actually trying to rid yourself of them. The U.S. Constitution was based upon a variety of governmental theories that were brought together for the unique purpose of governing a large and immigrant-populated republic. It is unreasonable to think that such a governmental form is well suited for all Indigenous societies.

While the increasing diversity of our nations may mean that many principles underlying U.S. government ultimately may be useful to us, if we are to preserve our distinct existence, we should begin with our own traditions. Where there remains a significant

population of elders to share an understanding of earlier times, those elders must be consulted. Even old politicians have important stores of unwritten knowledge about how tribal governing affairs are conducted. All of this information must be identified and recorded.

In addition, if any ancient texts about tribal life can be obtained, they too must be utilized. This includes some of the old anthropological reports written in terms suggesting that our ancestors were some kind of zoo animals. Regardless of how offensive you might find some of this work, some of it is quite helpful in understanding how society functioned in the past. The challenge is simply to sift through some of the disparaging conclusions about our ancestors to get to the core body of research.

In short, the starting point for any governmental precedent should be the unique governing traditions of the Indigenous nation itself. If this yields little information, the next best alternative is to look at the governing traditions of related Indian People. If that process too yields little information, the next source of information should be Indigenous communities that share many of the same size and demographic characteristics. Only as a last resort should the governing tradition of the United States be relied upon.

Step 4—Assess the degree to which historical notions of governance still apply. Once the historical review is complete, there should be a determination of which of the governing traditions continue to be relied upon by the people. This includes both the oral and written traditions. If any particular governing traditions within an Indian nation can be identified as surviving American colonization to the present day, then these practices undoubtedly must be the core of the political belief system. Especially in those nations that have previously undergone some form of constitutional development, the identification of political practices that have been carried on under both the traditional and constitutional forms of government is a revealing picture of previous governing traditions.

Step 5—Evaluate historical norms for continued usefulness. As part of the historical review process, there should be a deliberate effort to evaluate which of the traditional governing practices should be continued and/or revitalized. This may be the most difficult step because it requires a two-pronged approach. At one level, historical governing provisions must be viewed from the perspective of their literally being continued and/or revitalized. For example, a requirement under traditional governance that no action shall be taken until there is consensus could mean that the tribal council should not be able to act unless there is a unanimous vote. Thus, part of the inquiry should include whether any of the actual traditional governing practices should be continued.

At another level, however, there should be an assessment as to whether any of the values underlying a specific traditional governing provision should be continued and/or revitalized. Thus, to continue with the example above, the value underlying the requirement that no action shall be taken until "all of the people are in agreement" is simply that there should be widespread agreement as to the course of action. As a practical matter, this might be satisfied in a number of different ways other than by unanimous council votes. The council could only have to obtain a three-quarters or two-thirds majority, or it could have to vote twice, at least one week apart, and so on.

Focusing on traditional governing *values*, rather than *rules*, is tremendously important for the entire governmental reform process. It may be extremely difficult for some traditional people to relinquish time-honored procedures for doing things. Focusing on the fact that the underlying values and teachings of those time-honored procedures could be continued and expanded, albeit in a modern form, may be the key to gaining their support for any ultimate changes in governmental form. Similarly, many of the progressives might support traditional governing principles that they otherwise might reject if they are conveyed in a

> **"In order for the struggle to have meaning, the oppressed must not, in seeking to regain their humanity (which is a way to create it), become in turn oppressors of the oppressors, but rather restorers of the humanity of both."**
> **—Paulo Freire**

form that they can comprehend. In short, if the focus is on substance, and not exclusively on form, the seeds of compromise can be sown. This will be important when it comes time to address the difficult issue of how much, if any, of the new government structure should be committed to writing.

Step 6—Be creative when drafting a document on governing principles. Because of the many changes that have occurred within our nations, it seems inevitable that some important aspects of any governmental reform effort must be reduced to writing. If there are still nations that can sustain a wholly unwritten governing tradition, then obviously few, if any, changes should be made. In all of the others, however, drafting will take on a special role in the reform process.

Basing tribal governmental reform on historical notions of governance will have little impact unless drafting takes place with an eye towards creativity. Mindlessly borrowing language from federal, state, or even tribal constitutions will wholly undermine the historical research and will ensure that the reform process will have little positive long-term effect. If writing is to be done, it must be with original prose and devoid of legalese. Indeed, it may be the case that with some issues, no writing should be done at all. Cutting and pasting is simply too crude of a process for what needs to be done in decolonizing tribal governance. Only when a conscious decision has been made about adopting certain practices from the U.S. government should some of the "terms of art" under American law be adopted in the tribal constitutional text (for example, "due process," "equal protection," and so forth).

Step 7—Work deliberately and openly. For any governmental reform effort to be successful, the Native People themselves must understand and support what is happening. The only way I think that this can occur is if the reform process is approached like an educational process. If the tribal members are teaching each other about the governing traditions and working together to develop modern ways to perpetuate those traditions, then, when it comes time to put such changes into place, resistance should be minimal.

Sharing information about the reform process is critical to gaining acceptance. Often in tribal government there is a tendency to keep things close to the vest to minimize the opportunity for the opposition —whoever that might be at any given time—to undermine your efforts. Unless the process is open to all, the reality, or merely the perception, that something "fishy" is going on will condemn any possibility that honest reform can be achieved. Remember, legitimacy is the most important result from the process. If the ideas are worth doing, they will be accepted by the people. Good ideas will rise like cream; bad ideas will sink like stones. Allowing an open process will ensure that this natural process, and legitimacy, will result.

Step 8—Convince conservative opponents that good government is good politics. There is likely to be considerable resistance to governmental reform from conservatives within the tribal community. These conservatives may either be traditional people concerned that any change will undermine their position within the nation, or old-style politicians who are fearful of any change that may result in their demise. Of course, if there is one thing most Indian People can agree on, it is that they do not like what the tribal government is doing. The process of governmental reform is one that the people in any Indian nation will very likely support. Conservatives within the community, who may have the ability to halt changes desired by most of the people, must be convinced that reform is politically in their self-interest as well as the interests of all of the people.

Step 9—Exercise great patience and listen to the people. My working theory for dealing with change is based on my belief that people usually do not know what they want, but they usually know what they don't want. I think this is especially true when working with Indian People because we have developed such a good

defense mechanism against colonization over the years. In many ways, working with Indians is like working with a giant tortoise. At the slightest sign of danger, the head and legs retract to allow the protective shell to do its work. There is no movement and no progress, only the hope that the big shell will keep the threat away.

Well, the threat that we have been dealing with for all these years—American colonialism—has been both a poison in our food and an acid eating through our shell. We either have to have some faith that we can change our traditional eating patterns in the face of this danger, get a new shell, or do both. Unfortunately, this kind of change is difficult for many to accept, either because they do not perceive the problem, or because they are simply resistant to change. I think that the time for simply sitting with our head and legs tucked in is over. As things are going, our destruction will come from our failure to act.

E. The Need to Decolonize U.S. Indian Control Laws

No matter how much responsibility we assume for the redevelopment of our sovereignty, the United States remains a barrier to our progress. America, because of its geographic size, people, government, culture, media, and money, is an overwhelming influence on the Indigenous nations located within its borders. As a result, tremendous forces inhibit the preservation and strengthening of the unique fabric of our nations, and thus form considerable obstacles to our redevelopment.

One of the most significant barriers to our redevelopment lies in the body of American law. Since its founding, the United States has developed an extensive body of law—so-called federal Indian law—to define and regulate its relationship with the Indian nations remaining within its borders. While this law may seem to have a neutral purpose, it would be more accurate to say that "federal Indian law" is really "federal Indian control law" because it has the twofold mission of establishing the legal bases for American colonization of the continent, and perpetuating American power and control over the Indian nations.

There are specific American laws that inhibit the ability of Indian nations to self-govern. The most significant relate to the establishment of constitutional governments under the Indian Reorganization Act. These provisions are unnecessary and need to be repealed. While no Indian nation is actually restrained in its sovereign authority to change its form of government, leaving the U.S. law on the books serves as a practical barrier to this action occurring. Bureau of Indian Affairs officials rely on the existence of these laws and manipulate them to ensure control. While repealing these laws is much easier said than done, it should be kept in mind that decolonization has two dimensions. It is possible that an Indigenous People could go through the process described above and successfully decolonize their own government, but be prevented from achieving true freedom because of the limitations contained within American law. Being aware that these obstacles exist, and formulating strategies for neutralizing them, are important parts of decolonizing Indigenous governance.

ACTIVITY:

Find and read a copy of Title 25 of the United States Code. Do you think any of the laws contained therein should be eliminated?

_____

_____

_____

_____

_____

_____

Research how the United States Supreme Court has handled legal cases with Indians. Do you think that any specific decisions should be changed?

_____

_____

_____

F. Conclusion

It is important to remember that our many problems are related to the challenges that we face in trying to figure out how to survive in the modern world. Whether we realize it or not, each of our nations, as well as each of us personally, has undergone considerable change since the Europeans arrived to colonize our territories. What this means, for example, is that while we may desperately want to preserve our language and culture, we do not have the means to develop the educational and social structure that will allow it to readily happen. Or while we might worry about the disintegration of our traditional way of life, we have too many members who can only conceive of life in terms of what it means to be a part of American society. In short, in our personal and collective battle against cultural destruction, we face seemingly insurmountable odds and thus, often unleash our anger and frustration on the people closest to us—our families and fellow tribal citizens. In doing so, we jeopardize the very tribal sovereignty that we so desperately need to help us preserve our distinct Indigenous existence.

I believe that the challenge of tribal government is one that almost all Indigenous nations must be prepared to face in the coming years. While there may be a lucky few who have somehow maintained or developed a governing mechanism that has the support of their people, it seems that most are suffering from debilitating internal conflict that weakens them at a time when weakness can least be afforded.

Preserving and strengthening tribal sovereignty through decolonization should be the most important objective for any Native People who want to survive and grow stronger. While it may seem obvious to some that pursuing economic sovereignty should be the first order of business, it should be kept in mind that the cultural change and infighting associated with economic development ultimately may be more destructive than the poverty it seeks to replace. Over time, Indian nations that can develop a form of government to channel the passions and powers of their people into concerted action, will be able to handle any challenge thrown to them, whether of internal or external origin. Regardless of what the United States does from here on out, only we can make our nations stronger. While the United States might occasionally release its grip to give us some breathing room, unless we take the initiative to wiggle free, we will forever be under its destructive power. Knowing what we know about the world in which we live, we will have only ourselves to blame if we do nothing about it.

To assist you in conceptualizing how we need to decolonize how we govern ourselves, I would like to draw upon the teaching of the Gus-Wen-Tah, or the Two Row Wampum, of my people, the Haudenosaunee. The Two Row Wampum is a treaty belt that symbolizes the first formal agreement between the Haudenosaunee and the colonists to peacefully coexist. It is described as follows:

> When the Haudenosaunee first came into contact with the European nations, treaties of peace and friendship were made. Each was symbolized by the Gus-Wen-Tah, or Two Row Wampum. There is a bed of white wampum, which symbolizes the purity of the agreement. There are two rows of purple, and those two rows have the spirit of your ancestors and mine. There are three beads of wampum separating the two rows and they symbolize peace, friendship, and respect.
>
> These two rows will symbolize two paths or two vessels, traveling down the same river together. One, a birch bark canoe, will be for the Indian people, their laws, their customs, and their ways. The other, a ship, will be for the white people and their laws, their customs, and their ways. We shall each travel the river together, side by side, but in our own boat. Neither of us will try to steer the other's vessel.

If there is to be peaceful coexistence between the Indigenous nations and the United States into the future, then the balance in our relationship must be restored. For more than two hundred years, the United States has sought to "steer" our "vessel" and control our way of life. The argument that such actions were justified because they were for our own good is unacceptable. Our right to self-determination is one given to us by our Creator, and it is the spirit of that right that has allowed our people to survive to the present day. If we retain any regard for our survival as distinct peoples, we must commit to restoring the vision of the Two Row Wampum in our collective futures. An important part of that commitment is decolonizing our governments and unleashing the full power of our peoples.

G. Suggested Readings

There is very little written material that focuses on Indigenous governance, much less the decolonization of Indigenous governance. You may find the following materials that I have written helpful as you continue your studies.

"Building a New Longhouse: The Case for Government Reform Within the Six Nations of the Haudenosaunee," *Buffalo Law Review* 46, no. 805 (Fall 1998).

"Decolonizing Indigenous Governance: Observations on Restoring Greater Faith and Legitimacy in the Government of the Seneca Nation," *Kansas Journal of Law & Public Policy* 8, no. 97 (Winter 1999). Also available online at www.law.ku.edu/jrnl/index.htm.

"Decolonizing, Legalizing, and Modernizing New York State's Indian Law," *Albany Law Review* 63, no. 125 (1999).

"A Proposal to the Hanodaganyas to Decolonize Federal Indian Control Law," *University of Michigan Journal of Law Reform* 31, no. 899 (Summer 1998).

"Pursuing the Path of Indigenization in the Era of Emergent International Law Governing the Rights of Indigenous Peoples," *Yale Human Rights & Development Law Journal* 5, no. 123 (2002). Also available online at www.yale.edu/yhrdlj/index_enhanced.htm.

Sovereignty, Colonialism & the Indigenous Nations: A Reader (Durham, NC: Carolina Academic Press, 2005).

"Strengthening Tribal Sovereignty Through Government Reform: What Are the Issues?," *Kansas Journal of Law & Public Policy* 7, no. 72 (Winter 1998). This chapter is based upon this article; it's available online at www.law.ku.edu/jrnl/index.htm.

"Strengthening Tribal Sovereignty Through Peacemaking: How the Anglo-American Legal Tradition Destroys Indigenous Societies," *Columbia Human Rights Law Review* 28, no. 235 (Winter 1997).

H. Glossary

colonization: the process by which a people exploit and/or annex the lands and resources of another people without their consent and unilaterally expand political power over them. An advanced form of colonization is "auto-colonization," which is the process that the colonized people engage in when they try to implement solutions to their dilemma that have the effect of promoting the agenda of the colonists rather than remedying it.

colonization amnesia: what occurs when Indians don't have any knowledge of how they have been shaped by the colonists, because this knowledge has been denied to them by their education and even their family

government: the rules and procedures developed and used by a people to allow them to take collective action as a society

indigenization: the personal and collective process of decolonizing Indigenous life and restoring true self-determination based on traditional Indigenous values

politics: the activities that individuals engage in to obtain and use the power of government

self-determination: the right of all peoples to freely determine their political status and freely pursue their economic, social, and cultural development

social engineering: the process by which a colonizer strategically changes the culture, identity, and way of life of a colonized people to align the Native People more closely with the colonizers, with the final outcome being complete assimilation

sovereignty: the power of a people to control their own destiny. A nation's sovereignty is dependent upon three things: (1) the degree to which the people believe in the right to define their own future; (2) the degree to which the people have the ability to carry out those beliefs; and (3) the degree to which sovereign acts are recognized both within the nation and by the outside world.

Defying Colonization Through Language Survival

Waziyatawin

A. What Is at Stake

In the beginning, the Great Mystery gave us our languages. Through our languages we were given a way to name, categorize, conceptualize, and relate to the world around us. Through our languages we were given a way of life.

In the twenty-first century our languages are in a state of crisis. Many have already gone extinct and many others are dangerously close to extinction. Our ways of being are also threatened. If we are not able to save our languages, we will lose our ways of thinking and relating to the rest of the universe that distinguish us as Indigenous Peoples. We will lose our capacity to live as we were instructed. We will lose ourselves.

While our generation of Indigenous Peoples did not create the language crisis now before us, if we do not take immediate and dramatic action to save our languages, they may be lost from us forever. The generations living now must be the ones to recover and stabilize our languages so these millennia-old traditions do not die in our lifetimes. In saving our languages, we will be saving our ways of life and our ways of relating with the rest of the universe. We will save ourselves.

Until we really sit down to think about the status of our languages, it is easy to lull ourselves into the comfortable belief that our languages are not severely threatened. However, for most of us, even a brief examination of our families and our communities reveals that the situation is more serious than many of us have cared to admit. In the late 1990s, Michael Krauss, the director of the Native Alaska Language Center at the University of Alaska, Fairbanks, classified the surviving Indigenous languages in the United States into four categories.

Class A includes the 34 languages still spoken by all generations, including young children.

Class B includes the 35 languages spoken only by the parental generation and older.

Class C includes the 84 languages spoken only by the grandparental generation and older.

Class D includes the 57 languages spoken only by the very elderly, usually fewer than ten persons.

The 34 Class A languages are the only ones not in immediate danger, though if present trends continue they will likely also face diminishing use within the next few generations. When the issue of language loss is examined from this generational framework, it is easier to calculate how many years it might be before a language dies out because there are no living speakers remaining. Once the language decline begins and a generation emerges that can no longer speak the language, the language deteriorates rapidly. In examining the issue of language loss, it is important to accurately assess the status of your Indigenous language.

ACTIVITY:

To assess the status of your language, first examine the levels of language fluency within your immediate and extended family. It is important to first distinguish who are the fluent speakers of the language. This list of fluent speakers should include all those who can convey whatever thoughts they want to convey in your Indigenous language. This list should not include those individuals who may understand the language when it is spoken to them, but who cannot speak it themselves.

Who in your family's grandparental generation can speak the language fluently?

_____

_____

_____

_____

Who in your family's parental generation can speak the language fluently?

_____

_____

_____

_____

Who in your family's youngest generation can speak the language fluently?

_____

_____

_____

_____

If none of the above applies, who among the very elderly, perhaps in the great-grandparental generation, can still speak the language fluently?

_____

_____

_____

_____

Which one of Krauss's categories best describes the status of the language within your family?

Class A   Class B   Class C   Class D

Out of all the individuals listed above, now calculate which percentage of them speaks your Indigenous language. You may find the percentage by multiplying the number of speakers by 100 and then dividing that figure by the total number of people listed. For example, if you listed 12 speakers in your family of 57, the percentage would be figured like this:

$$12 \times 100 = 1200$$

$$1200 \div 57 = 21\%$$

In this case 21 percent of the family members speak the language.

Step 1: Multiply the number of speakers in your family by 100: _____

Step 2: Number of total family members listed: _____

Step 3: Divide the result from Step 1 by the figure in Step 2. _____

This is the percentage of speakers in your family.

This process may be repeated on a larger scale to more broadly calculate the status of language in your community or reservation. These simple questions could be asked in every household in your community as part of a door-to-door survey. While conducting a community-wide survey requires considerable time and energy, the data collected during the survey may help awaken the community to the dire need for language revitalization efforts. Furthermore, when seeking grants to fund language projects, this data will help justify the request for language monies.

B. My Experience with Dakota Language

I am a Dakota person who was not raised speaking our language. I grew up frequently hearing our language spoken and I learned to speak words and phrases, but my understanding and knowledge of the language was very limited. It was not until I began taking Dakota language classes at the University of Minnesota that the world of our language opened up to me. When it did, I learned to cherish everything about the language and, consequently, dedicated much of my time and energy to language work. I gained proficiency in the language after two years of daily instruction and continued to serve as a teaching assistant for the language until I graduated. I also spent considerable time outside of the classroom teaching and working with language. As president of the Dakota/Lakota Language Society, I helped organize and teach language classes for the Twin Cities urban community and I taught Dakota language in a variety of community education programs. My daily work on language continued over the next several years in my academic career as I worked with Dakota oral tradition, including a set of stories conveyed in Dakota by my grandfather, Eli Taylor. I believed firmly in the importance of our language and many of my efforts both professionally and personally revolved around this commitment to language. The more I learned about the language, the more I realized how little I knew and how important it was to save our language.

After completing my graduate coursework I returned to my home reservation of Pezihutazizi K'api Makoce (Land Where They Dig for Yellow Medicine, known as the Upper Sioux Reservation in southwestern Minnesota) to write my dissertation. I spent the next six years there, having children, writing my dissertation, and transcribing and translating Dakota with the help of my relatives. After a couple years of living back home, the tribal council asked me to develop and implement a comprehensive language preservation and revitalization plan for our community. I agreed, and that sent me on a language journey from which I am still reeling.

As a trained researcher, I believed it was important to find out how other Indigenous communities were attempting to address the language crisis in their communities. I looked at nearby Indigenous language efforts among the Anishinaabe and Hocak (Hochunk) as well as the extraordinarily successful programs among the Maori and Native Hawaiians. In this research phase I had a breakthrough moment that forever changed my attitude toward language recovery efforts. When a small group of us visited the Hocak Wazija Haci Language program in Mauston, Wisconsin, the cultural director at the time, Kenneth Funmaker, informed us that their goal was to produce a new generation of Hocak language speakers within the next twenty years. This statement blew my mind. I realized at that moment how my own mind had been impacted by colonialism and how limited my vision had become as a consequence. While I had dedicated much of my life to Dakota language work, I really had not even considered the possibility of producing a new generation of fluent speakers. Instead, I had contented myself with the end goal of simply increasing Dakota language usage and perhaps developing conversationally proficient speakers. Then when I began researching the language programs of the Maori and Native Hawaiians, particularly the language immersion preschools, I realized that regaining fluency was within our reach, if we would only grasp that possibility and embrace that vision. I dedicated the next couple of years toward that end.

We implemented several language projects in my community, including preservation efforts such as support of the existing Dakota-English Dictionary Project and the creation of a Dakota language CD-ROM, as well as major revitalization programs such as family language classes and the first Dakota language immersion preschool. These projects flourished until April 2000, and then they exploded and collapsed. That was by far the most heartbreaking experience of my life, but that experience did not come without some valuable lessons. The discussion and suggested activities to follow are drawn from those years of research and lived experience.

C. The Attacks on Indigenous Languages in the United States and Canada

The assaults on Indigenous languages were an indispensable part of the colonizing project, and efforts to eradicate Indigenous languages occurred simultaneously with sustained Indigenous-white contact. Indigenous languages were, in fact, not even recognized as legitimate languages. Indigenous languages were considered to be gibberish, gobbledygook, or backward by the European invaders and their descendants. Many of us who grew up in the twentieth century are well aware of the stereotypes associated with Indigenous languages. In movies, television shows, and cartoons we were frequently depicted as people with a limited vocabulary that primarily consisted of words such as "Ugh!" In fact, a favorite movie among schoolchildren through the end of the twentieth century, Walt Disney's *Peter Pan*, had these musical lyrics, "What makes the Red Man red? When did he first say 'Ugh!'?" Most Americans have assumed on some level that Indigenous languages are inferior to European languages, especially English. This is an assumption that can be traced all the way back to first contact.

While most invading Europeans never attempted to learn or understand Indigenous languages, when they did learn them, they often did so only to facilitate the conversion of Indigenous Peoples to Christianity. If missionaries could deliver sermons in an Indigenous language, more potential converts could be reached. Among such missionaries, Indigenous language

orthographies were often quickly created so that the Bible could be translated and printed in the Indigenous language. This practice was not developed out of love or respect for Indigenous languages; it was developed to more rapidly acquire souls for Christianity's kingdom. Thus, even with these laborious efforts, work in Indigenous languages was never conceived as a long-term project. When Indigenous people converted to Christianity, they were expected to learn the colonizer's language, whether it was Spanish, English, or French. The idea of supporting the maintenance of Indigenous languages was not seriously considered as a viable option among the colonizing population. Like every other aspect of Indigenous cultures and ways of life, Indigenous languages were perceived to be inherently inferior. The colonizers sincerely believed that Indigenous Peoples would only benefit from acquiring what they perceived to be superior European languages.

The eradication of Indigenous languages, then, was always a part of the "civilizing" and Christianizing campaigns of the United States and Canada. The negative attitude toward Indigenous languages only intensified in the nineteenth century, as educational institutions for Indigenous youth were created with the specific intent of carrying out these destructive and systematic campaigns.

From our own observations, most of us understand that the loss of our language in our communities is a direct consequence of boarding school experiences, yet colonial history has also taught us that the boarding schools were beneficial to Indigenous Peoples. The outrageousness of this perspective becomes apparent when the schools are examined by international standards. According to the United Nations Convention on the Prevention and Punishment of the Crime of Genocide, "forcibly transferring children of the group to another group" constitutes a form of genocide. When the United States and Canadian governments mandated that Indigenous children attend boarding or residential schools under the care and supervision of non-Indigenous government workers and missionaries, they were perpetrating acts of genocide by today's standards.

The violence done to Indigenous children in these schools ranged from ethnocide (the intentional and systematic destruction of our cultures) to torture, rape, and murder. The Truth Commission into Genocide in Canada estimates that 50,000 Indigenous children in Canada died as a consequence of this federally mandated "education." Estimates for the loss of life among Indigenous children in the U.S. boarding schools have not yet been realistically calculated, but stories of various forms of abuse are rampant. Given this atrocious reality, anyone arguing the benefits of boarding school education must also argue the benefits of the work camps for Jews in Nazi Germany. From both moral and logical perspectives, acts of genocide cannot be deemed beneficial to the victims.

It was in this context that the greatest attacks on Indigenous languages were perpetrated. The fact that the schools would achieve the most success at eradicating Indigenous cultures by turning their attention to the youngest possible population was not lost on white educators and politicians. They realized that the younger the children were brought to the "schools," the more quickly and thoroughly they would be stripped of their Indigenous languages and traditions. They could be made over into little brown-skinned white people, espousing the same values, beliefs, and worldviews as their teachers, clergy, and staff. Any and all measures were used to pressure the children into speaking English, including shaming, humiliating, beating, swatting, forcing them to kneel for hours on end or on marbles or broomstick handles, putting them in solitary confinement, and washing their mouths out with lye. In fall 2004 when I was explaining to my students the various methods used to punish children for speaking their Native languages, I told them that lye, a strong alkaline solution, is so powerful that when placed in the mouth it causes severe burn-

> "The choice of language and the use to which language is put is central to a people's definition of themselves in relation to their natural and social environment, indeed in relation to the entire universe."
> —Ngugi wa Thiong'o

ing. One of my elderly students in the class then shared with us that his Diné mother, who was sent to a day school in Arizona, was punished with lye soap when she was a child and that she still carries the burn scars in her mouth, more than a half-century later. How many punishments like this, either personally received or witnessed, would it take before an Indigenous child never wanted to speak his or her Native language again? The long-term ramifications of these U.S. and Canadian genocidal campaigns have yet to be quantified or even realized.

In 1990 Congress passed the Native American Languages Act, which recognizes that the United States has "the responsibility to act together with Native Americans to ensure the survival of these unique cultures and languages." While the act encourages the support and use of Native languages, nowhere does it specify which active steps the United States government will take to ensure the survival of Indigenous languages, there is no extensive plan for the government to support and fund Indigenous language immersion programs, or to implement a national campaign to revive Indigenous languages with the same gusto with which it tried to eradicate our languages in the first place. In fact, no mention is made of the systematic attempts at language and culture extermination by the United States government, except the comment "acts of suppression and extermination directed against Native American languages and cultures are in conflict with the United States policy of self-determination for Native Americans." This acknowledges the attacks on language and culture, but not that the United States was the perpetrator of these attacks, even suggesting that the attacks must have come from the outside because the United States is in the business of supporting Indigenous self-determination. While this act may be construed as some kind of progress in its expression of support for Indigenous languages, when the issue is examined in a broader context, it is clear that the act falls far short of any semblance of justice or action.

Furthermore, this act does not diminish the fact that in the twenty-first century we are still left with the legacy of generations of abuse to Indigenous children. As a consequence, many of us were not taught our Indigenous languages. If our parents or grandparents survived the boarding and residential schools with knowledge of our languages intact (that is, if the languages had not been beaten out of them), many of them chose not to teach us. This has been a cause of tremendous grief and even anger for those of us who grew up without our languages. As we lament the loss of our languages, or as we struggle to learn or revive our languages, let us keep in mind the wise words of language activist Darrell Kipp, co-founder of the Piegan Institute of the Blackfeet Nation, which implemented the Blackfeet immersion schools in Browning, Montana: "Parents did not teach the language because they loved us and they didn't want us to suffer, to be abused, or to have a tough life. Because our parents loved us and our grandparents loved us, they tried to protect us from the humiliation and suffering that they went through."

ACTIVITY:

When did language decline begin in your family and under what circumstances?

_____

_____

_____

_____

_____

_____

If your relatives attended boarding schools, what punishments were used to prevent them from speaking your Indigenous language? If you do not know the answer to this, attempt to find out either by asking older relatives or researching the schools they attended.

_____

_____

_____

_____

The impact of the boarding schools and day schools where Indigenous languages were forbidden continues to wreak havoc on our abilities to undo this damage. In general, the damage is more than the outright loss of our languages. The colonizers have taught us to devalue our languages, and this has greatly hampered both our desire and ability to save our languages. On the most basic level, we are faced with the outright loss of our languages and a reduction in the number of fluent speakers. That means that efforts to save our language will be limited by existing speakers' age, physical and mental capacities, and geography. As a language becomes more endangered, the struggle to save it becomes exponentially more challenging. For example, if all of the fluent speakers are over the age of 70, teaching a daily preschool immersion program would be extremely taxing on them. While participation in such an effort might still be a possibility, it would be unrealistic to expect these elders to be the primary teachers in such a school. Yet, the more endangered the language, the more likely it is that the younger generations also could not serve as primary teachers because they might not speak the language either. Or if the handful of speakers is spread over a wide geographical territory (for example, if your population experienced a diaspora because of forced removals or warfare), coordinating a unified language effort would be exceedingly difficult. These are real challenges that Indigenous language activists face every day.

On a more subtle level, the devaluation of the language may be present in the attitudes expressed in your community. While many people might express public support for language efforts, they may not be interested in a full recovery of the language. For example, they may still believe that Indigenous languages are not practical for the modern world (even while they promote the use of language in ceremonial contexts), or that their children might face a disadvantage if they are taught to speak the Indigenous language fluently. They may like the idea of children learning numbers, colors, and animal words, but they may be more uncomfortable with children speaking about computers,

microwave ovens, and convenience stores in the Indigenous language, especially if they have to create new words to do so. This thinking is the product of a couple factors.

First, because Euro-Americans and Euro-Canadians were concerned about establishing the dominance of English (or French in parts of Canada), all other languages needed to be subjugated, including languages indigenous to these lands and languages imported from other parts of the world. Among immigrant populations in the United States, for example, the language of their homeland generally dies within one or two generations of arriving in America. The practice of privileging English and emphasizing the need for one language may also be seen in the establishment of English-only laws in places such as Arizona. This practice is now reaching beyond the continent of North America. Because of the rapidity with which English is sweeping the globe and displacing other languages, it is considered to be an imperialistic language by those struggling to keep other languages alive. On the other side, those advancing the spread of English and the subjugation of other languages justify such action by linking English with modernity and emphasizing the convenience associated with a broadly used, common language. These are the same arguments that were used in nineteenth-century boarding schools. By attacking the viability of other languages or creating circumstances that make language survival unlikely, colonizing forces participate in and cause the decline of other languages. Furthermore, as television and media bring English (and sometimes French and Spanish) into Canadian and American households, this also contributes to Indigenous language decline. In a 1998 article, James Brooke states that within the next century, it is expected that half of the world's 6,000 languages will disappear. We are all taught that English is important to our survival in the modern world, while our Indigenous language has very limited or no usefulness.

Another factor that contributes to negative attitudes regarding the usefulness of Indigenous languages is the disruption in the natural evolution of languages. In communities where the Indigenous language stopped being spoken by the children, the language began to stagnate. This causes considerable harm to any language and might be considered the first phase of language death. What keeps languages living is their ability to adapt, change, and expand. This process occurs naturally as the people speaking a language are exposed to new stimuli. For example, while Indigenous Peoples in the Americas would not have had words for technological creations such as trains or airplanes, or for animals from other parts of the world such as giraffes or zebras, when fluent speakers encountered these things or animals they created words to describe them. Thus the world was named through the Indigenous lens and the language was expanded to accommodate the changing world and expanding environment. With many of our languages, this ability to adapt, change, and grow was violently interrupted when it was no longer taught to the children. As speakers of the language aged, they were less likely to create new words to accommodate the changing world and instead began to incorporate English into the Indigenous language. As a consequence, it is common in many of our communities to hear fluent-speaking elders talk in their Indigenous language with frequent interjections of English. This is an indication that the language is in jeopardy. Many fluent-speaking elders may not feel like they have the authority or right to make up new words, even though this was clearly an activity engaged in by every generation before them.

This is no coincidence. As Leanne Hinton points out, "A language that is not the language of government, nor a language of education, nor a language of commerce or of wider communication is a language whose very existence is threatened in the modern world." Because U.S. and Canadian colonization worked to systematically eradicate our Indigenous systems and institutions, which traditionally were means of maintaining Indigenous languages, while simultaneously attacking our languages in the youngest generations, they made the maintenance of our languages virtually impossible. Now all American and Canadian commerce and institutions conduct their business on Indigenous lands using the language of the colonizing societies to the detriment of Indigenous languages.

Whenever efforts to recover an Indigenous language are made, the impact of residential, boarding, or day schools on their survivors must be acknowledged. Many Indigenous adults who as children were punished or humiliated for speaking their languages may carry deep emotional scars from their school experiences. Even thinking about the language may be too painful, let alone talking about the language or teaching the language. And while these fluent speakers offer our best hope and possibilities for saving our languages since they remain the most knowledgeable about our languages, because of their schooling experiences they too may have internalized many of the attitudes and beliefs of the colonizers, including attitudes about the unimportance of our languages.

ACTIVITY:

What attitudes toward your Indigenous language currently exist in your family? In other words, do your family members value the language? If so, how? If not, how does your family devalue the language?

_____

_____

_____

_____

In what ways does your community value your language?

_____

_____

_____

_____

In what ways does your community devalue your language?

_____

_____

_____

_____

Which segment of your community population is most excited by and supportive of language recovery efforts? Why?

_____

_____

_____

_____

_____

The purpose in identifying these attitudes is in no way to discourage language recovery efforts. It is instead intended to help you gauge the levels of support and resistance to these efforts within your own community. Language recovery requires a tremendous amount of hard work and commitment, but it is also incredibly rewarding. Because of the particular challenges that will arise when you engage in this work, it is important to identify your allies as early as possible. In many communities the people most committed to language revitalization are young parents who would like their children to be raised with greater language abilities than themselves. These young parents may have had little or no exposure to their language growing up and as a consequence feel like they have suffered or at least missed out on important knowledge and teachings. Because they desire greater opportuni-

ties for their children, they may be the most enthusiastic population for language programming. Any language efforts should begin with the population of people who are most supportive and excited about language learning, as they will help sustain the momentum required for long-term language work.

Since you have already identified the segment of your population most excited about and supportive of Indigenous language recovery efforts, seek out those people, initiate a discussion about language, and brainstorm ways to save your language. This can be done among family members who are interested in revitalizing your language, or it can be done among a larger group of like-minded people with similar language goals. At this early stage I would recommend refraining from trying to convince naysayers about the significance of the language. As Indigenous Peoples we have an inherent right to our languages, especially since many of us consider our languages to be of divine origin. It requires tremendous energy to sustain depressing discussions with our own people who have bought into the colonizers' myth that our languages are irrelevant to our lives today. That energy could instead be put into launching new language projects.

Ultimately, a commitment to Indigenous language revitalization requires a clear understanding of why the language is important, what might be gained from its revitalization, and what the end goals are for revitalizing language. These questions need to be first addressed on an individual level and eventually on a small-group and community level.

ACTIVITY:

Why is language important to you personally?

_____
_____
_____
_____
_____

What do you think will be gained from language revitalization?

_____
_____
_____
_____

What is your end goal for a language recovery program? For example, do you hope to create a group of people conversant in your language? Proficient in ceremonial language use? Able to recite numbers and animals? Or do you hope to produce fluent speakers?

_____
_____
_____
_____
_____
_____

These questions will help determine what kind of language program might be most beneficial to your community.

D. A Summary of Language Models

A variety of language models exist for language learning and some may be more readily and easily employed than others. If you are interested in learning basic nouns (colors, numbers, animals) or conversational language, this may be done on an individual basis if some curriculum materials are available in your language (tapes, language books, CD-ROMs, DVDs) or through relatively easy-to-plan language classes that could be held once a week if you can find a willing teacher and community space. However, it is important to understand that language learning in this limited capacity will produce limited results. No one will become a fluent speaker using such tactics. Because of this, most language activists reject this kind of teaching as inadequate for language preservation or revitalization and would instead recommend language programming geared toward larger goals. Most would recommend creating a language immersion environment that would produce fluent speakers. It is the creation of this immersion environment that will be the focus of the rest of this chapter.

When babies are born, they are brought into a language immersion environment and they eventually learn to speak the language that surrounds them every day. If children are exposed to multiple languages on a daily basis, they will learn to speak multiple languages as long as they are required to respond in the languages that are spoken to them. This is the most natural and effective way for language learning to occur. Young children usually begin speaking only after they have been listening to a language for months, and when they do begin, they do not do so perfectly. But because we recognize that they are learning, we encourage any speech attempts and often simply respond with correct speech usage. For example, I remember when my older son first began putting words together in English to make sentences. He would say things like "Ball me," and he would reach for his ball. He had not yet learned to say "I want the ball" or "Please give me the ball," yet he effectively communicated his desire. Then we would ask him, "Do you want the ball?" and through such interaction he eventually learned to make his request in a full sentence. As he began to speak in Dakota a few years later in an immersion environment, he began very similarly. We frequently heard him and the other children at play begin with phrases like "Tapa mitawa" ("Ball mine"), to convey the same message instead of "Tapa wacin do/ye" ("I want the ball").

As we grow older, however, we rarely have a language environment where we are allowed to learn a second or third language in this way. Many adult language classes do not allow room for such "mistakes," and we often feel pressured to speak in complete, correct sentences. Furthermore, as we get older our capacity for language learning diminishes. At the time when we might need the most patience granted us in a language learning environment, we are the least likely to have it, despite the positive encouragement from committed teachers. Worries about good classroom grades or looking foolish in front of our peers actually hinder us from going through the natural process of language learning that includes a great deal of imperfect speech.

Language immersion education is about creating an environment in which it is safe to actively learn a language, to make "mistakes," and to practice speaking. Individuals learning a language within an immersion environment are likely to gain fluency within three to five years. One possible way of creating an immersion education on a smaller scale is through participation in what is now referred to as the Master-Apprentice Language Learning Program (MALLP). This model was developed in the 1990s to help save endangered Indigenous languages in California, but it may be applied in any context in which some fluent speakers of the endangered language remain. In this model, a fluent speaker of the language (the master) is

> "The most urgent claim of a group about to revive is certainly the liberation and restoration of its language."
> —Albert Memmi

matched one-on-one with a younger person eager to learn the language (the apprentice) to form a learning team. The two consciously create and interact in an immersion setting so that the apprentice can develop conversational proficiency and eventual fluency. For this model to work successfully, both the master and apprentice should agree to devote at least ten hours, but preferably twenty or more hours, to immersion interaction per week.

If a critical mass of language activists in your community is committed to saving the language, it may be possible to create an immersion environment on a broader scale. The Maoris of New Zealand and Native Hawaiians have established astoundingly successful immersion education programs from the preschool through the high school level. Indigenous children can receive an entire education in their Indigenous language. Both the Maoris and Native Hawaiians began with *language nests* for preschool-age children, and as the children advanced, the adults created more advanced programs to meet the children's needs. Their models of immersion education are increasingly used by Indigenous communities throughout the United States. Developing children's immersion programming requires a strong commitment to immersion education by a group of teachers, language speakers, students, and parents. While raising outside funds to support language programming is always a challenge, some federal programming dollars are dedicated to Indigenous language programming, and private foundations are becoming increasingly more aware of the necessity of supporting Indigenous language efforts. With any such programming efforts, because the costs can be prohibitive, it is important to start small and gradually expand. However, if you have teachers and students willing to work together to develop a program, do not wait to start. Immediately begin with whatever language activities you can, because it will never be wasted time and effort. As difficult as it may be to remember, the money should be a secondary concern.

If it is at all possible, establishing a nonprofit organization to support your language programming is preferable to working through tribal councils. As we all know, tribal politics can be quite tumultuous and nasty, and even if a tribal council is initially supportive of language programming, there is no guarantee that they will remain so, or that when the next election rolls around that the new council will be. Keeping language programming separated from tribal councils will help depoliticize it and make it more sustainable in the long term.

A note on parental concerns: If children are exposed to multiple languages it may take them longer to begin speaking, but they will eventually speak all the languages that are spoken to them and as a consequence, their brains will have developed greater intellectual capacity. A child learning an Indigenous language along with English (or French or Spanish) will not suffer ill effects, but will instead be intellectually and culturally enriched in the process. No one need fear that the revitalization of our Indigenous languages will have a detrimental effect on our children. Furthermore, even if a child receives an Indigenous language immersion education, the child will still learn the dominant society's language. Since we are surrounded (and therefore immersed) in the dominant society's language, all of our children will develop skill in that language even if they are learning an Indigenous language in the home or at school.

In a one-on-one immersion environment, the classroom is generally the home of the master, though it might also be outside, in the car, or in the supermarket. There is no formal curriculum required to create an immersion setting. Instead, teaching occurs through activity. This means that in the master-apprentice model, there is ample opportunity for the apprentice to participate with the master in normal household or outdoor activities and to help with chores so the master's normal schedule does not need to be disrupted. For example, if it is decided that three mornings a week the apprentice arrives at the teacher's house at eight o'clock and stays until one, during that time period the two might have the opportunity to share breakfast, wash the dishes, run errands, hoe the garden, prepare and eat lunch, and wash the dishes again. In addition to the ample language-learning materials surrounding all of these activities, the master and apprentice might also discuss such topics as what is happening in the community or the world, what their plans are for the evening or weekend, and the problems or joys in their lives. This helps to re-create the language environment that we were all born into. It allows the apprentice to learn and remember by doing, seeing, smelling, tasting, touching, and hearing.

The most important thing for the master to remember is that teaching the apprentice will take time and much repetition. It will take literally dozens of times of hearing most expressions for the apprentice to learn to speak and use them in an appropriate context.

The master can facilitate this learning by pointing to objects or pictures, using facial or hand gestures, or acting out the language with body movements. It is extremely difficult to learn to speak a language in an immersion environment if no context is ever provided, but there are many things both the master and apprentice can do to help this. By directly relating the language to activities at hand (for example, "I am slicing the tomatoes for our sandwiches," "The teapot is whistling," "You are pouring the tea"), the master can provide the relevant context. Similarly, the apprentice can help prompt dialogue to stimulate language learning that is faster, easier, and more fun.

ACTIVITY:

After identifying an elder willing to work with you in a master-apprentice–modeled program, meet with that elder to set a schedule and explain that your goal is to create an immersion environment during the time that you have together. Ideally you should try to meet at least twenty hours per week, but this has to be agreeable to both parties without creating a hardship. For the sake of flexibility, it may be helpful to leave some times purposefully vague. For example, you might agree to meet for two hours on Friday mornings, or four hours on Saturday afternoon. If specific times are not used, however, it is important to make sure that if you said afternoon and you come at three o'clock, that the elder has not been waiting ready to run errands since one. If you keep in frequent contact and are respectful about what the master teacher's needs are, this should not be a problem. What schedule did you decide on?

Day of the Week   Time

_____   _____

_____   _____

_____   _____

_____   _____   Once this schedule is decided upon, it might be helpful to create a monthly calendar for each of you to post in your homes.

_____   _____

_____   _____

_____   _____

ACTIVITY:

To help create a basic vocabulary for you to use once you are in your immersion environment, it is important to learn how to ask key questions and to be able to let the master know when you are having difficulty understanding. Work with your teacher to tape-record translations for the following list of questions and phrases that will be helpful to your learning and, if appropriate and acceptable, write the translations below. (If your language does not have an established writing system or you do not yet know how to use the one that exists, write the phrases phonetically in a way that makes sense to you and will help you with recall.)

How do you say _____?   _____

What is this?   _____

What is that?   _____

Who is that?   _____

What are you doing?   _____

What am I doing?   _____

What is she/he doing?   _____

Where are you going?   _____

Is that correct?   _____

What do you want to do?   _____

Please say that again.   _____

I understand.   _____

I do not understand.   _____

Please speak to me in our language. _____

What is appropriate to say now?   _____

Part of the initial work for the apprentice will be to memorize some of this basic speech, because these questions and statements will be used repeatedly. On the first day the apprentice can use many of these questions to prompt discussion and interact with the master language speaker. As a student, you can begin by greeting your teacher. If you do not know what a proper greeting in your language is, this is your opportunity to ask in your language, "What is appropriate to say now?" "How do you say 'Hello, how are you?'" Or "How do you say 'good morning'?" While it is important to listen carefully to the fluent speech, it is also important to try to repeat phrases as often as possible so that practice is gained in speaking. Adult language learners frequently are fearful of saying things incorrectly or of using the language inappropriately, yet these mistakes are unavoidable and they will actually help facilitate language learning. The earlier the apprentice learns this, and the master understands that this is part of the language learning process, the more quickly both parties will become comfortable and at ease with one another. It may be useful to also tape-record some of the initial immersion meetings so that the apprentice can replay those early days when some of the most basic information is covered, without relying as heavily on the master speaker's otherwise constant repetition. Now both parties are ready to experience an immersion environment.

It will be difficult initially for the master language speaker to continuously talk in your Indigenous language. Most of us are not used to providing a running narrative of all our actions for other adults, but many of us are used to it in other contexts. This is precisely what many of us do with our infant children. Mothers and fathers frequently carry their babies around and talk to them, describing what they are doing and what the baby is doing, asking the baby questions, and even providing the baby's end of the discussion (for example, "Oh, you're hungry now aren't you? Well, let me walk over and give you to your mother so that she can feed you. Say, 'Mama, I am hungry now.'") This kind of running narrative helps facilitate language learning because it is in context. In an immersion environment

this can be prompted by asking in your language, "What are you doing?" or "What do you want to do?" This method of language learning is always appropriate because it can expand to accommodate the apprentice's increasing level of language proficiency. The speaker can simply become more descriptive in the narrative. Instead of saying "You are pouring the tea," the master teacher might say, "When you are finished setting the table, please pour the hot tea into the flowered coffee cups on the shelf over there."

This format can also be used in a classroom immersion environment, though the response from the language learners may be different. Small children are unlikely to constantly repeat words and phrases back in the Indigenous language to a teacher initially, and if they have learned English (or Spanish or French) as their first language, they will also likely respond to all questions in that language. However, when these children are supplied with a constant stream of Indigenous language and when questions are asked of them in that language, they will eventually begin to use it. They may listen for a long time, but they are always learning. In the early months of our Dakota language immersion preschool, we were not sure how much the children were learning to actually speak our language because they were constantly responding to our questions in English. I still remember one of the first full sentence responses by one of the children. The children were painting at a table and after the teachers had been asking each of the children, "Taku yakaga he?" ("What are you making?"), one of the children excitedly said, "Kunsi, Kunsi, tipi wakage do!" ("Grandma, Grandma, I am making a house!"). This was a breakthrough moment for that child and for our preschool.

In an immersion classroom, the purpose is not to have language lessons, but rather to conduct all preschool activities in the Indigenous language so that everything becomes a language lesson. The daily routine might look very similar to routines in other preschools (though they should include more culturally appropriate and relevant activities), but the primary difference will be that all activities are conducted in the language. Monthly, daily, and seasonal calendar lessons, creative art and music activities, fine and gross motor-skill activities, snack time, outdoor play, lessons in oral tradition, history, and science are all appropriate activities and they should be taught and discussed in the Indigenous language. Even when children are in free play, there are ample opportunities for dialogue. Teachers should constantly describe what the children are doing and intersperse that commentary with questions. For example, "That is a scary growl sound you are making and I see that you are walking on all fours. Are you a dog? No? Are you a lion? Where are you going?" When language listening and speaking are emphasized, actual language curriculum becomes less important.

Immersion environments can also be created for community members of all ages and this can be a rewarding way for families to learn together. In my community we initially held family language classes on Wednesday nights to encourage parents of our preschool children to attend so that they could provide language support within the home. However, we quickly realized that the language classes were also of interest to community members who did not have preschool-age children. On any given Wednesday we had twenty to forty people attend, the vast majority of whom had little or no language speaking experience. We learned that if we played the same sort of games that we did with the children in our school, it quickly broke down inhibitions and created a fun, supportive language-learning environment. After sharing a potluck meal and learning about the food and utensils, we used hands-on, action-oriented games to teach the language. Initially we started with a form of Unktomi Eye (a version of Simon Says), to get everyone to follow directions in the language, and then we moved to other activities in which participants would be required to perform action and tell us what they were doing. For example, for one lesson we piled old clothes in the center of the floor and after teaching the basic vocabulary for the different pieces of clothing, we would then tell each person individually to get an article of clothing: "Cousin, go get the blue shirt and put it on." We would then help them tell us what they put on until they could tell us on their own: "I got the blue shirt

and I put it on." On another night we adapted an activity from Dr. Seuss's book *Ten Apples Up on Top!* We brought in a few bags of apples to see how many apples we could stack on our heads. While seemingly silly, this activity allowed the participants to easily learn and remember Dakota sentence structure (taspan wikcemna pa akan, literally "apples ten head on," but in English structure "ten apples on his head"). The children giggled when they saw their parents, aunts, uncles, and grandparents with apples on their head and delighted when they could provide proper pronunciation for words and phrases. The most important aspect of the family language nights was the sense of good feeling and well-being that participants began associating with language learning.

Although not necessary, curriculum materials can be useful to language learning, but only as tools to help supplement the teachings from fluent speakers of the language. We come from languages and cultures in which teachings were transmitted orally and minds were constantly sharpened and strengthened by the constant act of remembering. In the last century, in particular, we have become increasingly dependent on the written word and some would argue that our minds have become weakened as a consequence. Because the dominant society values the written over the spoken word and it has affected our own perceptions of reality, to decolonize our minds we must overturn this thinking. If we want to produce fluent speakers, we must reemphasize the importance of learning orally and decrease our dependence on the written word. Many fluent Indigenous elders believe our languages should only be taught orally, but others believe that the writing systems might also help us save our languages. Many language activists who teach Indigenous languages in classrooms emphasize oral teaching methods, but use written materials in a supplemental way. It may be possible to work cooperatively with such language teachers and their students to acquire curriculum that will meet your language needs and provide fruitful ideas that you can incorporate into your own language immersion environment, whether it is a master-apprentice–modeled program or a community language-immersion program.

ACTIVITY:

Identify all institutions or organizations where your Indigenous language is taught, including any tribal colleges or universities.

_____

_____

_____

_____

Contact these institutions and organizations to see if they would be willing to help you develop the kind of language curriculum you need to help you achieve your goals. For example, many university students taking Indigenous language classes are required to complete class projects as part of their grade requirements. Contact the professor or language instructor to see if you can suggest possible language projects for students who would be willing to create and share their projects while knowing they have developed something needed and useful to Indigenous communities.

The most important thing to remember is that any time and energy devoted to language work will never be wasted. You will never regret your efforts to learn to speak your language and as a consequence, you will feel a tremendous sense of accomplishment and well-being. When we speak the languages that were given us by the Creator, there is also a sense of serenity that comes from walking on the path that we know we are supposed to be following. If we can imagine a future in which our languages are flourishing, we have beaten the colonial mindset and we can begin the hard work that is necessary to save our languages. Our people shall live!

E. Suggested Readings

Leanne Hinton and Kenneth Hale, eds., _The Green Book of Language Revitalization in Practice_ (San Diego, CA: Academic Press, 2001).

Leanne Hinton, Matt Vera, and Nancy Steele, _How to Keep Your Language Alive: A Commonsense Approach to One-on-One Language Learning_ (Berkeley, CA: Heyday Books, 2002).

Darrell R. Kipp, _Encouragement, Guidance, Insights, and Lessons Learned for Native Language Activists Developing Their Own Tribal Language Programs_ (St. Paul, MN: Grotto Foundation, 2000).

Native American Languages Act (www.ncela.gwu.edu/pubs/stabilize/ii-policy/nala1990.htm, May 4, 2005).

Jon Allan Reyner (http://jan.ucc.nau.edu/~jar/, May 4, 2005). Includes excellent book collections produced from the Stabilizing Indigenous Languages Conferences (and published through Northern Arizona University) and other anthologies that cover a variety of language programs and models.

"United Nations Convention on the Prevention and Punishment of the Crime of Genocide" (www.un.org, May 4, 2005).

Andrew Wright, David Betteridge, and Michael Buckby, _Games for Language Learning_ (New York: Cambridge University Press, 1983).

Decolonizing Through Storytelling

Chi'XapKaid (Michael Pavel, Skokomish Nation)

As teachers, we are mentors of our children for all time. We labor to stand against anger, sadness, criticism, and defeat. Our hearts shall be full of peace and our minds filled with urgency for the welfare of our children. With endless patience, we embrace our duty. Our firmness shall be tempered with tenderness. Our words and actions shall be marked by calm deliberation.—Linda Sue Warner, Superintendent, Milwaukee Indian School, 2002

A. Purpose

B. Personal Narrative

C. Relevance and Support

D. At Least One Decolonization Strategy

E. Conclusion

F. Suggested Readings

A. Purpose

This chapter draws on personal experiences, selected literature, and ancestral teachings that provide a framework on how to decolonize our Native societies through education. It begins with a personal narrative to provide the reader with (a) my own personal awareness of decolonization, and (b) the methods of decolonization that I employ in my personal life and professional work. The methods of decolonization are illuminated in the section dealing with storytelling. Although pertinent literature will be reviewed and incorporated throughout, the primary information is derived from my elders and uncle, who work tirelessly to maintain the dignified presence of American Indian and Alaska Native people in today's society. I conclude with a summary and closing comments.

B. Personal Narrative

I was selected as the lead male dancer in the newly formed Twana Dance Group on the Skokomish Reservation back in 1973; it was a thirteen-year-old boy's first step into cultural renewal and celebration. No one could remember the last group of community members that had gathered together to sing the family songs and dance the family dances that are a part of our ancestral teachings. Although there was excitement, there was also doubt and resistance, even competing external interests within the group (for instance, people wanted to learn about their culture, others felt that traditional culture was not important, and people in the dance group had other responsibilities with school).

But my uncle, subiyay (Bruce Miller), would have none of it. We were either going to remember our culture, or our culture would be doomed to gradual dismemberment, until there would be nothing deeply rooted in our ancestry that we would be able to call our own. *If we failed to remember our ancestors, our freedom would be somebody's freedom, not our own. Our destiny, the destiny of someone else. Our ancestors will not even be able to recognize us on the other side: we would have changed so much.* My uncle is a gifted individual who knew that the words he spoke were the spirit of our ancestors. If we learned the songs, the dances, and the stories, then we would have a chance to retain the distinct social character that is uniquely us. Simply said, we would have a chance.

So Uncle gathered us together—my aunts, cousins, sisters, brothers, and anyone else who was interested—and begin introducing us to the ancestral teachings that would change all of our lives and the destiny of our community, and join us to the worldwide Indigenous movement to embrace one's cultural heritage. At the time, our world-renowned basketry was held in trust by only two elder women and one man; our language was spoken by only a handful of people; there was no evidence of contemporary ancestral-spiritual practices; and there were few traditional artists, and very little (if any) Native exposure in the school experience.

Our traditional culture at the time was embedded in intertribal athletic events, and we were reveling in the afterglow of pan-Indian participation in and appreciation for the civil rights movement. Redbone was

> **"Indeed this resistance will eventually succeed. And it will be finally successful when people are in total control of all the means of their physical, economical, political, cultural, psychological and spiritual survival, so we have to strengthen our capacity, and that of our children, to resist the evil."**
> **—Ngugi wa Thiong'o**

singing "Come and Get Your Love," and we were engaged in a struggle to assert our treaty rights. I remember one hot day during my fifteenth summer, the word got out that the state fish and game agents were confiscating a tribal member's fishing net. The first reaction among a few of us young rez men was that we were going to be part of the solution.

I rode shotgun with my cousin, who was seventeen, and we drove fast down a windy road in a rusted pickup headed to the fishing docks, *because we were going to be part of the solution.* All the while, I was firing off a Colt .22 pistol at vague passing targets of some imaginary enemy. We skidded into the dock's parking lot and jumped out in mid-stop to see that another one of my cousins was surrounded by several agents. He turned to us and shouted, "Let's take my net back, cuz!" Then he stiffed-armed two of the agents in the chest so hard, they fell to the ground.

We pushed our way past the third agent who shouted at me in a paternalistic manner, "You'd better not touch that net, boy!" I shouted back, "You're going to hell for what you're doing to our people," and even today, I remember how long I had been waiting to say that to somebody since I began to understand racial oppression and discrimination. It gave me strength as I leaped into the agents' patrol boat and started unloading a 200-fathom gill net, 120 meshes deep, out of the boat and into another tribal member's truck. Big-ass pile of net, believe me. It was a tangled mess made worse because the agents had hauled it in with seaweed, branches, fish, and all.

We managed to get the net, and all of us roared off, only to be followed by the police and game agents. My cousin and I were behind the truck with the net and were able to stall the authorities by blocking the road with our truck long enough to let the truck with the net get away. We relented when we faced shotgun barrels and pistols aimed at our heads, supported by threatening shouts of, "Get that goddamn vehicle out of the way." It was a strange feeling; even as we got in our truck to get out of the way, I remember vividly thinking, "I am not afraid to die for my country, and it's not right how they treat the Indian people."

All the while, I kept singing and dancing, and learning more from my ancestors who left the stories behind for us to hear, and trying to remember all that I could.

At sixteen, I joined four people to sponsor the first traditional naming ceremony on the Skokomish Reservation in more than eighty years. At seventeen, I was selected to prepare and carry the salmon that would be ceremonially returned to the river in the first Salmon Ceremony held on our reservation in more than 100 years. When I was eighteen, a local reporter asked to interview me, saying it would be for a feature article on senior students—the kind that showcases an outstanding student's achievements and aspirations. Days later a two-page article appeared in the county newspaper, with the headline, "Mike Pavel Hates White People." Well, my feature article was controversial given the headline, to say the least. It was asking a lot for the reader to overlook the headline and wade through the middle of the story, to find out that what I said was something like, "I hate white people who think that all Indians are drunk or lazy. I know a lot more white people who are worse drunks, drug addicts, and beat their women. I also know a lot of good Indian people."

All the while, I kept singing and dancing, and learning more from my ancestors who left the stories behind for us to hear, and trying to remember all that I could.

I went through a rigorous initiation into a traditional society when I was nineteen, shortly after the time when the American Indian Religious Freedom Act was passed (silly to think that one of this country's basic tenets is freedom of religion and that we needed such an act in the year of our Lord, 1978). At twenty-one, I graduated from a prestigious private university, and then took a low-paying job with an Indian

employment and training consortium of small tribes, only to move on to another low-paying tribal planning position after a few years.

All the while, I kept singing and dancing, and learning more from my ancestors who left the stories behind for us to hear, and trying to remember all that I could.

My professional experience began in 1985, the year I left the reservation in Washington State to attend graduate school in the Southwest. I earned my Ph.D. and graduated with awards, and got my first tenure-track faculty position at an esteemed university. During my first few years as a faculty member, I felt unwelcome and endured constant slights, my presence in the academy being continually questioned. You get the idea. If you don't, I am tired of telling much more because it plays out like a bad record, so you will just have to use your imagination. What I will tell you is that I met good people who encouraged me to remember who I was and what my purpose was as an American Indian faculty member in higher education: to fundamentally seek solutions that would promote the higher education of American Indian and Alaska Native People.

All the while, I kept singing and dancing, and learning more from my ancestors who left the stories behind for us to hear, and trying to remember all that I could.

I did well, ignoring the criticisms of those who said that Indians could not do research on Indians. I excelled, despite people telling me that I needed to publish in top-tier journals and not in the second-, third-, fourth-, and fifth-rate journals that focused on Native issues. I became a highly respected teacher while using unconventional and nontraditional forms of instruction. I enjoyed myself even when my colleagues did not invite me to their parties or acknowledge my contributions in faculty meetings.

"We" had a chance because the spirit of my ancestors was close to me. It was my decision to succeed in the mainstream higher-education establishment because it was very apparent that the success of American Indian and Alaska Native People is not at the highest priority level of those who fund, govern, administer, and teach in America's finest universities.

Note that I do not care who reads or hears what I just said. I live with it every day.

All the while, I kept singing and dancing, and learning more from my ancestors who left the stories behind for us to hear, and trying to remember all that I could.

C. Relevance and Support

While the storytelling of our ancestral and contemporary histories is important throughout and in every context of our lives, it possibly has our greatest opportunity for impact in the schooling of our children. In 2004, Pavel and Reyhner completed a review of literature for a national study of Native teacher preparation, entitled, *Research Review: Addressing the Language and Cultural Needs of Indigenous Communities.* Their historical overview describes the missionary, military, and political ill-treatment that was intended either to exterminate the Indians or wipe clear their minds of anything to do with their ancestral heritage. Assessment of early teacher knowledge as well as curricular and instructional developments had no application to Native Peoples or Native ways of knowing and learning. It was not until the emergence of tribal self-determination and self-governance that more sustained application of Native culture in the education of Native Peoples became more evident. This latter event in the Indigenous histories of Native Peoples has become part of our story: a story of struggle and success, of risk and rewards, of humor and sadness.

In the early 1990s, the Indian Nations at Risk (INAR) Task Force and the White House Conference on Indian Education made possible the gathering of personal stories by many Native students who attended schools that did not promote Indigenous cultural and spiritual development. Essentially, no Indigenous stories or gifted Native storytellers were in the schools or involved in educating the majority of our children. Overall, these government reports, in addition to a growing body of literature, lent strong support for the need for linguistically and culturally appropriate education for Native Peoples.

Whatever their training, teachers who have been responsive to their students have been more successful than those who have slavishly taught from textbooks and curriculums that may or may not reflect the culture of their students. It is long past the time to remember what Luther Standing Bear (1933–1978) declared about young Indians needing to be "doubly educated" so that they learned "to appreciate both their traditional life and modern life."

The Pavel and Reyhner review also provides a section on Native teacher preparation that offers additional insights regarding (a) curriculum and instruction, and (b) the importance of language and culture. Curricular and instructional practices in mainstream American schools career back and forth, from very restrictive teacher-centered approaches to anarchic child-centered focus, while public and political support for Native curricular and instructional approaches has wavered back and forth throughout U.S. history. The constant throughout this history is that teachers who develop effective classroom strategies for American Indian and Alaska Native students can do so by developing a better understanding of language and cultural factors that affect student-learning outcomes.

Whichever strategies are used, critical and caring reflection will help teachers show genuine respect for cultural teachings that relate to autonomy, authority, diversity, and joy in learning. To guide teachers of Native students, Reyhner and Jacobs advocate a wisdom-centered approach that embodies knowledge "that is possessed by elders, embedded in Native languages, revealed by plants and animals, and expressed mysteriously in ceremony." To help them in the process of receiving the wisdom of elders, Kincheloe recommends that "teachers must possess an anthropological view of the educational process. Such a perspective would help the teacher analyze and interpret society by providing a conceptual framework for raising questions and making observations." Simply put, teachers need to know the stories of the Indigenous Peoples.

Development of Native-oriented curriculum and instruction should be done in the context that cultural disintegration in Native societies has and will continue to inhibit the transformative and harmonic nature of knowledge sharing that comes from traditional Native culture. As Gordon and Boseker explain, "We Anglos can learn from Native Americans and how those understandings can improve education for all students, both Indian and non-Indian. Educators should be listening to Native American people more carefully and modifying their teaching accordingly."

The issue is no longer whether Native language and culture should have a role in developing educational strategies for American Indians and Alaska Natives. Rather, the prevailing sentiment throughout American Indian and Alaska Native communities— both rural and urban—is that Native language and culture should be an important part of the education system. The timeless knowledge inherent in the spirituality (a sense of interconnectedness with all) and reciprocity (a sense giving back to others or restoring balance) of Native culture are vital to Indian learning and to enjoying increased support from the public at large. "Guiding students toward a deep understanding about the values of their cultural worldview and how it applies to local and global issues is one way to facilitate a spiritual perspective that honors input from the community," say Reyhner and Jacobs.

In summary, there are two broad themes in the literature that can be tapped to gain further insights about the intersection between language and culture, and Native schooling. First is that to integrate Native language and culture into the public education system, teachers must grapple with the potential of language and cultural loss, look for alternative approaches to education, and recognize the incompatibility of Western mainstream public schooling and Native methods of education. The reality is that Native languages and traditional cultures are severely threatened. Most approaches incorporating Native language and culture into public schooling are alternative. Moreover, there are myriad governance and management differences that separate Native education from public schooling.

The second theme involves preserving Native language and culture, redefining Native education, understanding the ecology of Native education, and creating community- and place-based education that convey Native language and culture. These core values can be the foundation for (a) developing a philosophy, a mission, and purpose of schooling; (b) creating governance and administrative practices in collaboration with Native communities; and (c) training teachers to incorporate relevant and appropriate curriculum for Native students.

Research on holistic approaches to learning concludes that Native students are more successful academically when they can be active learners and when teachers act as facilitators and coaches. Educators should take a bottom-up approach that begins with them studying their students and their homes and communities. This approach can begin with a very brief history of Indian education, and then move on to reviewing how, why, what, and from whom American Indian students learn, including research on brain dominance, learning styles, whole language, testing, motivation, and discipline. I believe that storytelling is a natural approach to education and that much of what has been missing in the education of Indigenous children is the cultural knowledge and appropriateness that is embedded in the stories of their people.

D. At Least One Decolonization Strategy

It is both presumptuous and unrealistic of me to share an entire set of strategies that will decolonize the Native Peoples. However, my uncle taught me that for the ancestors of Indigenous Peoples, shared knowledge of cultural concepts was a tool for survival. The American Indian and Alaska Native People, for example, developed a belief in a story symbology to create a sophisticated educational system. My ancestors believed that the plants and animals were created first and became the first teachers of our people. Animals, in particular, experienced all the trials and tribulations necessary to survive. The plants' and animals' life experiences became the teachings upon which humans would base their culture; they would become the curriculum. The best way to convey that curriculum was through storytelling. Therefore, storytelling became an instructional technique, enabling the listeners to visualize the knowledge that needed to be preserved and passed on to future generations.

Before the introduction of written language, grandparents and gifted storytellers distributed all knowledge orally. It was through their living breath that the ancient tales of their ancestors were passed on and remembered. The stories taught the young people how to learn from the environment and their life experiences. This learning style promoted the same analytical, cognitive, and retentive skills that are necessary to succeed in the contemporary educational system. As the skills associated with this oral tradition have eroded, however, the old stories have almost disappeared, and along with them much of the people's cultural resiliency. *If we failed to remember our ancestors, our freedom would be somebody's freedom, not our own. Our destiny, the destiny of someone else. Our ancestors will not even be able to recognize us on the other side: we would have changed so much.* Their can be no sovereignty for Native People when there is no cultural distinctiveness, regardless of how important a person feels economic development and assimilation are to paying the bills. You cannot buy freedom with jobs, and you cannot protect the environment for future generations by cutting down the trees or using up the water today.

What to do? One of the many strategies to decolonize the Indigenous Peoples is to remember the ancestral teachings and master the art of storytelling. My uncle taught me that ritual and ceremony are important components to children being able to develop their visualization process. The visualization process is part of children's ability to construct a sense of reality that they could trust; Uncle often reinforcing the point by saying, "Seeing is believing."

The storytelling experience is also enhanced by our sense of smell and by songs that awaken the spirit. Our sense of smell, stimulated by the burning of incense,

> **"Peace is impossible in a world dominated by imperialism. Peace is impossible in a world guided by the ideology and practice of racism. Hence the struggle for peace in the world must be a concerted struggle against racism and imperialism."**
> **—Ngugi wa Thiong'o**

can induce a powerful learning experience because it prepares the mind to receive specific information. To our animal people, the sense of smell is still highly developed and a means of communication (for example, finding the faint trace of one's path hours or even days before, telling each when it is time to mate, and allowing the salmon to find their birthplace). To the human people, aromas invoke the memories of our past that transcend our own childhood to encompass the memories of our ancestors. We can associate a sense of smell to everything that deserves to be remembered, pleasant or unpleasant.

Songs help us to remember important teachings and events, and even help to identify who we are in the world. We often sing the most important concept of a story in compositions of four or fewer short lines. Before the invention of writing, singing and chanting allowed our ancestors to remember phenomenal amounts of information pertaining to our genealogy, family history, inherited rights, sacred ceremonies, and the great sagas of our ancestral heroes.

When my people, the Skokomish, are ready to perform a ceremony or relive the oral history of our ancestors, we use the aroma from sacred plants like the cedar to prepare the path as well as songs to help convey the teachings embedded in the words and work that take place. Uncle explained to me that to Native Peoples, the burning of incense before and during ritual and ceremony is a key element in the recognition of important information. These acts perform a validation to what is about to take place.

Uncle teaches that the basic components of storytelling are sacred words that are like ceremonial keys to another dimension. In some ways, we might compare them to magical incantations. What they are, are symbolic metaphors or verbal keys. Each one will unlock the spatial door to another dimension. We call them se'owa (the sacred words, words of law); something like "God is the word, and the word is God." Some of these words are:

- ha'bu (invokes the invitation to tell a story)
- sha'bu (the story itself)
- sha'but3d (storyteller)
- tu di tu hakW (from the ancient memories)
- sXW3XWiʔa'b (bringing back the breath of our ancestors)

I offer these knowing that most, if not all, who read these words may not be able to correctly pronounce the words; the lowercase and uppercase mean different things as well as the 3 and ' marks. However, there might be the gifted among you who naturally pronounce the terms correctly because the spirit has chosen you for something great. If not, Native People engaged in remembering their ancestors are free to visit us on the Skokomish Reservation and learn more. The main purpose of sharing these words is that, from my experience, every Indigenous culture has words that are sacred, open the way, and prepare the mind for storytelling. We sing the anthem of our traditional society throughout the year to keep the ancestors close to us:

- p3t t scH3lal (from the time of the ancestor—history, in the beginning)
- tulas 3b3b d3xW (received right where we are now)
- tid sHabu (my sacred stories)

There are other important techniques to storytelling, and Uncle has shared these as things to remember.

- Gesticulation, or the use of nonverbal gestures, adds more meaning to the spoken word. It allows us to shade, stretch, highlight, and add texture to the word. (Practice embellishing gestures.)
- Body language, or the use of facial expressions and eye contact, has a strong impact on storytelling. The facial expression exemplifies the mood of the moment. (Practice facial expressions like anger, sadness, worry, and happiness.)
- Articulation is essential because stories are important, and the storyteller must enunciate clearly, without running the words together or being too complicated. (Practice verbal exercises and saying things clearly.)
- Pauses allow time for the listener to visualize what has just been said and internalize it in one's memory. (Practice saying a sentence and waiting a few seconds before uttering another sentence.)
- Pace and repetition means that important information is never blurted out but is shared in a slow, enunciated, rhythmic, ceremonial speech pattern. (Practice saying something in a manner that conveys, "I am telling you something really important," and say it two or three times.)
- Voice is the great repertoire of things that you hear in nature or in your own personal experience and allow for a greater degree of voice characterizations. (Practice saying something from a variety of animals or what a tree might sound like.)

A primary reason Native students give for dropping out of school is that school is boring. I have never seen or experienced boredom when a gifted Indigenous storyteller is sharing knowledge through a story. On contrary, I have seen Indigenous children captivated by the gripping details of what was being conveyed by a good story. My guess is that all teachers, not just teachers of Indigenous children, would benefit from being good storytellers.

However, what about the Indigenous Peoples who have been so colonized that their ancestral stories are all but forgotten? This situation is so pervasive—so many stories have already been forgotten and more are on the verge of being forgotten—that it has to be addressed in a proactive and creative manner. I would say that we, as individuals and communities, need to begin documenting and telling our stories, much as I tried to do in the beginning of this chapter.

ACTIVITY:

Here is a general guide to creating our own stories; use the themes of love and relationships as an example. Identify all the experiences you have faced and align each along themes of important information you want to convey. (An example is provided.)

Experience

positive bedtime rituals

_____

_____

_____

_____

_____

_____

_____

_____

Theme

love of a parent

_____

_____

_____

_____

_____

_____

_____

_____

For example, love and companionship are vital to the health of our people. However, the effects of colonization have so disrupted our feelings of love, that our concept of a healthy relationship has often deteriorated to a point where our children grow up expecting that two people in a relationship is characterized by abuse. This does not have to be, and to change it will require that we start educating or training our youth about ideals of love and how this generates healthy companionship. To me this means developing a relationship that culminates in good parenting, where both parents make an effort to create a positive relationship that promotes good child-rearing practices.

ACTIVITY:

For stories we direct to our young, we can supplement the main characters with animals so that children can relate to the situations more readily. Animal characters in stories are a lot like puppets in theater, as children tend to focus more on puppets than real human characters. I think it is because children are more fascinated with imagined reality than concrete reality. In a story of love and companionship, I might choose animals that mate for life (for instance, swans, eagles, wolves) to model what it is like to develop healthy and sustainable relationships. The story on love and companionship can have contrasting animal characters that mimic some serious relationship issues in our society (such as animal fathers who abandon their mate soon after conception and never participate in raising the children). For this activity, compose a story based on one of your positive experiences surrounding the theme of love and companionship. What experience will your story address?

_____

_____

Who will your characters be?

_____

_____

_____

_____

_____

Break up the story into segments so that children can more easily remember and understand the plot. Continuing with the example of love and companionship, the first segment might be about respecting or not respecting yourself as demonstrated by good eating, grooming, and behavioral practices. What will your first segment be about?

_____

_____

_____

_____

The second segment could be about seeing and admiring the same qualities in other people, contrasted with situations where poor qualities are overlooked in hopes that you may be able to make things better. What will your second segment be about?

_____

_____

_____

_____

The third segment may be something about courtship, and about the expectations that being in love should cultivate a healthy relationship versus a one-night stand or tendency to move from one relationship to the next with no true love at all. What will your third segment be about?

_____

_____

_____

_____

The fourth or final segment to the story should center on the beauty of being in a loving relationship over time, and what that generally brings to the family and community. On the other hand, the story may show the things we might miss if there are no enduring relationships in our communities. What will your fourth segment be about?

_____

_____

_____

_____

I am sure that there are many ways to approach the compilation and retelling of stories concerning a particular Indigenous community. Indigenous writers, who have been creating a growing body of literature, serve as a rich resource of stories. I also have benefited from hearing or reading about such stories and have been able to use the stories in and out of class to convey lessons important to succeeding in life. We should be free to share our own stories with people to encourage them to create their own.

E. Conclusion

The living breath of our ancestors is kept alive through the stories we remember. In doing so, we remember who we are, what our history is, how we behave, how we treat other people, what is important in life, what our worldview is, who the future generations are, who our heroes are, and how to believe in the spirit. The first created (the plant people) taught us how to learn from the environment as well as our own life experiences. This learning style promoted the same analytical, cognitive, and retentive skills that are necessary to succeed in this contemporary society. The applied knowledge skills associated with the oral tradition have nearly eroded with the sovereignty of the Native Peoples. The old traditional stories that once honed these skills have almost disappeared under the oppressive weight of colonialism. Many Native Peoples refuse to be washed away and are strong enough to triumph over any burden.

However, life need not be so dismal. Storytelling can be a form of play, where our children learn to enjoy the life they are living and give light to ancestors who want to be remembered by future generations. It can be fun, exciting, entertaining, and challenging to the intellect, and serve to unite the people. This is especially important, because Native Peoples emphasize a group-oriented learning mode. Moreover, our destiny is inherently tied to the plants and animals; their fate is our fate, their solution our solution. Decolonizing our minds then becomes an epic journey, as we travel through time and folding space: a journey where we join together the past, present, and future all at the same moment. This magical moment is created through storytelling. An experience invoked by breathing the words of our ancestors to teach us today what we need to do to survive into tomorrow.

F. Suggested Readings

S. L. Gordon and B. J. Boseker, "Enriching Education for Indian and Non-Indian Students," *Journal of Thought* 19, no. 3 (1984):143–48.

T. S. Kincheloe, "The Wisdom of the Elders: Cross-Cultural Perspectives," *Journal of Thought* 19, no. 3 (1984):121–27.

D. M. Pavel and J. Reyhner, *Research Review: Addressing the Language and Culture Needs of Indigenous Communities* (Tempe, AZ: Center for Indian Education, Arizona State University, 2003).

J. Reyhner and D. Jacobs, "Preparing Teachers of American Indian and Alaska Native Students," *Action in Teacher Education* 24, no. 2 (2002):85–93.

Ideology, Power, and the Miseducation of Indigenous Peoples in the United States

Cornel Pewewardy

A. Introduction

This chapter illuminates the role that many white policy makers of Indian education have played in the design of education that is the *foundation of miseducation*. To help you process this story, this chapter has an overview, exercises, and reflective questions for you to consider and write about. Many of the exercises are group or partner activities designed for you to participate in collaboratively. However, if you are studying independently, you can always adapt them to suit your circumstances. I also invite you to personalize this chapter through journal keeping. Record your own reactions, reflections, confusions, and insights.

The objective of this chapter is to investigate the reasons behind the construction of colonial Indian education by examining the views, politics, and practices of the white policy makers (sometimes referred to as "white architects of Indian education") who funded, created, justified, and refined colonial educational policies. Ultimately, a manufactured romantic image of Indigenous Peoples has been used to justify the control of entire tribal communities. More specifically, white policy makers of Indian education represented the interests of Western expansion. White policy makers of Indian education designed educational strategies to foster the ideology of white supremacy.

Early Indian boarding schools have been used historically as educational instruments to ensure European domination through miseducation. The American educational system promotes a system-maintaining curriculum that perpetuates oppression through the strict control of all aspects of home living and the adoption of official curriculum. Students need to know that colonial educational practices and philosophies are still supported by the dominant educational power structure in this country. For example most K–12 schools in this country have been consistent in their original design by graduating students with a value system that is basically Eurocentric, individualistic, competitive, and materialistic.

ACTIVITY:

Before reading any further, take a few minutes and reflect on where you grew up. Think about daily interactions and relationships in terms of your tribal or national identity, especially as it relates to K–12 schools. Think about the racial boundaries in your community. What did you learn from your family about people who looked and spoke different from yourselves?

_____

_____

_____

_____

_____

As you explore these questions further during the exercises and discussions, return here to record any new memories or insights about growing up in multiracial schools.

_____

_____

_____

_____

_____

_____

B. Sociopolitical Analysis of Early "Indian" Education

Prior to the invasion of Indigenous communities in the Americas and the imposition of Euro-American educational systems, tribal nations had their own very diverse educational systems that were culturally responsive to their children. These traditional educational systems were culturally and linguistically designed to provide education informally through parents, extended families, elder members of the tribe, and religious and social groups. The focus of pre-European Indigenous education was to facilitate the child's acquisition of the spiritual and cultural knowledge necessary to meaningfully contribute to the overall socioeconomic welfare of the group (also known as tribalism), while also sharing their values, appropriate behaviors, and language. Indigenous perspectives are rooted in Indigenous experiences, cultural and political. One of the starting points for discussion might be how Indigenous Peoples were educated and socialized before European colonization and after colonization.

ACTIVITY:

At this stage in your reading, ask yourself the following question:

From your tribal perspective, what did the tribal educational system look like before white policy makers of Indian education took over the education of Indigenous Peoples?

_____

_____

_____

_____

The newly arrived Europeans' overall educational mission was to coerce Indigenous students to forget and to dispossess their cultural identity and the historical significance of their people. This objective was later delegated to the Bureau of Indian Affairs (BIA) in the form of boarding schools located far from the students' ancestral homelands.

The BIA was established in the late nineteenth century when the United States government first negotiated its responsibility for educating Indigenous students. These early efforts at "civilizing" Indigenous Peoples involved attempts at deculturalization—the destruction of Indigenous cultures and languages and the replacement of Indigenous cultures and languages with Anglo-American Protestant culture and the English language.

Overall, the basic theme of this chapter is that Europe's colonial conquest of Indigenous Peoples focused on two fronts. One front involved the political and military strategy to drive Indigenous Peoples from their ancestral lands to make room for European settlers. Earlier in this chapter, this action was referred to as Western expansion. The second front involved the spiritual and cultural strategy pursued by the United States government as well as European and Euro-American missionaries of all denominations. Education was an important component of this second front of colonial conquest.

Throughout U.S. history, Indigenous Peoples have been characterized as "problems" and as having "cultural deficits" or having something wrong with them that shaped the theoretical rationale for educational and curriculum policymaking. Such a description falls within the "deficit theory" model—the dominant position of Western research on minorities through the 1960s.

The conventional "deficit syndrome" as an educational practice has been used historically to address the needs of Indigenous students despite evidence suggesting that Indigenous learners have definite cultural values and traits that affect learning and academic achievement. For example, Lucien Levy-Bruhl's (1926) *How Natives Think (Les Fonctions Mentales dans les Sociétes Inferieures*, which in French means "the mental functions within the inferior societies") hypothesized that Indigenous Peoples came from undeveloped and uncivilized peoples; were inferior races; had primitive, savage, and unintelligible mentalities; and had simple and artless logical-reasoning processes.

This deficit perspective explored the "problems" faced by Indigenous learners and their family, including societal dislocation, poverty, and language acquisition, and saw in these deficits the origins of the unsatisfactory outcomes that Indigenous students experience primarily in mainstream, public schools as well as higher education. By using the Eurocentric schooling and curriculum, white policy makers have failed Indigenous Peoples by not providing the cultural foundation for authentic, natural learning. An example of this design was to leave out the essence of the "spirit" in the educational process of the children. White policy makers have relied on negative pathology theories regarding Indigenous students, such as being "uncivilized," "culturally deficient," "disadvantaged," "at-risk," and part of a "permanent underclass," as theoretical rationale for educational policymaking.

> "Decolonization never takes place unnoticed, for it influences individuals and modifies them fundamentally."
> —Frantz Fanon

A curriculum of genocide has been a defining feature of Indigenous education. From the outset the white policy makers of Indian education understood the power of ideas. They carefully selected and sponsored teaching that contributed to obedience, subservience, and political docility. The strategy was not technical, but mostly political. For example, the creation of BIA boarding schools was a statement of political philosophy. It taught Indigenous Peoples the transition from a vocational and agricultural training to mechanical industrialization. It addressed the vexing questions of how Indigenous Peoples should fit into the new social order without disruptions. The battle over content knowledge for which Indigenous Peoples learn has been longstanding and inextricably connected to tribal sovereignty, national politics, civil rights, labor economics, and social justice.

Why are there disproportionate numbers of ethnic minority youth (Indigenous children included) in special education today? An article in the 2004 issue of *Multiple Voices* documents the ways special education is overrepresented by a large percentage of poor and ethnic minority students. I believe the major reason why there is an overrepresentation of poor and ethnic minority youth in special education is because there is a lack of appreciation for different cultural learning styles. Moreover, if Indigenous children cannot fit the norm, they are placed in special education. Many studies report that ethnic minority children are nearly twice as likely to be assigned to ineffective teachers. Moreover, many ethnic minority children who are referred to special education were very often coming from classrooms in which teachers exhibited poor behavioral management and instructional skills.

ACTIVITY:

Name individuals and/or books that challenged your consciousness in your lifetime (that is, knowledge that expanded the way you analyzed issues and problems) about Indigenous Peoples.

_____

_____

_____

What are some possible reasons that some people have more cultural awareness and/or a more critical consciousness than others?

_____

_____

Conscientization is the ability to challenge current oppression and make reparations for past injustices based on the understanding that a just society is in the best interest of all people, not just the oppressed. Why would a just society be of benefit to all people?

_____

_____

_____

_____

C. White Architects of Indian Education

To begin this discussion, we might want to look at a few examples of white policy makers of Indian education. To start, one must ensure that the goal of Indigenous education and the tribal socialization process are important. Historically, the Western notion of education for Indigenous Peoples has been, for the most part, a curriculum designed to deculturalize (that is, destroy a people's culture while replacing it with a new culture) and to disconnect Indigenous Peoples from a tribal perspective and worldview.

The following biographical sketches of white educators and researchers (also referred to as professionals) in no way exhausts the considerable list of policy makers of Indigenous education, but this is an ideologically representative group. I have tried to profile a few professionals whose educational and research roles and impact have been obscured in the mainstream education literature.

General Samuel Chapman Armstrong

As a theorist and founder of Hampton Institute, General Samuel Chapman Armstrong (1839–1893) can be considered a classical example of a white policy maker of Indian education. Hampton Institute was a statement of political philosophy of the times. It first taught Africans the transition from agricultural slavery to mechanical industrialization. It was about nation building in the United States—carefully situating newly freed Africans together with Indigenous Peoples forced from their tribal homelands to form a new sociopolitical and economic order. It was about reshaping delicate race relations. Finally, and most important, it was about forging a social order rooted in cultural genocide, apartheid, economic exploitation, oppression, and inequality. The Hampton model of education and societal development dramatically influenced 100 years of Indigenous schooling. Hampton education came to exemplify colonial education for African Americans and Indigenous Peoples in the United States and in the rest of the world.

Armstrong and Hampton displayed the same colonial mentality toward Indigenous Peoples as toward freed African American slaves. Even Hampton's African students were convinced that Indigenous Peoples were lower on the social ladder than themselves. The Hampton educational idea for Indigenous students was to become Richard Henry Pratt's Carlisle Indian School.

Richard Henry Pratt

In the seventeenth century, mission schools run by religious organizations were the first non-Indigenous schools to educate Indigenous children. Eventually, the U.S. government, from 1810 to 1917, financed these mission schools. In the 1860s the U.S. government created a federal school system for Indigenous children. In 1879 the U.S. government opened the first off-reservation boarding school in Carlisle, Pennsylvania. It was called Carlisle Indian School and was founded by a U.S. Army officer, Richard Henry Pratt.

Pratt's theory and infamous motto for "taming" Indigenous Peoples was "Kill the Indian and save the man." He requested that the U.S. government support Carlisle Indian School with the goals of assimilating and acculturating Indigenous children by removing them from their tribal families and communities and submersing them in a totally Eurocentric learning environment. Carlisle Indian School was considered the premier model of schooling for Indigenous students by federal government officials. It also served as the idea model in the U.S. government's creation of BIA boarding schools in the nineteenth century.

Estelle Reel

According to Brenda J. Child and K. Tsianina Lomawaima, in "Part One: A Uniform Course of Study (Life at School)" of *Away From Home: American Indian Boarding School Experiences, 1879–2000* (Phoenix, AZ: Heard Museum, 2000), at the end of the nineteenth century, the Indian Service attempted to standardize the boarding school curriculum. The academic instruction was largely remedial and restricted to early childhood levels. The official curriculum, the Uniform Course of Student for the Indian Schools of the United States, was developed in 1901 by Estelle Reel (1862–1959). In 1898, President McKinley appointed Estelle Reel to superintendent of "Indian" schools, a position she held until 1910. Reel's goal was to train Indigenous students to meet the demands of U.S. citizenry, making them willing workers as well as good citizens of the United States. Child and Lomawaima report that Reel believed in the racist ideology of her time, that Indigenous Peoples (and other ethnic minority populations) were inescapably conditioned by heredity and environment to be inferior to whites. She believed that "Indians" were intellectually incapable of excelling in academic school programs—the deficit syndrome.

Estelle Reel's educational philosophy for Indigenous students was to design a curriculum that focused on trades and domestic training, military discipline, and regimentation of student life. White policy makers like Reel were from the outset horrified by the power and place of song, dance, and ceremonial activities in the spiritual lives of Indigenous Peoples.

Armstrong, Pratt, and Reel were all purporting to solve the so-called Indian question. Their educational ideologies and practices would transform how they perceived Indigenous Peoples as inferior to Euro-Americans and designed educational programs for their place in the new order of their times. Other white policy makers of Indian education worked feverishly in the field of science, trying to prove that Indigenous Peoples were intellectually and biologically inferior to European Americans.

ACTIVITY:

Strategies for Making Connections Between Colonization and Your Own Experience: Sitting with a partner, make a list of four examples of how you have been impacted by colonization in your own schooling experience. Then consider how you would undo (or decolonize) this effect of colonialism. (An example has been provided.)

Examples of Educational Colonialism	Decolonization Strategy
I was not taught my Indigenous language.	Learn the language.

_____

_____

_____

_____

D. The Mismeasurement of Indigenous Students

It is evident from the theories of the nineteenth-century intellectuals that the inhibiting influence of both Galen and the Catholic Church had been profound. Galen (second century CE) thought that memory and mental processes were part of the lower order of animal spirits. In the fourth century CE, St. Augustine accepted the Church's idea that memory was a function of the soul and that the soul was located in the brain. Practically all of these great thinkers accepted without question such unorthodox ideas on memory.

Europeans and European Americans have long debated the mental capacities of Indigenous Peoples, most of which positioned their rationale in racial hierarchy. At the turn of the twentieth century, many psychologists had a keen interest in scientifically proving that Indigenous Peoples had low mental abilities. Through intelligence testing, many researchers presented their studies as valid and objective assessments of Indigenous mental capacity. Based on the confluence of racist ideologies that included evolutionary anthro-pology, eugenics, and psychometrics, intelligence testing promised to measure the differential distribution of traits and capabilities among racial groups. Early psychometric instruments suggested that intelligence was a single, fixed, and measurable entity.

The assault on Indigenous Peoples by the misuse of tools of psychometry and racist scientific theory is longstanding. As early as the turn of the twentieth century, white psychologists and educators were amassing their psychometric armaments to justify the continued oppression of Indigenous Peoples. Walter Ashby Plecker from Virginia was a fervent eugenicist. He detested the notion of racial and social mixing in any form. Moreover, the concept of Indigenous racial inferiority attained credence with a publication by Lewis Terman (who was appointed to Stanford University) in 1916 that stated that certain racial types would benefit from education minimally at best. In essence, Indigenous Peoples were reputed to be racially inferior. This presumption of inferiority was widely held by the general public and concomitantly in the public school systems. Consequently, schools in the United States have been used as a tool to prevent ethnic minority educational advancement and to ensure white domination. Another misuse of tools of psychometry is the story of the Hiawatha Insane Asylum, and the Cherokee School for the Deaf, Dumb, Blind, and Insane Asylum.

In 1873 the Cherokee Nation of Oklahoma created the Home for the Insane, Dumb, and Blind of the Cherokee Nation. Located south of Tahlequah, Oklahoma, the home was established for the "insane and mentally defective." The building design for this insane asylum seemed also suitable for jail purposes. Therefore, in 1904 the Insane Asylum was converted into the National Jail at Tahlequah. The Hiawatha Insane Asylum was created in 1899 by the U.S. Congress, and its short but brutal existence ended in 1933. Located in Canton, South Dakota, the Hiawatha Insane Asylum became the first and only federally funded mental institution for Indigenous Peoples in the United States. Overall, both stories of these insane asylums are tangled in a horrific web of greed, political opportunism, and racist oppression.

New and expanded historical materials that formed scientific precursors to racial stereotypes and negative views toward Indigenous Peoples are also a critical part of the history of Indigenous Peoples' education. For example, scientist and physician Samuel George

Morton's conclusion about the inferiority of cranial capacity in Indigenous Peoples impacted the debates about westward expansion in early U.S. history. Morton rose to notoriety in mainstream academe of his time for his studies on human cranial capacity. He hypothesized that the bigger the skull, the bigger the brain. For example, Morton asserted that because American Indian brains were smaller than those of Malays and Mongolians, Indian intelligence must therefore be correspondingly inferior. This strategy is the ultimate in the process of dehumanization and cultural genocide. The heavy emphasis placed upon the categorization of races, and the subsequent psychological testing of various groups of people, often led to incorrect conclusions of the racial superiority of whites and the inferiority of people distinguished outside the role of whiteness.

Like Morton, Benjamin Rush's work had important political implications for he too worked to reinforce the notion that Indigenous Peoples were inferior to European Americans. Intellectually and politically opposed to slavery, Benjamin Rush nevertheless advocated a segregated America. Over the years, psychologists have issued disclaimers in an attempt to erase the interpretations made from mainstream psychological testing data.

ACTIVITY:

At this point in your reading, let's reflect on your thoughts about how early scientists used Western research to justify inferiority and superiority based on racial groups. Why do you think it was important to establish the inferiority of Indigenous Peoples?

_____

_____

_____

What would the colonizers gain from such a project?

_____

_____

Give three examples of how this idea has been taught to you in your life.

1. _____

2. _____

3. _____

_____

E. Patterns of Miseducation

Historically, most Indigenous Peoples have encountered a Machiavellian model of teaching and learning. Attempts to defeat Indigenous Peoples were not so much by military force but by politically restructuring the institution of education to mold a colonial belief system. Colonialism that imprisons young minds with the concept of racial or ethnic inferiority is by far more tyrannical than brute force. As an outgrowth of explorers' observations and the deductions by some European philosophers, a concept emerged (circa 1730) arguing that, although nature is created innocent, all things degenerate when touched by civilization. The idea became a double-edged sword for Indigenous Peoples in that, while the concept suggests inherent evils of so-called civilization, it labels Indigenous Peoples as savage (that is, subhuman), thus lending them to Eurocentric investigations, measurements, and studies. The myth of the noble savage emerged and moderated somewhat the disapproving European attitudes toward Indigenous Peoples in general but did not prevent most Europeans from maintaining a view of Indigenous Peoples as barbaric and liable to genocide.

The ideas of superior and inferior races that permeated mainstream American thinking about continental and world mission also often permeated the thinking of the English and of Western Europeans in general by the mid-nineteenth century. Fabricated (civilized/uncivilized) ascribed identities are the results of multidisciplinary academic falsification of the human record. Historians have denied, distorted, or ignored the history of subordinated groups, and magnified, embellished, and glorified, even deified, the histories of their own people. Western anthropologists fabricated savage and uncivilized people. Theologians in seminaries even debated the existence of whether Indigenous Peoples had souls. Biologists created races and ranks among races.

As an early educational practice with Indigenous students, deculturalization is one aspect of this strange mixture of democratic thought and intolerance that exists in minds of Euro-American policy makers. The concept of deculturalization demonstrates how cultural prejudice and religious bigotry can be intertwined with democratic beliefs. The mastery of such a Eurocentric curriculum by Indigenous children who have no knowledge of their tribal identity is merely an advanced form of programmed cultural destruction. Deculturalization combines education for democracy and political equality with cultural genocide—the attempt to destroy cultures.

In early BIA boarding schools, Indigenous youngsters were easily identifiable and were segregated. Boarding schools grouped Indigenous children along tribal lines that later facilitated intertribal comparison. The added variable of language differences offered still another dimension for educational psychologists in their discussions and debates of mental capacities; opinions expressing the need for Indigenous students to absorb the white culture in order to improve their "innate inferiority" (as measured by the tests) were frequently discussed. The BIA boarding-school experience is just one example of how the educational system has not met the needs of Indigenous Peoples.

Overall, federal educational policy to educate Indigenous Peoples has largely ignored the fact that Indigenous Peoples had a sophisticated and powerful educational process prior to contact with Europeans. The ultimate proof of European superiority was not offered as subjective opinion or personal desire but "scientific fact." Thirty years of research in educational anthropology and sociology represent a legacy of deficit thought guided by assimilation ideology. Thus, the overall schooling of Indigenous children is a shameful history of domination by missionaries and the federal government. Young children taken from their families, stripped of their customs, and forbidden to speak their languages, passively withdrew within the hostile environments of BIA boarding schools and missionary domiciles.

The manufacturing of the history of any group of people causes them to forget their authentic histories. Indigenous Peoples were not ignorant "savages" or "pagans" as described in early U.S. history books. These were negative, stereotypical terms and concepts created by European American politicians and historians. Many Indigenous Peoples knew their creation stories from memory and could recite them in various types of ceremony. All were highly educated in their tribal perspectives and profoundly spiritual, sharing in a complex culture that had granted survival for thousands of years before 1492.

It took white policy makers of Indian education to construct an educational system, unparalleled in the history of the world to erase the tribal memories, to cloud vision, to impair hearing, and to impede the operation of the critical capacities of Indigenous Peoples. Once creation stories were lost, Indigenous Peoples became programmed by white policy makers to follow a pattern of historical lies.

In general Indigenous Peoples need to understand the systematic miseducation of Indigenous Peoples. It makes no difference whether Indigenous educators were driven by Indigenous intellectual self-determination. The only education allowable was education for pacification, servitude, and inferiorization.

Teachers who want to teach Indigenous students must have an agenda for the transformation of Indigenous Peoples based on sound information. To set the agenda, however, we must ask and answer two questions.

- What happened to the independent Indigenous education process as a consequence of disturbances through invasion, colonization, and white supremacist ideology and behavior?
- What is the nature of Indigenous resistance to domination and interference and the nature of efforts to reconstruct tribal-based systems? In particular, what roles do Western education and socialization play in resistance to oppression and in the creation of solidarity?

When people are educated to respect the knowledge, the scholarship, and the history and the background of everybody except themselves, then those people are miseducated. It is important to remember that there have been many oppositional voices over the years. Unfortunately, the miseducation has not ceased. In fact, it has increased and we are now more highly miseducated than we ever were before. Why do you suppose I said this?

ACTIVITY:

Many K–12 schools, particularly public schools, have a feel-good approach to Indigenous education. For example, having an Indian week or month to celebrate Indigenous Peoples in schools is a very popular approach, especially in many schools' efforts to integrate multiculturalism into their curriculum. Think about the types of schools that you attended in your K–12 experience. Do you feel your schooling helped you to affirm your tribal identity as well as integrate your tribal histories into its official curriculum? Briefly explain your response.

_____

_____

_____

_____

F. Two Hundred Years of Indigenous Protest

There has always been a difference of opinions among Indigenous Peoples and European Americans regarding the nature of the education problem and the remedies that should be sought in schools. There has always been opposition to integration of Indigenous Peoples into the mainstream society.

Intercultural encounters between white policy makers and Indigenous educators have been the predominant characteristic of race relations for half a millennium. Indigenous theorists have been trying to explain what the invasion of this continent has meant to both Indigenous Peoples and white educators.

Current battles against the miseducation of the poor and people of color are being waged on different fronts. In local schools and communities, heroic teachers, involved parents, caring administrators, and students themselves reject the alienating formulas and rigidities of the past. Correspondingly, a new group of Indigenous scholars and researchers participate in this battle.

A persistent demand of Indigenous protest thought has been education. All understand that the future belongs to the young and that education is a necessity in the struggle for uplift and equality.

Historically, there have always been oppositional voices protesting how white policy makers designed educational programs for Indigenous Peoples. Racial uplift, improvement, and separatism continue as common themes in Indigenous protest.

A historical example may help us understand today's work. In the 1930s and 1940s, although Indigenous Peoples had long contributed to literature, fiction, poetry, and theater, the Reservation Period represented the coming together of a new and large group of Indigenous writers and artists. They told the story of Indigenous literature, music, plays, and so forth through the eyes of Indigenous Peoples. Similarly, we now have a renaissance of indigenizing and writing from an Indigenous perspective. History and time have rendered this new group of scholars, practitioners, and researchers distinct. Some are in a position to inform policymaking and the policy makers. Many have been in the classroom, many have been in the "movement," and many have been in both. All, without exception, have been tempered and shaped by the modern American Indian Movement (AIM) and accompanying struggles. This group has the advantage of all the great work that preceded them. They are able to stand on the shoulders of giants.

They (we) were weaned on militancy and the

discourses (that is, verbal interchange of ideas) and struggles for human dignity, social justice, and racial equality. Theirs is a "post-AIM" scholarship and these are "post-AIM" scholars. Rejecting the canon of the academy, this scholarship is not "objective." Rather is it a discourse for Indigenous Peoples. This scholarship is unapologetically partisan. It opposes racism, colonialism, oppression, and inequality. It opposes any social system that desires to subjugate one people to another. It stands for the uplift of oppressed people.

Today's Indigenous scholar lives in a dynamic setting, unimagined by former generations. It is a crossroads in history. If equitably shared, advanced technology and the creation of great wealth can reconfigure the world, improving the lives of all. If not, the continuation of racism, ignorance, privilege, and greed will condemn us all. If societies are judged by their lowest strata, then this workbook is important. Will we break through ethnocentrism, racism, and the colonial practices of the past? Can schools really change? Can teaching practices, the curriculum, and the school organization be made to serve Indigenous students and other underserved populations? These are the critical questions addressed in this chapter.

ACTIVITY:

Take a moment and write down the names of individuals you know as educational warriors (teachers, researchers, writers, and so forth) who have always been oppositional to European colonization.

_____

_____

_____

How have these individuals inspired you to move forward in your decolonization work? Briefly explain.

_____

_____

_____

_____

_____

_____

G. Toward Traditional Models of Curriculum and Teaching

Indigenous Peoples' culture anchors them to reality and it must be the starting point for all learning. Therefore, beginning with a tribal-specific, tribal-centered education within the context of familiar cultural and social references, from their own historical settings, is key to fostering educational excellence.

The effects of colonization did not only occur to the Indigenous Peoples of the Americas, but to other Indigenous Peoples throughout the world. Transformational researchers and educators have united and are working together to find solutions for improving the condition of Indigenous education. From this collaboration, many Indigenous populations are provided with strength and hope because of their shared history of survival.

Transformational researchers reject the "colonizing mission" of schools. Some of the most interesting recent research has explored the roles of teachers and culture. For example, Jeanette Haynes Writer focuses on teacher success and instruction delivery. The corpus of her work has broad curriculum implications, casting the teacher as central to the processes of learning. It explores the effects of cultural background and belief systems of teaching. Culturally responsive teachers are effective teachers who embrace Indigenous cultural norms; establish close personal ties with students, parents, and elders; are socially and politically conscious; and attempt to arm students for an alienating world, among other things. Culturally responsive appears more important and transcendent over partisan models (for example, direct instruction, experientialism, and so forth). Most effective teachers of Indigenous children utilize cultural referents to impact knowledge.

Other Indigenous researchers have been active in the prescriptive holistic curriculum discourse over the past three decades. Devon Mihesuah has taken up such topics as suggesting research guidelines in higher education as well as indigenizing the academy, while Linda Tuhiwai Smith issues a clarion call for decolonization of research methods. Karen Swisher and Michael Pavel provide a literature review of learning styles, Karen Cornelius introduces culture-based curriculum, and Gregory Cajete introduces an Indigenous perspective to science teaching and learning. Duane Champagne and Jay Stauss examine the collaboration between universities and Indigenous nations. Finally, Eduardo and Bonnie Duran analyze intergenerational grief and suggest tribal psychological interventions.

These scholars (some in cross-cultural collaborations) are providing the next transformational steps for continuing pedagogical traditions and empowering communities. The remnants of this tradition remain to be seen in the form of culturally responsive teaching practices for Indigenous students. However, during the past five hundred years, white policy makers of Indian education have attempted to dismember many revolutionary Indigenous educational attempts and to defame and stigmatize anything that survives in order to disconnect Indigenous Peoples from the traditional teachings of their ancestors.

This chapter is intended to bring together the critical thinking of many Indigenous scholars in the educational field. These scholars believe that the educational achievement of Indigenous children will not be improved by narrowing the curriculum or achieving desegregation of schools, or through better funding alone. Rather, the best chance for significant improvement in the performance of low-achieving Indigenous students lies in innovations based on replacing constructs rooted in past white hegemony and its current vestiges, and building educational programs and communities consistent with children's ethnic, cultural, social, and developmental needs.

H. Additional Activities

ACTIVITY:

How can you begin to decolonize Indigenous education?

_____

_____

_____

_____

_____

What do you bring to the work of decolonizing Indigenous education?

_____

_____

_____

_____

_____

What do you hope to gain in the work of decolonizing Indigenous education?

_____

_____

_____

_____

_____

_____

ACTIVITY:

Individuals can be held back from transformational action in many ways as they begin the decolonization process. Now take some time to try to list all the barriers—external and internal—that can get in the way of decolonization struggle in your life. For example, "I'm overcome by all the things going on in my life right now," "I don't know what to do or where to start," or "I'm afraid I'll lose my job or lose respect from my family and friends." Then strategize ways to move through them. For every barrier listed, identify at least one strategy for taking action. (An example is provided.)

Barriers to Action

I don't know what to do.

_____

_____

_____

_____

_____

Strategy for Taking Action

I will be willing to make mistakes.

_____

_____

_____

_____

_____

ACTIVITY:

Thinking back to the readings, discuss with a partner the questions below.

Do you feel capable of the commitment to honesty that several educators believe decolonization struggle requires? What are some examples of honesty? (Remember, verbal honesty may not be the only kind of honesty.)

What is your reaction to being urged to celebrate and welcome tribal difference instead of looking for tribal commonalities?

Do you see a difference between personal and political action? Describe both political and personal action.

Do Indigenous Peoples have to come into conflict with other Indigenous Peoples in order to deconstruct colonization?

ACTIVITY:

What is your commitment to action? What changes could you make in your life over the next few months to continue the journey into understanding colonization and decolonization? For example, you could learn to read critically, noticing how non-Indigenous people are characterized in comparison to Indigenous Peoples. What are some larger actions you could take? For example, if you are Indigenous, hold a series of study groups with some non-Indigenous friends to discuss how to use decolonization to be better allies to Indigenous Peoples in your community. Make a list of the next possible steps in your journey.

Steps I Can Take

_____

_____

_____

_____

_____

_____

After completing your list, choose two actions—one small daily action and one larger action—to commit to.

Small Daily Action: _____

Larger Action: _____

State your commitments aloud to a friend to affirm your intention. Write the two actions down on a separate piece of paper and post them where they are visible to you every day. Revisit your list regularly and continue to incorporate other actions into your daily life.

FINAL ACTIVITY:

Having nearly completed the questions in this chapter, think about the following questions and make some notes. What did this journey stir up in you?

_____

_____

_____

_____

_____

_____

_____

_____

Which of the issues that you read about and reflected on do you need to explore more deeply?

_____

_____

_____

_____

_____

_____

_____

What are some ways you can work to deconstruct colonization in your personal relationships as a social activist?

_____

_____

_____

_____

_____

_____

_____

I. Conclusion

White policy makers of Indian education created educational programs to miseducate as well as implement white-supremacy structures of domination. Indigenous Peoples and their independent systems were and are part of a genocidal process—the American holocaust. Colonial and slave structures as well as apartheid and general white-supremacy structures were created, including BIA boarding schools to separate Indigenous children from their parents and tribal communities and cultures, especially mission schools that sought to destroy tribal worldviews. This provided the theological base for the doctrine of Manifest Destiny and served to stigmatize Indigenous Peoples as savages, primitives, and pagans. As a law school dean, Rennard Strickland regrets that this holocaust was, too often, a "genocide-at-law."

In this chapter I wanted to demonstrate how powerful forces influenced education of Indigenous Peoples. The selected policy makers indeed possessed the colonial mentality, and their ideological stance can be attributed to the sociopolitical history of this country.

White policy makers of Indian education have been training primarily to reinforce the deculturalization of Indigenous Peoples and ultimately to disconnect us from the power of the holistic mind. Moreover, it is important to understand the systemic miseducation of a tribal-centered philosophy and thought—an externally imposed European education based in pedagogical fear tactics. The overall schooling production becomes a manufactured monocultural reality. The failure to acknowledge and to respect the multiple cultures of others, as well as the multitribal realities, is at the base of the newest forms of inequality.

Ultimately, the strategy of Indigenous Peoples against colonization should be to deconstruct it (through the decolonization process) and replace it with the struggle for tribal community. Many Eurocentric educational systems are set up to detach us from our tribal communities. Exerting self-determination today is building nationhood. Building tribal nations opposes European domination and injustice. In this effort, we can also find allies and build cross-cultural coalitions of friends and colleagues who will join us in the struggle for self-determination. In essence, coalitions become critical for cultural survival as Indigenous Peoples. Countering white policy makers and their ideology about how to educate Indigenous Peoples today makes this chapter very dynamic as well as politically charged, because it deconstructs an externally imposed educational system that caused a five-hundred-year-long miseducation of authentic Indigenous Peoples' teaching and learning practices.

J. Glossary

deculturalize: To destroy a people's culture while replacing it with a new culture.

deficit theory model: This model shaped the theoretical rationale for educational and curriculum policymaking and was the dominant position of Western research on minorities through the 1960s. It is based on the notion that Indigenous Peoples may be characterized as having "problems," "cultural deficits," or something wrong with them.

Indian education: It is important to understand that the term "Indian education" is an externally imposed concept that was created and sustained by white architects of Indigenous education. This refers to the dominant society's educational system as applied to Indigenous Peoples rather than the Indigenous forms of education existent in Indigenous societies prior to colonization.

Indigenous Peoples: This is my preferred term for describing ourselves and our nations. Previous research focusing on aboriginal peoples in the United States has used the terms *American Indian, Indian,* and *Native American* as the primary nomenclature for this population. This chapter subverts this tradition by instead using the terms "Indigenous Peoples" or "Indigenous." These terms are capitalized to signify and recognize the cultural heterogeneity and political sovereignty of Indigenous Peoples in the Western hemisphere.

Machiavellian model: This is used here to refer to the idea that people feel good about doing well at whatever position or employment they occupy without asking why and what—not asking critical questions and challenging authority.

white architects of Indian education: These are the white policy makers who funded, created, justified, and refined colonial educational policies.

Organizing Indigenous Governance to Invent the Future

T'hohahoken

A. Introduction: Freeing the Sovereign Spirit

My Indigenous name sits as the byline for this chapter. Though registered as Michael George Doxtater in St. Mary's Hospital in Niagara Falls, New York, I use both aksennahonwe (my real name) "T'hohahoken" and my colonized name "Michael" interchangeably. Also, our people are called the colonized "Mohawk," but our real name pertains to the flinty country in northeast America. We call ourselves "Kaniienkehaka."

I use the discussion of identity to mark the difference between self-determination and self-government. Government agencies registered me under colonized names Michael and Mohawk. However, inside my country I am known as T'hohahoken and Kaniienkehaka. Thus, I determine myself by using terms I choose.

Colonized people are self-governed. Free people are self-determined.

In this chapter I challenge Indigenous Peoples to reenable themselves in the area of self-determination and self-government by doing something simple and something only they can do.

Think for themselves.

Here is the challenge. Use the rich heritage of joint problem solving based on the unique collective memory of the ancestors' thinking. Take this intellectual estate as an inheritance for your use. Freeing the sovereign spirit is no simple or easy task. However, there is no good reason not to try.

This chapter describes processes, systems, and pathways for sovereign spirits who seek to do good work for their people. Consequently, my task is to review a particular heritage for group decision-making processes in the modern age. Through this review process we decolonize our thinking, and then our Indigenous Peoples. Indigenous Peoples invent the future by embracing a rich heritage for governing their affairs.

B. The Way to FEEL Good

My work with elders focuses on the contemporary recital of the Iroquoian understanding of how things came to be called the Kaiianereserakowa (Great Law of Peace). The Great Law is the Iroquois Peoples' master narrative. Over the years I have helped Chief Jacob E. Thomas organize and conduct the recital of the Iroquoian Great Law of Peace on three occasions. I assisted Mohawk elder Chief Richard Maracle organize Six Nations people at the grassroots level on numerous issues, including treaty rights, environmental protection, and conflict resolution. The humbling experience of working for contemporary elders makes even more humbling the thought of Iroquoian collective memory. Realizing how much my elders knew and I didn't, reduced my self-importance. Even more, standing by these elders and hearing how humbled they felt by how much our ancient ancestors knew and they didn't, is doubly unsettling.

Using the Iroquois master narrative to teach governance has four purposes. First, this Indigenous knowledge shows that a group of people organized to learn how to make their lives better. Second, I show that belief and reason exist side by side. In most instances experts on our culture from Europe only value our religions and not our reasonable selves. We never argued about religion before. Why do it now?

Third, the narrative sets into place what I call the *Four Circles* of Indigenous life identified by one of our elders. "Things seem to happen in fours," an Onondaga chief once said. Fourth, the narrative reveals key functions of *organizational learning, collaborative decision making, co-generated mission*, and *quality assurance* systems. The narrative urges Indigenous Peoples to invoke and enact ancient knowledge in the present time. I review learning outcomes throughout this chapter.

Finally, in Kaniienkehaka (Mohawk) I am identified as T'hohahoken (Near the Road) of the Iensohake niwakataroten (soft-shelled turtle clan), born to the Kaniienkehaka (People of the Flint) from the Kanonsiionikon (Indigenous People of the Americas). In addition, my family name is Sha'tekariwate. This name means "mediator," our family's role in the vaunted Iroquois Confederacy. As such, I've thought a lot about the need for coping with change and how we learn to do that. This consciousness of identity aids my work in grassroots organizing, mediation, and working with bereaved families. That's what I feel.

FEEL for Yourself

When Indigenous Peoples organize to act on issues like land rights, environmental health, crime, or social injustice, it originates with true feelings. In addition, families organize to face obstacles, like a death in the family, which carry tremendously burdensome emotions. In almost all instances of our ordinary lives, we feel fears, worries, and threats to the successful completion of our duties and responsibilities.

"How will we ever raise enough money for our kid's baseball team?" "How can we get parents more involved in the lacrosse league?" "Where will we get funding for our after-school programs?" "Why can't we get our leaders to protect our rights?"

The questions go on and on.

Look closely though. You will see that behind each question, feelings abound. Many of these feelings directly attach themselves to what individuals feel is important. Mostly these feelings relate to the happiness and nurture of our children. In this way, I say that our highest good comes from feelings for our children. Not too bad a place to start.

The FEEL model sprang from my thinking about

the Iroquoian understanding of how things came to be derived from our narrative called the Great Law. The four main sections of the Great Law project are the processes of Formation, Education, Expectation, and Liberation. These four processes derive from what I learned from hearing and thinking about what the ancestors knew. I explain them in more detail throughout this chapter.

The Iroquois master narrative reveals an example of Indigenous knowledge that I call the FEEL model. Stages described in the Great Law provide a model for organizational learning, planning, evaluation, and decision making. I use the acronym FEEL to encourage human action based on having feelings. It is okay to feel okay about what you're doing.

> Formation: The mission describes corruption followed by healing, everything has a gift, and everyone gets to eat. We should acknowledge our understanding of how things came to be.

> Education: The learning mission expands to reveal everyone's personal gift rooted in the idea that everyone gets to be healed. We have the right to ask questions, and the right to be answered.

> Expectation: To fulfill our mission we use everyone's gifts when enacted through principles we expect, such as trust, respect, mutual aid, and defense. We have the right to expect things from each other.

> Liberation: To renew the mission we reflect on our performance and see if we have become corrupted, and are in need of healing to free ourselves to think clearly once again. We have the right to be free.

No one individual can implement an organizational mission. There is nothing wrong with humanity collaborating in coping with change. We can FEEL our humanity.

Take some time and participate in the exercises at the end of each section. These activities are designed to refocus our attention on our own governance processes and systems. The organizational learning exercises

derive from Indigenous governance systems. After thinking about Iroquois organizational learning, adapt these exercises to your culture's master narrative and your organization. I think you'll see things you didn't know were there.

C. Sharing Our History: Kaiianereserakowa

Ultimate Truths told in slogans, maxims, and proverbs derive from a people's collective memory. For example, the Ultimate Truth held by many Iroquois people is suggested in the phrase, "the good message of peace, and the power of good thinking." This Ultimate Truth derives from the Iroquois' conception of the good life that everyone gets to eat. Now, however, we also know that everyone gets to be happy. This conception of the good life is communicated through the Kaiianereserakowa, more commonly known as the Great Law of Peace.

Kaiianereserakowa can be broken down into English syllables; *kaiianere* or "it is good"; *sera* or "ness"; and *kowa* idiomatically expressed as "magnificent." The concept of "a-magnificent-good" has been called in other cultures "summum bonum" or "highest good." As a highest good, the Great Law of Peace describes how the Iroquois People are constituted, our history, inheritances, and warnings for potential dangers. This history includes four distinct sections. First, the Sky Woman's story is told up to the advent of war. Second, the Dark Times of malevolence by men is interrupted by the arrival of a Peacemaker named Tekanawite, with a story that begins with his birth. Third, governing practices and processes are described in terms that are more deliberate. Fourth, portents are described for Iroquois People that require them to reform themselves to meet changed times. The Great Law is recited as an epic narrative that is consistent with the transposed meaning of Kaiianereserakowa.

D. The Formation of Humanity

The purpose of this section is to describe processes for understanding how things came to be. We can use this understanding to identify our peoples' conception of the good life. In order to work together on this exercise, I will use my people's creation story as a common reference point. By focusing on this story, questions will spring to mind. Keep track of these questions. Later I offer some helpful tips for honing our research skills and for learning that how things came to be, has been passed down to us by our forbears. Usually our Indigenous knowledge is passed down to us in stories, songs, dances, and art. Reading these signs and symbols of culture improves our ability to accept the knowledge that has been passed down to us by our honorable ancestors. Our collective memory improves as we remind each other of what our ancestors said.

The following Iroquois creation story illustrates one people's understanding of how things came to be. While there may be variations on origins among various Iroquoian People, there also are variations across the land. However, note that I use the term Great Spirit, though most Indigenous Peoples in the Americas know that Being by many names. Nonetheless, this story has important lessons that we can learn about coping with life on Earth, which I describe later. I realize everyone has a creation story. The point here is to work through this exercise, then apply the same study skills to your understanding of how things came to be.

Formation: How Things Came to Be

Human beings dwell in a cold, dark world. Without hope and in despair, human beings exist without a conception of the good life. Horrible creatures abound and the savagery of early human life engenders harsh realities. According to the telling of this era of human life, Sky World dwellers (including a Divine Being) look down and feel pity for the miserable existence of human beings. In the Sky World no one is hungry. In the Sky World there is no fear, death, or tears. So, a Sky Woman is sent to the earth. And in the formation of the world order, Sky Woman also delivers a conception of the good life.

The conception of the good life derived from the Sky World model includes aspects of hope and happiness. These aspects of the good life are portrayed by

Sky World dwellers engaged endlessly in dance, song, games, feasting, talking, laughing, and comfort. Food, shelter, and healing derive from these heavenly pursuits. Sky Woman gives human beings Indigenous knowledge of food, shelter, and healing that forms our humanity. After healing, in particular, is the recognition of cycles of corruption followed by healing. The consequences of corruption are marked within the context of human development. We derive our special knowledge of the way things came to be in terms of our ability to heal our corruption. The cycles are depicted in specific terms.

The recital of the Great Law begins with the account of Sky Woman's story that forms the basis of human life through the Kanohnweratonsera (thanksgiving address), or being thankful for all that we are given. However, the inciting incident for Kaiianereserakowa begins with the conflict between the Sky Woman's grandsons. The right-handed twin is known as Teharonhiawakon—"Upholding the Sky," or "heaven," as inferred in the word shakoiatanonstaton (upper sanctuary). Born normally, Teharonhiawakon is considered a messenger of Divine Being. Conversely, Tawiskaron is called "flint." This left-handed sibling forces his way into the world by kicking through his mother's abdominal cavity. Causing her death, Tawiskaron engages in a bloody feud with Teharonhiawakon. Prior to being relegated to the lower world after his defeat by his right-handed brother, during their conflict Teharonhiawakon assaults Tawiskaron and bloodies his mouth. The blood droplets fell to earth as flint stone, and form the material source of arrowheads. Thus, so the mythopoeic epic contends, were humans provided with the weapons of war.

Beginnings

Human life begins in the pristine Sky World. The Sky World is populated by beings similar to humans. These humans dance, play games like lacrosse, and revel in the comfort and safety of their world. Populated by animals, plants, and birds, the Sky World is also populated by spirit entities. In the Sky World there is no hunger. Happiness is the most important quality of that life. In the sheltering embrace of the Great Spirit, the Sky World is sheltered from dark forces, cold, hunger and death. Thus, describing the Sky World provides our conception of the good life.

There are three versions of Sky Woman's descent to Earth. In one version a hole appears under the Celestial Tree and the pregnant Sky Woman slips and falls through. She grasps a tobacco plant and a strawberry plant to rescue herself. Another version has Sky Woman and her husband digging and planting around the Celestial Tree. He digs too deeply and creates a hole in the sky through which Sky Woman is pushed. The Celestial Tree plays a function in both accounts. Both accounts describe the husband or Great Spirit pushing her through a hole dug under the tree. Divine Being might also have placed Sky Woman through the hole in the sky. Thus, Sky Woman either jumps, falls, or is pushed through the celestial hole. Generally, we begin with the admission that the Great Spirit sees how miserable human life is on Earth. Thus, Creator sends Sky Woman to Earth to improve human well-being, and so that the humans will be fed, happy, and safe.

The origins of human life begin with Sky Woman's fall. However, when the corruption of the sky was created, the corruption is healed when birds fly to cushion Sky Woman's fall. As birds place her gently on a turtle's back, she has nowhere to put her plants. So animals try to bring her soil from the bottom of the sea. Muskrat dies though finally reaching the surface with a soiled paw. Sky Woman plants the tobacco and the strawberry in the muskrat's soil and shuffles her feet on the soil, performing the first Woman's Dance to honor the muskrat. Eventually Sky Woman gives birth to a daughter. This daughter becomes pregnant by the North Wind. Sky Woman helps her daughter give birth to two sons, but the daughter dies in childbirth when the left-handed twin corrupts the mother's abdomen. Grandmother and grandsons bury the

> **"For a colonized people the most essential value, because the most concrete, is first and foremost the land: the land which will bring them bread and, above all, dignity."**
> **—Frantz Fanon**

daughter, and from the mound of her grave grow all the vegetable and fruit plants. The daughter's sacrifice is remembered by human beings in appreciation—all food is medicine to restore human happiness and life.

Most significantly for humanity, the sons fight each other after their mother's death. Blamed for the mother's death, the left-handed twin is defeated by the right-handed twin. However, during the battle, the left-handed son is bloodied. His blood drops to the ground and turns into flint. Flint is used by humanity to produce weapons of war. Humanity is corrupted.

The era between Sky World and Creation is associated with the rise of agriculture. Women are elevated within Indigenous society for discovering agriculture, an event described through the Sky Woman's deceased daughter's grave sprouting the food plants necessary for human life. Each day, ideally at dawn, the thanksgiving prayer thanks all the forces of the natural world that give us our happiness and health. Consistent with the creation story, thanksgiving is chanted to all creation: beginning with mother earth, medicine plants, food plants, trees, insects, small fur-bearing animals, larger mammals, birds, fishes, elements like water and air, meteorological presences like thunderstorms and northern lights, and also celestial bodies like the stars, moon, and sun. Thanksgiving also addresses lizards, snakes, thistles, and insects, remembered for their gifts.

Human beings have pledged to commemorate all of the forces working for human life. In fact, the thanksgiving prayer is considered to be a treaty or covenant between the Great Spirit and people. This covenant has one theme—sometimes individuals are asked to sacrifice themselves for the happiness, health, and safety of others. So included in thanksgiving are human beings, who nurture their children and are mindful of the future generations.

ACTIVITY:

Take some time and list questions you might ask the ancestors about our origins. Then answer your questions.

Question 1:_____

Answer 1:_____

Question 2:_____

Answer 2:_____

Question 3:_____

Answer 3:_____

Question 4: _____

Answer 4:_____

Question 5:_____

Answer 5:_____

Don't be intimidated by the complexity of the story. There are degrees of difficulty with the concepts, but these complex notions evoke complex thinking. Thinking begins with questions.

Questions That Came to My Mind

When my students ask questions, I know that there's a lot of thinking going on. I say to my students, "That's a good question. What did you have in mind?" Moreover, as they explain their thinking, they usually come up with the answer to their own question.

Here are the lessons that come from the questions I asked.

Lesson One: What does it mean if Sky Woman was pushed, jumped, or fell through the corrupted sky?

Some days I feel like life is all a big mistake (fell). Some days I feel like the forces of life are beyond my control (pushed). Mostly, though, I feel happy. However, Sky Woman got here, I am thankful for all that has been given to me for my happiness and health (jumped).

Lesson Two: What does it mean when after something bad happens, something good always seems to happen?

Corruption happens throughout the story. The sky becomes corrupted. There is corruption in the muskrat's death. The daughter dies. The sons fight. In every example, a healing event takes place. The birds rescue the Sky Woman. Muskrat is honored with the first Woman's Dance. Sky Woman's daughter produces all our food plants. The weapons of war are finally buried under a pine tree when our nations pledged friendship and peace. So I realize that there are cycles of corruption that should always be followed by healing. When we expect corruption and healing, we also have the knowledge for coping with changes to our life.

Lesson Three: Does our covenant with the Great Spirit mean that we try to make a Sky World on Earth?

It seems that everything we need to be happy has been provided on Earth. When we buried our weapons of war under a tree, we made a commitment to try and live good lives. But we also know we might become corrupted. So we also pledged to help each other. We promised the Great Spirit we would be mindful of each other.

Lesson Four: How do we make sure that everyone is fed and is happy?

Our ancestors have passed down to us many practices that we know today. We have many foods such as corn, beans, squash, tomatoes, and potatoes that are good and nutritious. We have sap and juice from plants like cactus and maple trees. There are apples, berries, peaches, and grapes growing throughout the land. There are fish, deer, buffalo, geese, and ducks. One reason people came here in 1492 is because we had lots to eat. But we also had medicines. Our healers are world famous. Healing grief is one important medicine we use to restore happiness to the people we care about. Through the Sky Woman's story, our ancestors tell us that no one eats until we all eat, no one is happy until we are all happy. Lastly, no one is healed until we are all healed.

Lesson Five: Does everything have a gift?

Everything on Earth has a purpose. There are uses for plants, animals, and minerals. However, these things can become corrupted when not used wisely. Psychotropic plants can be used recklessly for recreational purposes. Using minerals to construct weapons of war is a corrupt practice. A poisoned environment affects the health of the creatures living there. Yet we know that all things have a gift. Even thistles, snakes, and vultures are said to possess gifts that help human life. So we also know that every human being has a gift. Our role as humanity is to help each individual find his or her gift. Then, we encourage people to give their gift.

Lesson Six: Ask what you want answered.

This section may appear to be an exercise in cultural literacy. However, don't overlook the process we used. We presented a series of questions with various degrees of difficulty. Our inquiry into the meaning of Sky Woman's story began with questions. Groups learn by asking questions. Ask the questions you want answered.

E. The Education of Humanity

Contemporary Indigenous society is a wonderful forest of life. Our communities rustle with activity, like the sound of the wind through trees, whether summer or winter. Our people tend to the business of organizing the lacrosse, basketball, baseball, and soccer leagues and teams. We also organize home and school groups, after-school activities, even lunch and breakfast programs. We have singing groups, dancing groups, theatre groups that perform our culture. In addition, we continue to marry and bury our own people. We have families. So we also tend to the business of our spiritual life with groups organized to keep our faith, whether that be our heritage societies, or even the newer organized religions (Indigenous or not). Sometimes people participate in social service commissions, police commissions, and tribal or band councils.

Yet, there are times when we get lost in this forest.

Throughout life we face changes in our pathways. Sometimes our journey becomes so repetitive that we become bored with the same old scenery. Our trails become travails. Our roadways become filled with potholes and ruts. For some, dead end after dead end replaces hope with despair. For others, the endless journey becomes a march. Our paths cross Turtle Island, searching endlessly for spiritual and emotional release from our wandering. So often, we despair and lose hope that we shall ever find our spiritual families.

Indigenous Peoples live scattered in diverse places in our country. This family has suffered through many tragedies. Our suffering, and the ruin served on us by agents of despair throughout history, has been told in many places. "Our people have suffered a great trauma from which we have not recovered," an elder named Babe told a Six Nations gathering in 1992. "You won't be able to help your people unless you heal that trauma." This legacy need not be repeated here. Our collective memory of the Great Tragedy of Earth—the near complete genocide of the Real People—affects Indigenous individuals in subtle ways. But what needs saying concerns individual human beings. Saying the effects out loud can help clear the air.

Around 1992 Indigenous Peoples began to connect ideas about healing the trauma. One connection was the association of acute stress disorder (ASD) and post-traumatic stress disorder (PTSD) with historical unresolved grieving. Psychologists Maria Yellow Horse Brave Heart and Lemyra DeBruyn identified the relationship between war veterans' experiences from the battlefield and the attempted annihilation of Indigenous Peoples of the Americas. However, Brave Heart and DeBruyn also describe how PTSD could be transmitted across generations and time. The effects of the American Revolution are still felt today among the Iroquois. Even more acutely, the effects of tragedies like Wounded Knee keep our relatives in the Dakotas gripped by unresolved grief. Uncertainty is the least of those effects. However, family violence, substance abuse, crime, poor parenting skills, and poverty are substantive realities.

In this section I discuss the knowledge and understanding of challenges to our mission. The stages for achieving enlightenment seem complex, but once practiced, come to mind as uncomplicated. In fact, the notion that we complicate matters ourselves is the basis of looking at our individual thinking. Then we proceed

> **"As long as the oppressed remain unaware of the causes of their condition, they fatalistically 'accept' their exploitation."**
> **—Paulo Freire**

to think clearly, but first we clear our minds in order to focus on the task at hand. I use the Iroquois master narrative as a learning tool for clearing the mind.

Tekanawite's story contains many lessons, but I focus on how people learn from this special man. The story of Tekanawite's birth and childhood prepare him for his mission of peace. His grandmother Kahentoktha attempts to murder the baby, because she believes that her daughter Kahentehsohn lied about Tekanawite's virgin birth. After being taught by a celestial messenger of the child's dangerous mission as peacemaker in a war-torn world, Kahentoktha becomes his teacher. In his childhood, Tekanawite displays a knack for mediation. He confounds other children with his penchant for magic. Peacemaker leaves Kahentoktha and Kahentehsohn as a man, with a bittersweet farewell because of the air of tragedy that was foretold at his birth.

A reign of terror by an oligarchy of Iroquoian men characterizes Iroquois civilization. The example of Aiionwatha best illustrates how brutal the Dark Times were for the weak and defenseless. In short fashion, Aiionwatha's enemies destroy his city, kill his wife and daughters, and force the defenseless women and children to flee as refugees into the hills. Tyrants serve despair and ruin to the innocent.

Tekanawite arrives in Iroquoia as the tragedy of Aiionwatha unfolds. The Great Law epic concentrates on Peacemaker's mediation of the Iroquois conflict. When the Peacemaker begins his mission among five warring nations, his relationship with Aiionwatha is a story of restoration through the Condolence Ceremony. The ceremony teaches the grieving that many generations of Iroquois ancestors join them in condolence, are present at all times, and can even be heard. The destruction of Aiionwatha's people leads to Aiionwatha's redemption when he accepts the Great Peace teachings of the Peacemaker. Peacemaker's mission is to teach the Good Message of Peace and the

Preternatural Force of Reason (stated in Mohawk as Karihwiio, Skennon, Kanikonriio, and Kashastensera). Acceptance of these founding principles leads to the confederation of the Five Nations when twelve warlords, sorcerers, and cannibals accept the Great Peace.

The Peacemaker challenges these twelve founding Iroquois leaders to link their arms together and act as a fence around the tree. War between these relations is symbolized by a war club. The despotic oligarchy cast their weapons of war into a river running under a Great Tree, to be carried away forever. Now women, men, and individuals collaborate collectively in the Iroquois decision-making process:

1. The decision makers are charged with the Great Law *mission* of peace as symbolized by white roots of peace emanating from a white pine tree.
2. This circle of decision makers protects Iroquoian cultural *properties*—their language, customs, spirituality, and lands.
3. The decision makers teach how the Great Law protects the rights and freedoms that insure the safety and happiness of *individuals.*

The principal duties of decision makers include the protection of the mission, properties, and people. However, with a new mission, the ancestors recognized the human need to overcome the past. The idea of *condolence* prepares the individuals to undertake their duties and responsibilities.

Clearing at the Wood's Edge

An innovation used by ancestors to clear their minds is found in formal ceremonies. The respectful use by modern Indigenous Peoples of these cultural innovations seems necessary. After five hundred years of occupation, Indigenous Peoples began again to affirm our heritage to invent the future. With certain intimidation, and with plenty of renewed hope, we began listening to the voices of our ancestors. We began to accept that the Indigenous knowledge of survival is communicated through signs and symbols of culture that had somehow survived to the present time.

One example of the sophistication of our ancestors' Indigenous knowledge comes from the Iroquois ceremony called At the Wood's Edge. This ceremony is part of a larger ceremony called They Shall Wipe Each Other's Tears. However, this particular passage is important to our discussion about how the mind works. These words illustrate our ancestors' understanding of the complex nature of the thinking used for human understanding and coping with change.

…and then One will say…
Now then today, I was suddenly aware of your voices
Across the forest as you confronted obstacles
And you could barely see the pathway of our
     Ancestors.
And this is weighing on your minds,
You could see the smoke rising.
For this is where the Ancestors smoked and held
     council.
Everywhere you looked you saw the footprints of our
     Ancestors.
For, how could it be well with your mind
For you to be going along with tears in your eyes,
     Ancestors.
Great thanks that you have crossed through the forest
     and
we are sitting together now with the Ancestors.
For you might have drowned in the water.
Or there may have been Evil Forces to strike you down.
Or you have become trapped in the thorns.
Or something may have blocked your path.
Or you may have stumbled on the pathway.
Or one would see dead bodies and say in horror
"We see our dead Ancestors and wonder what happened."
So, great thanks that you have arrived here safely.
Our forbears decided that we kindle a fire
And as we console each other with few words
We will mingle our tears together.

The ancestors provided their children with what seem to be simple ideas for looking at the human mind. Yet within this simplicity are complex ideas that can help Indigenous Peoples now.

ACTIVITY:

Why do we mingle our tears together?

_____

_____

Add some questions of your own. Answer those questions.

_____

_____

_____

_____

What remedy did the ancestors provide to heal?

_____

_____

What does it mean to leave the forest and kindle a fire by the wood's edge?

_____

_____

Mission Statement

The idea of condolence describes the need for people to clear the air, cool off, relax, and regain strength. Once that occurs, we renew or invent our mission. I suggest that we begin with the following text that shows one view of the Iroquois mission. Though your club, association, organization, or agency may have a modest mission, the pledge below implies ethics and principles of a good life. Note that the following mission statement implies the conception of the good life we described in the Great Law of Peace.

Many Indigenous Peoples offer similar sentiments to recognize their honorable ancestors.

Akwekon Akenkweten (All My Relations)

The Children of the Great Spirit are a free and independent People governed by Covenants made in very Ancient Times by our Forbears and handed down to us their Children. These Covenants describe our rights and freedoms to govern over our own affairs in our own way. And we consider these covenants to be a precious inheritance for our Children and future generations with which no one can interfere. We say these words before the Children of the Great Spirit who have gone before us. We say these words before the Children of the Great Spirit who are with us yet. We say these words before the Children of the Great Spirit yet to be born.

ACTIVITY:

Take some time and write down your own people's pledge. You could also translate the text written above into your Indigenous language.

All My Relations

_____

_____

_____

_____

_____

_____

_____

_____

F. The Expectation of Humanity

The purpose of this exercise is to become familiar with a process for balancing power. More pointedly, the Great Law codifies expectations for dispute and conflict resolution. Iroquois dispute and conflict resolution includes a system for *balancing power*. Power balancing is necessary in case one area of power overrules the others areas of power, especially when the organization is confronted with changes.

The Great Law reveals guidelines to cope with expected changes. The Great Law teaches people to expect change. Coping with change becomes easier when change becomes part of the organizational system.

Power is balanced in the Iroquois system between three identified areas of power. First, the Great Law describes the *judiciary* function of the chiefs. Second, the *executive* governance of nation's affairs under the clanmothers is examined. Third, the people's rights are explored, including their responsibility to expect that their rights and freedoms are protected and that actions taken by the nation are *representative* of their will.

The object of power balancing comes from the idea of consensus. All three areas of power agree on actions to be taken. Consensus building is required, and consequently, building consensus focuses the organization on finding solutions. Then, finally, the exercise of joint problem solving creates interdependency—our strength comes from our unity.

Tripod of Power

Peacemaker encounters key historical figures and asks three basic questions: "Who are you?"; "What are you doing?"; "Why are you doing what you're doing?" Iroquoian historical and cultural development is based on episodes retelling these dialogues. Each episode describes chiefs, clanmothers, and people accepting the idea of power balancing through the process of answering those questions. There is the bawdy-house operator Tsikonsase, the first woman and first Iroquois to accept the Great Law. The handsome cannibal looks critically at his reflection in his own cauldron and leaves the forest to raise a family. Aiionwatha is recruited. Warlords Tsatekariwate and Tekarihoken, and the sorcerer Atotarho are reformed. In each encounter Tekanawite questions these people about their motives, encourages their critical reflection on their actions, and using only logic and reason, convinces them to expect change. Learning is essentially the basis of the confederation of the wisk nihohnowentsiiake, or the League of Five Nations (as it is still legally known).

The judiciary role of the chiefs is described first. Roles, responsibilities, and limitations on the powers of chiefs are characterized by the symbolic Circle Wampum (teiionkwarihastohn). The chiefs have authority around the tree, but with arms linked, their main function is to keep watch over each other. They say what they think but are no longer able to tell anyone what to do. Remember: These powerful yet dangerous men have extraordinary talents.

The Great Law defines the sovereignty (tewata-towiiehake) of the league's members. The mission of peace is the central image of the terrestrial Great Tree of Peace. The wampum belts of confederation are also explained. Narratives of the formation and functioning of the Five Nation councils and the League council are described. Mohawks are principal initiators of all League matters, but are colloquially described as "the well." Oneidas cooperate in the promotion of peace. The Cayugas' covenant with the Peacemaker is to support the Mohawks and Oneidas as they promote peace. The Onondagas have a duty to tend and host council. Protecting the western entrance to Iroquoia, the Senecas maintain a dominating presence in relations with western nations. Consequently, as keepers of the eastern door, Mohawks sponsor nations to the east (including Europeans later on). Also described is the process for removing a chief from office and conferring of chieftainships, as well as funeral rites and condolence.

The Great Law describes the executive preeminence of clanmothers in mediating and facilitating Iroquois government. Women are the focal point in the conferring of a chieftainship following the death or removal of a chief. Also described is the sovereignty of the clanships to govern their affairs. Extending from the authority of the mothers, there are many options for conferring authority on individuals to carry out the nation's work. There are the "real names of the big people," secular chiefs (like Cornplanter and

Thaienteneka, kasennahonwe ronwatikowanen). There are those "who have sprung up," the so-called Pine Trees (though gender is not inferred by the word onkanetoten). Coincidentally, there are a male and a female "who have a duty" (raterihonte), who are also called faithkeepers. The "tobacco hanging" (oiienkohn-toh) are usually called "the runners," but are more likely sentries. The clanmother has an *aide de camp*, as does the chief (shakotiyenawase). Finally, there is a local law-enforcement officer called "he watches the log" (rarontarone). There are also official conferring rituals for these people, as well as funeral rites and condolence.

Under the Great Law, Indigenous governance must be representative of the covenants that protect equal rights and freedoms of all individuals (i:katatariwasnie). Symbolically represented by the Aiionwatha Belt and the Circle Wampum, no individual, clan, or nation is above the law. They have become one family of many relations, akwekon akenkweten. The Kaiianereserakowa describes clans, international relations, national sovereignty, democracy, and the importance of condolence or basic human compassion. These features are represented by a clan's hearth (oiienkwara; otara); human compassion as rafters and braces for the rafters (konoronhkwasera); sovereignty (tewatatoweiiehake); democracy (owennasohnhake); and the strengthening of our minds (ionkwanikonhraniron) in order to be self-governed individuals (i:katatariwasnie). The list of laws includes property rights, cultural practices, religious practices, customs such as marriage and adoption, self-defense, and freedom of expression and speech or "having a voice" as Iroquois democracy is known ("many voices" or owennasohnhake). Also described are the condolence and funeral rites that are administered when one of the people dies.

The word kanonhsionikon is translated as the "people of one long house," but connotes the cooperation between the builders; hence, "many built the house." Not only has the law become the estate of the people, peace is a universal principle. The nature of human interactions is described in the Kaiianereserakowa as intrinsic human compassion (…esi:entakene konoronhkwasera, esahrihowanektenhake oniionkwe) as taught by the Peacemaker. The equality of rafters is a model for humans (…atonhets tewahawe tsi nonkwetatseh akwekon nithshakan Shonkwaiiatison thotkaoh atonhoh antwenthaoiake). All humans carry the same spirit. In addition, "tohsa sasewa'nikohnra'ne skennon, kasa'sthensera tahnon karihwiio" represents the principle message for human social stability and harmony. As if to summarize the intent of the Great Law, the longhouse takes on features of kanonhstaten and becomes a sanctuary, a veritable heaven on Earth. By burying the weapons of internecine war under the roots of a tree and then standing the tree upright, Peacemaker restores the corruption from far into the past, even including the corruption of the Sky World in antiquity. The Great Law describes the people of one longhouse, including rafters, as braces for the rafters bound together using untangled vines. The simple compassionate act of wiping each other's tears strengthens the house by retying the vines on the rafters to make the house new again. According to the elders, respect (ontatekhweniohnstak)

and compassion (konoronhkwasera) are the sources of our humanity and power. Our unity begins with the expectation of human decency.

Democracy and Individuals

According to the Iroquois system, democracy begins with thoughtful individuals. These individuals question their actions to help understand themselves. Therefore, Peacemaker asks three questions that have the effect of causing individuals to look at themselves, which is called *critical reflection*. Consequently, we look inwardly and ask:

1. Who am I?
2. What am I doing?
3. Why am I doing what I am doing?

These three questions form a good starting place for critical reflection. The three questions can be asked of ourselves, of each other, and of our work as an organization.

ACTIVITY:

In terms of your own organization, answer the following questions.

Who am I in my organization?

_____

_____

What do I do for my organization?

_____

_____

_____

Why do I do what I do in my organization?

_____

_____

_____

_____

Democracy and Collaboration

We have seen that individuals should think about themselves. Upon due reflection, these individuals may see something they think is important. They also may discover there are others of a similar mind. As they begin to discuss why what they see is important, they may also uncover and refine ways of participating together in the valuing of what they consider their common good. The process involves:

1. People who agree something is important;
2. People who question why something is important;
3. People who collaborate in answering the questions;
4. People who act on the answers to the questions.

ACTIVITY:

Thinking and action do not function independently. Take time to answer the following questions.

How important is your organization?

_____

_____

What is important about your organization?

_____

_____

_____

What is important to your organization?

_____

_____

_____

What important work does your organization do?

_____

_____

_____

_____

Democracy as Consensus Building

Modern democratic societies view democracy as majority rule—the end result of voting. The Iroquois master narrative describes Indigenous participatory democracy as a process. The governing processes described throughout the narrative reinforce learning to cope with change through consensus building.

Organizations have three areas of governance support. In this section we have reviewed the three parts of Iroquoian political and social organization. I have labeled these the judiciary, executive, and representative areas of power. The interdependency of this triune decision-making system portends to the equal power vested in each area. These areas correspond to many organizational systems.

Judiciary

Longstanding members of the organization care for the collective memory of the organization. Similar to the Iroquois chieftainships, longstanding members of organizations carry with them the collective memory of past deeds, incidents, rules, regulations, duties, and responsibilities. This collective memory helps others involved in governing the organization.

Executive

Members of organizations who are identified for specific gifts and talents are nominated and mandated to use those gifts for the benefit of the organization.

Similar to officers of the Iroquois system, organizational officers execute the program for which they receive a governing mandate. An organization varies its executive officers based on the number of individual gifts needed to respond to the mandate.

Representative

Organizations work on social, political, economic, spiritual, or cultural issues that have been deemed important by stakeholders in those issues. Organizations rely on collective memory to refine their opinion. The organization's stakeholders recruit, appoint, and mandate people to enact their wishes. They also maintain vigilance over their organization's officers to make sure that actions taken are representative of their mandate. This vigilance is the basis of governing.

Quality Assurance

In democratic systems, all members may participate in the performance assessment of the organization. While there are three groups listed above who support the organization, essential principles of respect and compassion between these areas create an environment for mutual aid. In other words, the organization learns to help itself. We achieve consensus when we agree how to do our important work better—something called *quality assurance.*

ACTIVITY:

One method for evaluation involves layering the assessment. Answer the following questions within your organization. See if this builds consensus and identifies how you can assure quality work.

What am I doing well?

1._____

2._____

3._____

What can I do better?

1._____
2._____

What can I do differently now?

1._____

What are you doing well?

1._____
2._____
3._____

What can you do better?

1._____
2._____

What can do you differently now?

1._____

What are we doing well?

1._____
2._____
3._____

What can we do better?

1._____
2._____

What can we do differently now?

1._____

Constantly refining your lists serves two purposes. First, we see three positive things that are done well. Second, we see a couple of things where help might be needed. Third, we identify one thing that can be fixed right away. Be positive.

Also, note that action is a requirement at all times.

G. The Liberation of Humanity

After his mission among the Iroquois, Tekanawite is said to have traveled overseas. In these depictions, once peace was achieved in Iroquoia, Peacemaker travels to the Middle East, where he is killed. After this episode he returns to Iroquoia one last time before leaving for the Sky World. Peacemaker's return is shrouded in mystery—he arrives in a stone canoe, his hands and feet pierced, slashes on his forehead, with a wound to his side. He tells the gathered Iroquois not to touch him, but he has returned as promised.

Peacemaker issues several warnings about potential dangers awaiting Indigenous Peoples in the future. Affirming the covenants that are made by "our forbears in very ancient times, which are handed to us their children" may diminish these dangers. In the future our leaders (the chiefs) will possibly again fall into disarray. During these times despair and ruin befall the Indigenous Peoples. Although Iroquois People have a mission to spread the message of Peace through the extension of the White Roots of Peace worldwide, Peacemaker says that the world's people would chop the white roots. These destructive people would follow the white roots back to the tree. At this time the Iroquois originators of the peace message would be attacked. And so would all their relations.

During this turbulent future, a path chosen by the People is called okaratsikowa (elm-magnificent). During these times the chiefs' heads will be rolling around in the road. Their eyes will be filled with tears. Destructive people and their allies who have hacked and mocked the White Roots of Peace will be stricken with convulsions. The confusion and tumult are manifested in the chiefs' heads, which will be kicked. At this time the people will gather, sort out their clans, and reform their leaders. The word okaratsikowa refers to the slippery-elm birthing medicine used by Iroquois wa'eriwatsehnri (midwives). According to the Peacemaker, there will be a rebirth and the Iroquois People will emancipate their mission from tyranny. Okaratsikowa refers to a "Great Rebirth." We will start over.

Finally, before departing on his stone canoe, Peacemaker consoles the Iroquois people. In those days, he says, when times are uncertain and dark, "burn tobacco and call my name." Tekanawite tells the Iroquois People: "For I will be with you always, under the ground with the coming faces." As he drifts away in the stone canoe, he says he will be listening: "Just call my name, and I will be there." We will be liberated.

Clearing the Air

The era of the Great Rebirth begins at the beginning. Recall earlier in this chapter that a corrupted humanity had to clear the tangles from their minds. When confronted with organizational change—adding people to the organizational family, losing a member of that family, or some other unexpected circumstance—there is a need to cool off, calm down, take a breath, and clear the air. In this case, the organization is comprised of many parts, but works as a collective system. Working properly, like the human mind, this self-taught system remembers. The collective memory engages the obstacles and we start again.

ACTIVITY:

What changes are confusing our organization?

_____

_____

_____

_____

What kind of obstacles does the organization face?

_____

_____

_____

_____

What dangers has the organization overcome?

_____

_____

_____

_____

How do we find our way through these changes?

_____

_____

_____

What did our predecessors do to start again?

_____

_____

_____

How do we regain our passion for our good work?

_____

_____

_____

Perhaps these questions are only a starting place. There may be other questions you need to ask, but work collectively. Remember: Collective memory makes you strong.

Our unity comes from respect and compassion.

H. Conclusion: Free to Invent the Future

Theories and practices already exist that help mediate the difficult contradictions surrounding Indigenous governance. These modern theories and practices include such high-sounding methodologies as action research, board policy governance, and total quality management. However, all of these methodologies strive for participation by stakeholders in achieving desired results. Specifically, these methodologies advance principles of integrity, accountability, and guardianship.

Indigenous governance revives Indigenous democracy to provide a foundation for stable organizational change that includes integrity, accountability, and protecting the public trust. However, foundational ethical principles get lost along the way—respect and compassion. The Great Rebirth comes about because people accept the need to invoke principles. In the process of invoking respect and compassion for the ancestors, each other, and our future generations, we invent our future.

Studying Indigenous governance builds capacity for organizational learning. For example, we have transferred Indigenous governance principles into modern terminology quite easily. The following areas are drawn from the Iroquoian Great Law. However, instead of chiefs, clanmothers, and citizens, these basic guiding principles are directed toward *decision makers*.

1. The decision makers protect the integrity of the *mission*.
2. The decision makers are trustees of our *properties*.
3. The decision makers guard the rights and freedoms of *individuals*.

Committee members, directors, trustees, administrators, managers, and elected officials use the following Criteria for Excellence in the performance of these duties.

- Protecting the Integrity of Our Mission

  Organizations operate under mission statements that frame their mandates. Therefore, we have a duty and responsibility to protect the integrity of our self-determined mission. We serve a constituency, which accepts the integrity of that mission. Thus, an organization exists because of the integrity of their good work. Sometimes all we have is our good name.

- Protecting Our Trust

  Organizations rely largely on the public and philanthropy for their financial resources. Implicitly, the nature of the funding requires the public's trust. In order to accomplish our good work, diligent accountability comprises the heart of self-governance. Many hardworking people support varieties of missions with their hard-earned wages. We protect that trust through responsible use of those funds for buildings, salaries, operations, and program expenses.

- Protecting Our Constituency

  The stakeholders in organizations include the public being served, funders, and service personnel. Stakeholders have specific self-interests, but we protect the interests of all stakeholders equally, a difficult but necessary task in a democracy. Consequently, this protocol suggests that democracy is a process, not an end; that consensus building, not majority rule, becomes the guiding principle for democratized self-governance.

Anyone who comes in conflict with these Criteria for Excellence will be in conflict with the decision makers. Stakeholders delegate the duty and responsibility to protect our mission to these decision makers. We only complicate our role as decision makers when we go beyond the parameters of our mandates. Plenty of examples exist that safeguard against irresponsible governance.

Indigenous governance applies democratic principles in the conducting of its affairs. Numerous extant Indigenous governance methodologies can be recovered. In the Indigenous context, democracy is a process, not an end. Thus, the ideal of consensus is not an idealized invention. Rather, according to historian Philip Deloria, the guilds, unions, and societies of North America emulated the Indigenous model for participatory democratic process. Consensus driven by purpose is the outcome of processes whose characteristics are fundamental to democracy.

These characteristics are referred to as guiding principles. To adapt the Indigenous model of governance to self-governance is not difficult. In fact, Indigenous leadership is based on principled adherence to ethical guidelines in the administration of our mission.

Here are six maxims for Indigenous governance.

1. Organizations are purpose-driven and participatory processes in achieving the mission, goals, and mandate of their public.

2. Organizations have stakeholders who are included in the process because of their significant interest in the mission, goals, and mandate of their public.

3. Organizations are collaboratively co-designed and co-generated by all stakeholders in the delivery of their mandate.

4. Organizations' stakeholders require equal access to relevant information and the opportunity to participate effectively.

5. Organizations respect the diverse values, interests, and knowledge of their stakeholders.

6. Organizations resonate with accountability among all stakeholders.

The only guarantors of the integrity of democratic processes are the participants themselves. Democratic systems create an environment for stability. Democracy can be taught. Organizations become democracy's principal advocates, and thus, its teachers. Ironically, affirming these principles also affirms the Indigenous heritage of democracy. In the process we decolonize our thinking of what it means to govern over our affairs in our own way. Decolonization means thinking for yourself.

I. Suggested Readings

Maria Yellow Horse Brave Heart and Lemyra M. DeBruyn, "The American Indian Holocaust: Healing Historical Unresolved Grief," *American Indian and Alaska Native Mental Health Research: The Journal of the National Center* 8, no. 2 (1998).

Stephen R. Covey, *The 7 Habits of Highly Effective People* (New York: Simon and Schuster, Inc., 1990).

Philip J. Deloria, *Playing Indian* (New Haven, CT: Yale University Press, 1998).

Lloyd Dobyns and Clare Crawford Mason, *Thinking About Quality: Progress, Wisdom, and the Deming Philosophy* (New York: Random House, Inc., 1994).

Robert L. Flood and Norma R. A. Romm, *Diversity Management: Triple Loop Learning* (New York: John Wiley and Sons, Inc., 1996).

William Glasser, M.D., *Choice Theory: A New Psychology of Personal Freedom* (New York: HarperCollins Publishers, Inc., 1998).

Peter Reason and Hilary Bradbury, eds., *Handbook of Action Research* (Thousand Oaks, CA: SAGE Publications, Inc., 2001).

Peter M. Senge, *The Fifth Discipline: The Art and Practice of the Learning Organization* (New York: Doubleday, Inc., 1990).

J. Glossary

collective memory: Knowledge remembered by people with an understanding of the interdependencies of their social, political, economic, and spiritual environment. Local knowledge includes practical wisdom to protect that world. Local knowledge and practical wisdom together form Indigenous knowledge. Holders of Indigenous knowledge are valued by their people for their collective memory.

conception of the good life: People express a highest good as the basis of their society. Usually people value a Holder of Ultimate Truth who expresses these goods in parables, proverbs, and legends.

critical reflection: The ability to analyze, interpret, and evaluate one's personal adherence to moral, ethical, and principled actions.

cultural presuppositions: A person sees the world based on conceptions that become presupposed. A person's "mother culture" teaches presuppositions that are communicated through *slogans, maxims, and proverbs as well-known facts.*

culture: Culture has two parts. What people from one society do for each other *goes without saying.* When one society is compared to another, culture becomes what *needs to be said.*

executive preeminence: Leaders who are usually selected because they possess outstanding gifts to achieve the good life.

Indigenous Peoples: People who have an ability to survive in their place. Inventories of human and natural resources that have helped people remain Indigenous are characterized as local resources. Preserving and protecting those resources insure peoples' indigenism.

Indigenous democracy: A heritage in the Americas for making decisions through participatory processes by all judicial, executive, and representative stakeholders and not by majority rule.

Indigenous governance: Governing over local knowledge and local resources derives from assorted interdependencies. People are interdependent with others. People are interdependent with what else lives in their place. People are aware of interdependence with their honourable ancestors and the knowledge they passed down.

judicial, executive, representative: Describes the people whose job is to protect the mission, those who enact the mission, and those who make sure the mission represents their will.

master narrative: A people's understanding of how things came to be that are told through parables, maxims, proverbs, and slogans.

organizational learning: How a collective or group learns to accomplish their good work.

power balancing: Resolving a dispute begins with making all things equal, and all things being equal the powerful sometimes need to be convinced they need to give away some of their power.

Preternatural Force of Reason, Good Message of Peace: A maxim from Iroquois People that describes the power of the minds that seems to defy the normal bounds of nature.

self-determined: A conception of what it means to have a good life.

self-governed: Adherence to moral, ethical, and principled actions to achieve the good life.

signs and symbols: Signs and symbols communicate infrastructure systems, dispute resolution mechanisms, performative expression—styles of roads, bridges, urban planning, policing, courts, anthems, and mythologies. Signs and symbols communicate a people's concept of what they prize as good. These goods are *what goes without saying.*

Decolonizing Tribal Enrollment

Michael Yellow Bird

A. Introduction

The present rules of tribal enrollment systems, which determine who is a citizen of an Indigenous nation based on a required blood quantum, are one of the touchiest of all issues among Indigenous Peoples. In this chapter, I provide an overview of the current state of tribal enrollment, discuss why it is in great need of reform, and offer possible methods for its decolonization.

In 1995, I coordinated and participated in a tribal elders' conference at Haskell Indian Nations University. This meeting focused on creating a dialogue on important contemporary issues facing Indigenous Peoples. The topics discussed included substance abuse, elders and youth, sovereignty, land rights, preservation of tribal languages, and repatriation of the remains of our ancestors and their sacred possessions. The gathering brought together elders who shared traditional teachings and knowledge, and advised the attendees on how to address these issues and the other concerns. The turnout had been light to moderate, yet the audience and panelists were very inspiring and interesting until we began discussing the relationship between tribal enrollment and who was considered Native.

After the elders' panel of former tribal council members, spiritual leaders, and grassroots activists had given their remarks regarding this last topic, I approached the audience microphone and made the following comments, questions, and proposals:

I'm concerned about tribes that use an enrollment criterion that requires our people to have a certain amount of blood degree in order to be considered a tribal member. The reason for my concern is that the 1980 U.S. Census shows we have among the highest out-marriage rates of all races in the United States. Huge numbers of our people have, and keep on, marrying others outside our tribes and race. If this continues, the tribal blood of each generation will get thinner and thinner, and there will come a day when the majority of our people will have less than one-quarter blood, the magic number that many tribes use as a standard for tribal enrollment and identity. In fact, Professor C. Matthew Snipp (Cherokee) and I examined this issue when we wrote a paper called "American Indian Families," which was published in book entitled *Minority Families in the United States.* We found that estimates done in 1986 by the U.S. Office of Technology Assessment projected that by the year 2080, only 8.2 percent of the entire Native population will have 50 percent or more tribal blood. Approximately 32.9 percent will have one-quarter to less than half Native blood, and 58.9 percent of the entire Native population will have less than one-quarter blood.

Given these numbers, the blood quantum method appears to be very shortsighted and dangerous to the survival of our identity, which I think should be determined by more than our blood "pedigree." The blood quantum method reminds me of the term "statistical genocide," which was part of the title of an article written by Professor Jack Forbes (Lenapi). In his essay, Professor Forbes says that the method of enumerating (counting) Native Peoples by the U.S. Census Bureau in 1990 is greatly flawed since it undercounted large numbers of our people. He believes this practice amounts to a form of genocide for tribal peoples. I agree with his logic and think we can apply it to tribal enrollment systems that use blood quantum criteria, which fail to acknowledge, or exclude, our people who are less than a certain amount of blood. I think we should abandon this type of system before we enroll ourselves out of existence.

So, my questions to you are: What would you elders say to a system that used citizenship criteria created by our own individual tribes rather than a bureaucratic enrollment method that was forced upon us by the federal government? What do you think of the idea of enrolling our people into our tribes according to several requirements rather than only blood content? For instance, I would propose a tribal citizenship criterion that would not allow full citizenship or tribal constitutional rights to members until they:

1) Provide a required level of (years of) community service to our people on our reservation or traditional homelands. For instance, tribal members who become physicians would bring their medical practice to the community for a specified period of time for the good of the people. Successful teachers in a metropolitan area would be required to come home and teach the children from their community.

2) Possess a required level of knowledge and understanding of their tribal history, culture, and politics.

3) Possess a required level of tribal language, writing, and reading fluency.

4) Take an oath of allegiance to the tribal nation to protect our lands, governments, constitutions, culture, resources, and way of life.

5) Prove they are of good character according to the tribe's traditional code of morality.

I know that this plan I am proposing is not perfect but I think it is a good place to start a discussion on whether the present enrollment system or systems are fair, ensure the survival of our cultures, and foster a more honest, capable, and committed tribal citizenry. I think the basic idea behind my proposed citizenship plan is rational since points two through five are similar to the citizenship and naturalization requirements used by different nations around the world. I believe we are nations and have the right to require our people to fulfill citizenship criteria set forth by our tribal constitutions; these criteria are more relevant than how much "Indian" blood one has.

While I think tribal blood is important and do not totally discount its importance, I do not believe that love, loyalty, and service to one's tribal nation can be exclusively measured by the degree of one's blood quantum. I will close by repeating that we have very large rates of out-marriage and childbirth that are producing tribal children that are often less than one-half or one-quarter Native blood. It seems to me that if tribes are determined to maintain the blood quantum system, we must do either of the two following things to avoid ending up with the majority of our tribal population having less than the "required" level of Native blood: (1) institute an arranged marriage system that ensures our children and grandchildren, who want to have children, marry within the race and tribe so they can produce more "little Indians," with the "proper" blood quantum required by our tribes; or (2) adopt citizenship criteria that do not care whether our children or grandchildren are quarter, half, or full blood but, instead, that they are productive, happy, committed, contributing members of our nations, who will keep our languages alive, protect our homelands and resources, and maintain a tribal way of life based upon the teachings of our ancestors. I personally vote for number two.

During my discussion of these two points I also had thought about mentioning my idea of developing a national tribal sperm and egg bank that would collect specimens from all tribes wishing to preserve their tribal blood/genetic/cultural traits. However, I decided not to say anything about this plan because of the raised eyebrows, half smiles, and other displeased facial expressions of several panel members during my short presentation.

I sat down amid murmurs and polite smiles from the audience. The members of the panel responded to my remarks by focusing only on my comments relating to the blood quantum issue and not to my citizenship idea or to the other issues I had mentioned. Most of them said that it was a very bad idea to forget about blood, and one individual even told me that my plan sounded like I wanted to "weaken and discount the blood of our tribes." According to him, if people were to follow my thinking, it would not be long before our "tribes would be made up of and run by white people." When he finished his statements, I looked around to

see if anyone else from the audience would join in. No one did, so I stood up and said, in the most diplomatic tone I could muster, "I understand what you are saying and can see how it might be possible, but can you, or anyone on the panel, comment further about the pros and cons of tribal enrollment versus tribal citizenship?" He pulled the table microphone closer to himself, leaned forward, and answered me a little more forcefully repeating what he said moments earlier. So ended the dialogue on this topic.

This encounter was, and remains, very troubling for me, especially as I consider the silence from the very well-educated Indigenous audience and a quote from a white American Studies professor, who after reading a 1986 *Washington Post* article that discussed the subject of health care delivered to Indigenous Peoples through the Indian Health Service, sardonically noted, "Set the blood quantum at one-quarter, hold it as a rigid definition of Indians, let intermarriage proceed as it had for centuries, and eventually Indians will be defined out of existence. When that happens, the federal government will be freed of its persistent 'Indian problem.'"

B. Who Is Indigenous?

Defining who is a tribal member varies among different tribal groups. Professor Russell Thornton (Cherokee) found that the most common methods of identification include language, residence, cultural affiliation, recognition by a community, blood quantum, genealogical lines of descent, and self-identification. Many tribes require their members to have at least one-eighth Indigenous blood, while others call for one-fourth to one-half. Some do not have a blood requirement rule and members only need to be able to document proof of ancestry. Professor Thornton reported in 1994 that twenty-one tribes had a blood requirement of more than one-fourth, 183 required one-fourth or less, and 98 had no minimum requirement. Stephan Pevar, author of the book *The Rights of Indians and Tribes: The Basic ACLU Guide to Indian and Tribal Rights*, has found that most federal laws require that a person have one-fourth Indigenous blood in order to receive federal services and be considered Native (he says "Indian").

Who is Indigenous is also discussed outside conferences and official bureaucratic settings. From my experience, there exist "unofficial" street standards, established by various identity gatekeepers (both young and old) in the tribal population, that determine not only who is or is not Native, but also what is the "necessary degree" of Native-ness needed to be considered Indigenous within the community. For instance, some individuals are judged as not-Native because they have "sold out" by marrying outside the race (or culture), have high socioeconomic status according to the "white way of life," are Native only when convenient, and/or do not practice certain "universal" Native values. Others who may actually have enough blood or can prove their ancestry are sometimes not considered Native if they do not have the "proper" Indigenous cultural phenotype profile: that is, they have skin pigment color that is too light or dark, hair too light or curly, or facial features that seem too white or African American. Finally, there are individuals who are called "Indian wannabes"; these individuals are not considered Native because they are accused of having dubious credentials or using discredited or unknown nations to prove their claims of Indigenous identity.

Who is Indigenous has become such an important issue that it is discussed in many different circles: in tribal newspaper editorials, at tribal and major mainstream colleges, at powwows and other ceremonies, on tribal radio, on websites and news shows, in chat rooms and forums on the Internet, and in contemporary Native music. For example, in a call to Native youth to empower themselves by maintaining and thinking critically about their Indigenous identity, pride, and loyalty to the tribal nation, a popular Native hip-hop group called Savage Family/Fully Loaded Game (FLG) articulated their thoughts on this topic in the following lyrics:

…get a hold of your life man;
you ain't really native, just white guys with a nice tan..
what good does it do for us to survive if we don't know who we are…

we sell our people out to survive in this white world.
Native women disrespected, fathers marrying white girls….
It's quite real, we now follow their perceptions like we're spectacles
portraying the myth and we accept it….

("Relying on Lies," from the CD,
Theories of (r)Evolution)

C. An Overview to Tribal Enrollment

One of the earliest official U.S. federal government policy statements, identifying who would be considered to be "Indian," is detailed in Section 19 of the Wheeler-Howard Act (Indian Reorganization Act) of June 18, 1934:

The term "Indian" as used in this Act shall include all persons of Indian descent who are members of any recognized Indian tribe now under Federal jurisdiction, and all persons who are descendants of such members who were, on June 1, 1934, residing within the present boundaries of any Indian reservation and shall further include all other persons of one-half or more Indian blood. For the purposes of this Act, Eskimos and other aboriginal peoples of Alaska shall be considered Indians.

Nora Livesay, writing for the American Indian Policy Center says, "Tribal enrollment raises thorny issues in Indian communities, not the least of which is identity. Should federally imposed blood quantum requirements be thrown out? If they are, how does one ensure that only 'real' Indians are enrolled? If they aren't thrown out, how can Indians avoid fulfilling the federal government's original objective of defining themselves out of existence?" She goes on to say that "today there are many different criteria for determining who is Indigenous. The census bureau, state governments, various federal program and agencies, and tribal governments all have different definitions."

The U.S. Department of Interior's Bureau of Indian Affairs webpage (http://www.doi.gov/enroll ment.html) provides a short overview about "Indian Ancestry—Enrollment in a Federally Recognized Tribe." Four points are briefly elaborated upon.

1) What is the purpose of tribal enrollment?
2) What are tribal membership requirements?
3) How do I enroll in a tribe?
4) How do I locate the tribe I may have Indian ancestry from?

The answer to the first point is, "Tribal enrollment requirements preserve the unique character and traditions of each tribe. The tribes establish membership criteria based on shared customs, traditions, language and tribal blood." In response to the second point, the website says, "Tribal enrollment criteria are set forth in tribal constitutions, articles of incorporation or ordinances. The criterion varies from tribe to tribe, so uniform membership requirements do not exist. Two common requirements for membership are lineal descendency from someone named on the tribe's base roll or relationship to a tribal member who descended from someone named on the base roll (a 'base roll' is the original list of members as designated in a tribal constitution or other document specifying enrollment criteria). Other conditions such as tribal blood quantum, tribal residency, or continued contact with the tribe are common."

D. Problems with Blood Quantum Methods

Required blood-quantum enrollment systems can be distressingly exclusive because they do not allow individuals who may have a "large" degree of Native blood to become enrolled members of a tribe. For instance (true stories follow), a person who is born of Native parents from different tribes, who are each half Native, would produce a child who is also half Native in total blood quantum: one-quarter from the mother's tribe and one-quarter from the father's tribe. However, this child can still be denied enrollment if both parents' tribes require their members to be at least one-half blood quantum from their respective tribes.

> **"Truth is that which hurries on the break-up of the colonialist regime; it is that which promotes the emergence of the nation; it is all that protects the natives, and ruins the foreigners."**
> **—Frantz Fanon**

The same situation occurs when a child is born of parents who are each one-quarter Native blood and enrolled in separate tribes that require their members to have one-quarter blood from their tribe. Again, the child will receive one-eighth tribal blood from each parent, making one-quarter blood in total. However, since he or she does not meet the one-fourth blood rule from either tribe, the child will be denied from becoming a tribal member in either tribe.

There are other reasons and situations that children and adults with Native blood are denied membership in a tribe. Some of these situations are, but not limited to, (1) when individuals are born to parents who lack proof of Native blood because they had been adopted out as babies or small children or because their parents moved to urban areas and did not get their children enrolled; (2) when retaliatory tribal politics occurs and tribal council government members deny an individual membership because of dislike of the individual or a family; and (3) when the tribe does not want to add more members because it will further divide already inadequate federal services and resources, and/or split up financial dividends given to the current membership from per capita profits from treaty settlements, the tribal casino, and so forth.

The tribal enrollment process has had supporters and detractors within the Native population. One reason many Indigenous Peoples appear to support tribal enrollment is because it provides a system that can control the number of individuals who want to become, or claim to be, tribal members. For many tribes, a large population may be good for various reasons (for instance, large numbers can help influence local, state, and national policies and elections to reflect the priorities of the tribe). However, large numbers can also be a liability since they can overstretch the already inadequate resources and opportunities in the tribal community. Rapidly increasing numbers present a special challenge to tribal enrollment since they can overwhelm tribes that do not have the human or technological resource capacity to carefully verify who is or is not Native according to their community definition. This problem has caused some to take the position that certain individuals who become, or claim that they are, tribal members are not really valid members and that their enrollment or claim actually hurts those who are "legitimate" members. For instance, the former editor of the newspaper *Indian Country Today*, and current editor of the *Lakota Times*, Tim Giago, wrote an article in the *Lakota Times* on March 12, 1991, called "Big Increases in 1990 Census Not Necessarily Good for Tribes," where he presents his criticisms of this situation.

> It was in the 1970s that people claiming to be Indian began to take jobs intended for Indians and to write books claiming to be authorities on Indians. These instant "wannabes" did us far more harm than good. Not only did they give out misleading information about Indians, they also took jobs that left many qualified genuine Native Americans out in the cold…[B]efore you can truly be considered an Indian you must become an enrolled member of a tribe. I think most Indians would agree that this is the only way you can truly be accepted as Indian.

Today, resources and services remain scarce among many tribes, which may make an enrollment system using blood quantum necessary in order to provide benefits to individuals who are considered "real Indians." Tribal enrollment is a critical issue that demands immediate attention, clear visionary thinking, and thoughtful leadership if it is to be resolved in a just and intelligent manner.

E. Tribal Disenrollment

A January 31, 2005, article from the *Indian Country Today* reminds us that tribal disenrollment is an extremely important issue that needs immediate attention in the tribal decolonization movement. In the article, "Disenrolled Tribal Members Recall Their Tribal Council," staff writer James May writes that removal of tribal members from the tribal rolls has become "an increasingly widespread problem with tribes in California." According to May, the Estom Yumeka Maidu tribal council disenrolled seventy-two members of the tribe after those members attempted to recall members of the tribal council because of "alleged mismanagement of funds." The article goes on to say that most tribal councils involved in disenrollment have kept their actions "shrouded in secrecy."

Disenrollment has been said to be influenced by the steady, and sometimes large, buildup of resources by some gaming tribes. For example, on World Talk Radio, a show called *The American Indian Movement Today*, recorded on January 19, 2005, discussed the problem of removal of members from the tribal rolls in a segment called "Indian Disenrollment and Enrollment Regulations: Disenrollment—Is It Justified or Simply Greed?" During the show, it was noted that about 1,200 people have been taken off the tribal rolls in twelve different tribes in California and that disenrollment "is a very real part of Indian life today." The program guest—John Gomez, a disenrolled member from the Penchanga Band of Luiseno Indians—and hosts, Joseph Redbear and Marty FireRider, concluded that taking people off the tribal rolls began to occur more frequently when tribes began to be very successful in their gaming activities. They say that, greed takes over and causes disenrollment; the people in power misuse their authority to get a bigger piece of the gaming profits than the rest of the tribal membership. Disenrollment happens when others stand up to them. Gomez pointed out that when tribal members are disenrolled, they lose their rights and health-care insurance; elders lose services; and children are kicked out of tribal schools because they are no longer tribal members.

The program hosts and guest raised important issues, including (1) disenrollment does not seem to be an valid legal action since it is done by a tribal council and not by the tribal membership; (2) disenrollment is not mentioned or supported in tribal constitutions; and (3) disenrollment has caused a serious backlash among those removed from the tribal rolls, which has resulted in national movements to organize disenrolled tribal members who will go to the U.S. Congress for remedy. The program hosts and guest argued that such actions will lead to further erosion in tribal sovereignty since the BIA likely would be called in to become involved in deciding who should or should not be a member of the tribe.

I want to remind readers that not all tribes practice disenrollment, and it is not only tribal governments who are accused of "mismanaging" the money of their constituents. For instance, many people believe that their local, state, or federal governments mismanage and overspend tax dollars.

F. Conclusion

The decolonizing of tribal enrollment and addressing disenrollment are two exceptionally important issues that Indigenous communities must immediately undertake. It is important that tribal people bring these issues to the forefront of their decolonizing discussions and activities, and work together to find creative, visionary, and intelligent solutions that will best service their tribal nations. Below are several activities that I believe are helpful to begin a decolonizing dialogue on the issue of tribal enrollment and disenrollment. I suggest working with others within your community to find innovative, just solutions to these two issues.

G. Activities for Decolonizing Tribal Enrollment

ACTIVITY:

1. In the past, what was your tribe's traditional way to make people members of your nation (whether Native or non-Native or born or adopted into the tribe)?

_____
_____
_____
_____
_____
_____
_____
_____

2. What are the reason(s) for allowing people outside your tribe to become members of your nation? And why did your traditional form of enrollment work?

_____
_____
_____
_____
_____
_____
_____

3. What are the strengths and drawbacks of your traditional way of making people members of your nation?

Strengths:_____

_____

_____

_____

_____

Drawbacks:_____

_____

_____

_____

_____

4. Which enrollment criteria does your tribe currently use to determine who can be a member? Do you consider it to be a just system?

_____

_____

_____

_____

_____

5. Discuss with others whether your present enrollment system leads to a strong membership and love for the culture and nation, and promotes healthy, positive identity, and a commitment of service to the nation by the tribal members.

_____

_____

_____

_____

_____

_____

6. What do you think are the major strengths and drawbacks of your current tribal enrollment system?

Strengths:_____

_____

_____

_____

_____

Drawbacks:_____

_____

_____

_____

_____

7. If you could design your own tribal enrollment criteria, what would they look like? What would be the strengths of your system and what would make it decolonized?

_____

_____

_____

_____

_____

_____

_____

_____

_____

_____

_____

_____

_____

_____

_____

_____

_____

_____

_____

H. Suggested Resources

American Indian Movement Today. "Tribal Government, Economics, and Gaming." World Talk Radio (www.worldtalk radio.com/category.asp?cid=276, January 19, 2005).

Bureau of Indian Affairs. "Indian Ancestry—Enrollment in a Federally Recognized Tribe." Department of the Interior (www.doi.gov/enrollment.html, October 9, 2003).

Tim Giago, "Big Increases in 1990 Census Not Necessarily Good for Tribes," *Lakota Times* (March 12, 1991).

Nora Livesay, "Understanding the History of Tribal Enrollment," American Indian Policy Center (www.airpi.org/pubs/enroll. html, December 30, 2003).

Patricia Limerick, *The Legacy of Conquest: The Unbroken Past of the American West* (New York: Norton, 1987).

James May, "Disenrolled Tribal Members Recall Tribal Council." *Indian Country Today* (www.indiancountry.com/content. cfm?id=1096410268, January 31, 2005).

Stephan Pevar, *The Rights of Indians and Tribes: The Basic ACLU Guide to Indian and Tribal Rights* (Carbondale, IL: Southern Illinois University Press, 1992).

Savage Family, "Relying on Lies," *Theories of (r)Evolution* (www.savagefam.com).

Russell Thornton, *American Indian Holocaust and Survival: A Population History since 1492* (Norman: University of Oklahoma Press, 1987).

Michael Yellow Bird and Mathew Snipp, "American Indian Families." In *Minority Families in the United States: A Multicultural Perspective*, edited by Ronald C. Taylor (Upper Saddle River, NJ: Prentice Hall, Inc., 1994).

Online Resources

Bureau of Indian Affairs Federal Acknowledgement Decision Compilation (www.indianz.com/adc/adc.html).

Debra Faria, "Disenrollment" (www.bureau-of-indian-affairs.com). Note that this is not the official BIA website.

Gregg L. Lewis, "Enrollment Procedures and Recourse," Native American Constitution and Law Digitization Project, University of Oklahoma (http://thorpe.ou.edu/OILS/enroll.html).

National Indian Law Library, "Resources About Native American Tribal Enrollment," Native American Rights Fund (www.narf.org/nill/enrollment.htm).

Author's Note

Special thanks to Julia GoodFox for her comments and suggestions.

Relieving Our Suffering

Indigenous Decolonization and a United States Truth Commission

Waziyatawin

> "The colonized seems condemned to lose his memory....The memory which is assigned him is certainly not that of his people."
>
> —Albert Memmi

A. Contemporary American and Indigenous Context

On September 24, 2001, less than two weeks after the 9-11 tragedy, the September 11th Victim Compensation Fund was enacted by Congress and signed into law by President George W. Bush. This law was designed "to provide compensation for economic and non-economic loss to individuals or relatives of deceased individuals who were killed or physically injured as a result of the terrorist-related aircraft crashes of September 11, 2001." This was an unparalleled attempt to compensate families for their pain and suffering, but also, because recipients of the compensation relinquish their right to sue, it was also an offer clearly designed to protect the airline industry and others from costly litigation and thousands of potential lawsuits. Kenneth Feinberg, fund administrator, commented on the tax-free compensation paid by the

American people, saying, "This is an unprecedented, unique program and exhibits I think the best in the American people." By the time the deadline for filing passed, 95 percent of the victims applied for their piece of the government compensation program. Save the voices who rejected the government offer and are pursuing lawsuits seeking accountability for their suffering, there has been no public outcry regarding the use of federal funds to compensate these families. Indeed, the victims of 9-11 have been deemed worthy, their suffering understandable, and their need for compensation justified.

If American compensation to victims of suffering is a measure of worthiness, then the Indigenous Peoples in the United States who have suffered acts of terrorism on our lands, persons, and resources too numerous to count are apparently considered unworthy. The victims of 9-11 will never recover their losses, but they will begin to heal from their wounds, not so much because of the financial support, but because of the recognition by the rest of the country that they have suffered. On the contrary, the pain suffered by Indigenous Peoples in the United States has been forgotten, considered a thing of the past, and become normalized. Rather than acknowledging that there has been a terrible wrong, colonization has imposed on us responsibility for our own pain. We have been taught that our current predicament is a consequence of our own shortcomings, that we are to blame. While policies of genocide, ethnic cleansing, and ethnocide have been perpetrated against us and our lands, and resources have been threatened decade after decade, century after century, not only are we taught that we are to blame, we are taught that we should just get over it. There has been no adequate formal body to address our suffering or acknowledgment that we have been wronged by the policies of the United States.

B. Preparing Evidence for a Truth Commission

This chapter explores the importance of preparing a formal body of evidence for eventual submission to a committee in the United States to hear our grievances,

to listen to our stories of suffering, and to allow the truth of our experiences of human injustice to be told. It lays out a plan of action for the creation of a United States truth commission. This project will be radically different from government-initiated and -sanctioned truth commissions in other parts of the world because it will be organized and pursued without the support of the colonizing government. This commission is a worthwhile venture, however, since the purpose of such work is to seek truth about the injustices perpetrated against us, to contribute to a state of well-being among our people, and to promote justice in our lands.

Roy Brooks, a law professor and scholar on the reparations issue, provides a useful and comprehensive definition for purposes here of a human injustice:

> …[T]he violation or suppression of human rights or fundamental freedoms recognized by international law, including but not limited to genocide; slavery; extrajudicial killings; torture and other cruel or degrading treatment; arbitrary detention; rape; the denial of due process of law; forced refugee movements; the deprivation of a means of subsistence; the denial of universal suffrage; and discrimination, distinction, exclusion, or preference based on race, sex, descent, religion, or other identifying factor with the purpose or effect of impairing the recognition, enjoyment, or exercise, on an equal footing, of human rights and fundamental freedoms in the political, social, economic, cultural, or any other field of public life. In sum, a human injustice is simply the violation or suppression of human rights or fundamental freedoms recognized by international law.

A few of the human injustices endured by today's Indigenous Peoples (either as a legacy of suffering resulting from the experiences of our ancestors or as experienced by us directly) include such experiences as slavery, policies of extermination and forced removal, brutal compulsory educational systems, abuses perpetrated by church and governmental officials, numerous policies of cultural genocide, thousands of involuntary sterilizations committed as part of a federal family-planning program, theft of homelands, discriminatory practices in the U.S. penal system, and the targeting of Indigenous communities for toxic and nuclear production and waste. The truths of these experiences need to be publicly disclosed, the carriers of this suffering need a validating and supportive forum in which to tell their stories, and much work needs to be done to carry out a plan of reparative justice.

ACTIVITY:

What human injustices has your nation or community endured in the last several centuries?

_____

_____

_____

_____

_____

How have these injustices impacted your life?

_____

_____

_____

_____

C. My Experience with Historical Memory and Trauma

The process of the South African Truth and Reconciliation Commission during the 1990s has had a positive transformative effect upon a significant portion of South Africans, both black and white. Therefore, it seemed that the implementation of a similar process would be a worthwhile and indispensable project for addressing the varied and numerous forms of oppression and violations of human rights perpetrated by the United States government and its citizens upon Indigenous Peoples. However, it was my recent experience on our Dakota Commemorative March in November of 2002 in Minnesota, that I experienced firsthand the value and transformative power of telling the truth about an aspect of our past that had been previously silenced and suppressed. During this seven-day event, we retraced the 150-mile path our ancestors (primarily women and children) were forcibly marched in 1862 as the first phase of expulsion from our homeland. While this was a grueling and exhausting experience for those of us who opened up the floodgates of the pain associated with this event, it was also uplifting and healing. By the time we completed the march, arriving at the Fort Snelling concentration-camp site where our people were imprisoned during the winter of 1862–63, as a collective group, we felt that we had taken a significant step in our own healing and recovery and that this experience set us upon a path of continued healing.

This event has caused me, and I think many who participated in the event, to reflect upon the specific aspects of this experience that propelled this healing transformation into motion. Several key components profoundly affected our experience. First, we had an opportunity to tell our stories about the event in an environment that was validating and empowering. With this event, suddenly our stories that had been relegated to the shadows were brought into the light and privileged above all others. In the colonialist version of this removal, the march is depicted as an unfortunate consequence of Dakota violence and savagery during the Sioux Uprising of 1862. Our stories provided a new framework for viewing the same event, one that emphasized the brutality of the true reason for our forced removal: desire for our lands on the part of the United States government and white settlers. As we were decolonizing our history, so too were we validating Dakota perceptions of our experiences and our pain.

In addition, as part of this event we had spiritual help along the way. Not only did we have spiritual leaders there to offer prayers and conduct ceremonies, we had literally hundreds, if not thousands, of prayers offered on our behalf and on behalf of our ancestors who suffered during the forced march in 1862. We were allowed an opportunity to grieve for the spirits of our ancestors who suffered and died along the way. Though the whereabouts of many of the bodies of those murdered along that 150-mile stretch is still unknown to us, we were able to begin a culturally appropriate grieving process. The close communion we were afforded with the spirits of our ancestors, feeling their presence the length of the march, also strengthened and nourished us. We felt the strength of our own survival demonstrated in the long lineages we represented, as well as a sense of hope for our children yet unborn. As we finally reached the Fort Snelling concentration-camp site, the sense of collective grief was, for a time, almost debilitating. However, with the strength and support of our people surrounding us through the prayers, honoring songs, and ceremonies, the sense of grief began to lift and we were overwhelmed with a sense of love, compassion, and resiliency.

Finally, we also felt a sense of empowerment in taking long-overdue action. The march became an opportunity for us to physically and spiritually reclaim our ancestral homeland with our tears, sweat, footsteps, and the memorial stakes we placed along the way. We were uplifted in the experience of taking action and, in honoring and remembering the pain of our ancestors, we were empowering ourselves. By challenging the colonial vision of our past, we were validating our claim to the future. In walking the path of our ancestors, we were realizing our right to walk these lands in the future. Those who were involved in the march came to the realization that this was just the beginning. An outpouring of creative and political expression followed the commemorative event, and many of us were inspired to continue efforts in furthering our claims to our ancient homeland.

D. Decolonization and Healing

The challenging of colonialist versions of history, the restoration of Indigenous spirituality to facilitate healing and draw on the strength of our ancestors, and the resistance we offer to the ongoing occupation of our lands and resources are all part of a larger decolonizing agenda. Ultimately, our freedom from colonization will not be achieved until there is an overturning of the colonial structure, but while we seek to achieve that agenda we must begin by decolonizing our minds.

Decolonization, which necessarily requires an overturning of the institutions and systems that continue to subjugate and exploit Indigenous Peoples and our resources, must occur at the individual, collective, and structural levels. Individuals might develop a critical consciousness from which they can call into question the colonizing institutions and begin a program of meaningful resistance to the colonizing forces affecting everyone's daily lives, but true decolonization cannot exist only at the individual level, nor can it occur only among the colonized. While we may individually liberate our minds from colonization, true liberation cannot occur until we can live our lives free from the constraints of colonization. Indeed, not only must the colonized rise up, the colonizers must eventually abandon their illegitimate status and liberate themselves from the injustices they have perpetrated and the systems of subjugation they have created. The colonizers must also take responsibility for and own the injustices that they have helped directly or indirectly perpetrate.

How is truth-telling an act of decolonization?

The act of truth-telling is as an essential component of collective decolonization for several key reasons:

As we empower ourselves by telling the stories of our own suffering that have been diminished, silenced, or ignored, we are validating not just our individual experiences, but also the truth about our status as colonized peoples in a country that continues to deny its colonial reality.

Breaking the silence about our experiences and recognizing among ourselves the reality of this relationship is basic to the decolonization of our individual minds.

As we tell our stories of oppression and suffering, we are educating each other and encouraging one another to candidly view the magnitude and calculated precision of our own subjugation. While this is a difficult and taxing process, the starkness of this venture promotes an increasingly critical consciousness.

In promoting an increasingly critical consciousness, we will likely create a crucial mass of activists dedicated to working toward decolonization more expansively.

E. A United States Truth Commission

How will the United States respond? Advocates of a truth-telling forum, such as a commission to hear Indigenous grievances, will be resisted greatly by the United States government and perhaps by much of its citizenry. As a disruption of the status quo would be detrimental to the power base currently enjoyed by U.S. leadership, any forum in which U.S. atrocities and crimes against humanity were illuminated would be adamantly resisted. If the truth were indeed told, it would upset the relationship between the colonizer and the colonized. As Frantz Fanon points out, the truth about Indigenous experience would be an enemy of the colonizers: "Truth is that which hurries on the break-up of the colonialist regime; it is that which promotes the emergence of the nation; it is all that protects the natives, and ruins the foreigners." Particularly in a society that has touted its own moral righteousness and relegated itself to the position of world policeman, the United States has much to lose by acknowledging its historical and contemporary treatment of Indigenous Peoples. In spite of these realities, truth and justice are more compelling and liberating powers than those of force and domination. This realization will inevitably come even to the United States.

The need for some form of a truth commission in the United States is based on several key, but debatable, assumptions:

1. As Indigenous Peoples of the United States, we are carriers of tremendous suffering; we possess wounded spirits.

2. This suffering is creating harm to us as individuals, communities, and nations.

3. We can facilitate our own healing independent of an acknowledgment from the perpetrator.

As Indigenous Peoples of the United States, we are carriers of tremendous suffering; we possess wounded spirits. While some Indigenous individuals may believe they have sufficiently risen above historical pain and suffering, current social conditions in Indigenous communities would suggest that as collective entities, there still exists significant pain and grief. Even if we have achieved some semblance of peace and well-being as individuals, the suffering of our brothers and sisters must be recognized and addressed.

This leads to the second assumption, which is that suffering is creating harm to us as individuals, communities, and nations. Indigenous scholars have articulated the argument that "alcoholism, poverty, learned helplessness and dependence, violence, and the breakdown of values that correlate with healthy living" are symptoms of historical and intergenerational trauma. Certainly, the effects of the initial traumas suffered have been compounded by the fact that many of our communities' traditional grieving practices were interrupted through colonizing influences. Rather than coping with loss and pain in a culturally appropriate manner and context, our people have continued to struggle unsuccessfully with expressing, processing, and releasing the powerful emotions associated with trauma. Because our feelings of loss have been invalidated and/or ignored by the dominant society, we have continued to suffer further trauma, intensifying our pain and blaming ourselves for our own grief. Furthermore, the sheer magnitude of loss facing Indigenous Peoples in the last five hundred years would seemingly be prohibitive of healing, even if our healing traditions were left entirely intact. The fact that these traditions were jeopardized and even outlawed only further served to exacerbate our seeming inability to cope with our loss and to facilitate healing. The question that then arises is: How do we relieve ourselves of the pain we carry in order to restore a sense of well-being and happiness among ourselves, even as we continue to suffer ongoing loss and oppression?

This question can potentially be addressed through a truth-telling process (as of yet unsanctioned by the state), but placing faith in such a process requires subscribing to a third assumption. As Indigenous Peoples, we can begin to facilitate our own healing independent of an acknowledgment from the perpetrator. Far more contestable than the first two, this assumption is at the heart of the issue. For if we continue to meet resistance from an unwilling government and citizenry to listen to, acknowledge, atone, and compensate for the wrongs perpetrated against us, are we destined to live in a perpetual state of pain? In discussing this issue, Archbishop Desmond Tutu, chairman of South Africa's Truth and Reconciliation Commission, states, "But if the process of forgiveness and healing is to succeed, ultimately acknowledgment by the culprit is indispensable—not completely so but nearly so." Similarly, in his work on the Canadian truth commission, which has not been supported by the Canadian government or churches (the primary perpetrators of crimes against First Nations Peoples in the residential schools), Reverend Kevin Annett laments, "Any wrong can be overcome, any scar healed, but only if there is first genuine lamentation and sorrow by the perpetrators." Perhaps a *complete* healing can only occur with the perpetrators' contrition and even acts of reparation, but in a decolonization movement with an empowering agenda, a state of complete victimage must be challenged. As Tutu further points out, "If the victim could forgive only when the culprit confessed, then the victim would be locked into the culprit's whim, locked into victimhood, whatever her own attitude or intention." If we are to facilitate our own healing so that we can strengthen ourselves for the long struggles for justice ahead of us, we must consider actions we can take on our own behalf.

> "Revolt. The mere existence of the colonizer creates oppression and only the complete liquidation of colonization permits the colonized to be freed."
> —Albert Memmi

ACTIVITY:

Can you identify evidence of pain and grief in your family and community? What does it look like?

_____

_____

_____

_____

How is this suffering harming your family or community?

_____

_____

_____

_____

Long-Term Goals and Gains

At this point a couple of clarifications must be made. While arguing for a United States truth commission, it is with the hope that Indigenous Peoples will ultimately achieve reparative justice. Borrowing definitions from Janna Thompson's book *Taking Responsibility for the Past*, "Reparative justice concerns itself with what ought to be done in reparation for injustice, and the obligation of the wrong-doers, or their descendants or successors, for making this repair. It is distinct from retributive justice, which focuses on the punishment of wrong-doers...." However, rather than focusing on reparation as the end goal (it is assumed that reparations will eventually occur), healing of both Indigenous Peoples and the perpetrators is the end goal. This may be deemed as a combined legalistic and theological approach. It is legalistic because it is concerned with rights, obligations, restoration, and compensation as is generally associated with the Reparations Movement, and it is also a theological approach to wrongdoing because "[i]t is concerned with apology, forgiveness, contrition, atonement and reconciliation." Both are components of a long-term, peaceful end goal. Reparations, however, will not likely be an immediate part of the process because of the current political climate, yet they are envisioned as a necessary part to the fulfillment of long-range objectives.

In light of this we must ask: What good might be gained from a truth-telling campaign, which may not immediately include a recognition from the perpetrators? It is here that work in the area of trauma and recovery is useful to explore. In the book *Trauma and Recovery*, Judith Herman argues, "True forgiveness cannot be granted until the perpetrator has sought and earned it through confession, repentance, and restitution," but that the survivor of trauma does not need to wait for it because "[h]er healing depends on the discovery of restorative love in her own life; it does not require that this love be extended to the perpetrator." She also acknowledges that seeking fair compensation may be an important part of recovery, but that "[m]ourning is the only way to give due honor to loss; there is no adequate compensation."

Having made that argument, she also suggests that those victims of trauma who are the most successful at facilitating their own healing, may not ever receive acknowledgment from the perpetrator or justice in their particular case. Yet, they can continue to gain strength and a sense of empowerment when they "rediscover an abstract principle of social justice" that connects their fate to the fate of others, and they are then able to participate in meaningful social action. While the act of true forgiveness, a seemingly final step in the healing process, may be beyond the reach of most Indigenous Peoples until the perpetrator contributes to the process, individuals and communities can make significant strides towards overcoming our grief and pain.

To overcome this psychological trauma, Michael Yellow Bird, an Indigenous scholar who has studied and connected the effects of colonialism to psychological trauma, suggests that along with a critical assessment of how this trauma relates to colonialism, communities can institute aggressive treatment and healing programs. Developing such programs based on culturally specific healing traditions would not only go a long way towards community healing, it would additionally support the broader decolonization agenda of recovery and revitalization of traditional knowledge. A truth-telling process would be an essential component of the critical examination of our psychological condition, as we must identify and understand what it is we need to recover from and the relationship of our trauma to colonialism. An acknowledgment of trauma or loss and the need for a period of mourning, such as with the loss of a loved one, is inherent to most Indigenous cultural traditions. Furthermore, when individuals suffered physically, spiritually, emotionally, or psychologically, our cultures often had ceremonial ways of addressing this suffering to promote healing, often with the knowledge and support of the community. Because many of these cultural traditions have been lost, are no longer accessible by entire communities, or have been supplanted by imposed religions (which may have further contributed to trauma), this loss itself may be associated with deep grief. The process of reclaiming these traditions becomes in itself a healing and empowering project.

The recognition of the need to alleviate suffering and institute healing is certainly not distinct to the Indigenous Peoples of the Americas. Zen Buddhist Thich Nhat Hanh reminds us that the Four Noble Truths of Buddhism acknowledge that:

1. There is suffering.
2. There is an origin of suffering.
3. The end of suffering is possible.
4. There is a path to the end of suffering.

In following a path to end suffering according to Buddhist teachings, he encourages deep listening and loving speech as positive methods of relieving suffering. "You listen deeply for only one purpose—to allow the other person to empty his or her heart. This is already an act of relieving suffering." Recognizing that the suffering of individuals can compromise the integrity and well-being of entire nations, he also proposes establishing a Council of Sages in the United States.

"I propose that the people of the United States ask Congress to form a Council of Sages that can listen deeply to people who feel they are victims of discrimination, exploitation, and social injustice. America is suffering greatly. The destiny of a nation is too important to leave to politicians alone.

"The First Noble Truth of Buddhism is the recognition of suffering, or ill-being. The first step in curing ill-being is to understand the situation and find its roots. This is the practice recommended by the Buddha. Members of the Council of Sages would have the duty of inviting people who suffer to speak out. They would have the responsibility of listening deeply to them."

While Thich Nhat Hanh is talking about the destiny of the nation of the United States, in this discussion we must also consider the destiny of Indigenous nations residing within the borders of the United States. Furthermore, any attempt to alleviate suffering is compromised and/or contaminated if the acts that caused the suffering are ongoing. Addressing the cause of the suffering, then, becomes a necessary part of the healing.

In considering the current situation in the United States, Archbishop Tutu came up with a similar conclusion: "It may be, for instance, that race relations in the United States will not improve significantly until Native Americans and African Americans get the opportunity to tell their stories and reveal the pain that sits in the pit of their stomachs as a baneful legacy of dispossession and slavery. We saw in the Truth and Reconciliation Commission how the act of telling one's story has a cathartic, healing effect."

ACTIVITY:

What is your Indigenous nation's philosophy about suffering? Is there a means to end suffering? Is this practiced today?

_____

_____

_____

_____

_____

_____

_____

_____

F. Reparations Versus Truth Commission

While committed to the act of truth-telling about the atrocities and crimes against humanity perpetrated against them, African Americans in the United States are gaining momentum in the United States for their reparations movement, rather than a movement towards a truth commission. The truth commission processes most successfully employed in other countries occurred with governmental sanctioning after an oppressive regime was overthrown. Because no such overthrow has yet been achieved in the United States, reparations to the black community in the United States are seen by advocates of this movement as a precondition for healing and racial justice. The truth-telling in this movement will be carried out in America's courtrooms. Here also, however, is a denial of victimage and an embracing of a strategy of empowerment, as Martha Biondi, a reparations advocate has described, "Reparations changes the discursive image of African Americans from victims to creditors and revises the dominant narrative of American social, political, economic history in order to emphasize the debt owed to African Americans."

Indeed, the same strategy could be employed by Indigenous Peoples for a parallel reparations movement. Certainly, the debt to Indigenous Peoples, from land wealth alone, is a debt of gargantuan proportions. Many of the policies of genocide perpetrated against Indigenous Peoples were carried out as a means to an end: to acquire Indigenous land. Kevin Annett documented the powerful words of Canadian residential school survivor, Harriet Nahanee:

> We were keepers of the Land; that is the special job given to our people by the Creator. And the whites wanted the land, the trees and the fish. So they had to brainwash us to forget we had to guard and preserve the land for our Creator. That's why they put us in the residential schools, and terrorized us, so we'd forget our language and our laws, and allow the land to be stolen. And it worked. The whites have 99% of the land now, and our people are dying off. That's why it's never been about God, or "civilizing" us. It's always been about the land.

Though many human rights abuses perpetrated against Indigenous Peoples are worthy of reparations, loss of land remains the most tangible and clearest example of injustice begging restitution or restoration. Though almost all lands in what is now the United States were "purchased" through treaty, as Indigenous scholars Vine Deloria Jr. and David Wilkins point out, "There is no question that no Indian tribe ever received anything approaching just compensation for its lands from the United States. Even the most carefully negotiated treaty only returned to the tribes pennies on the dollar, and some treaties had terms so outrageous as to shock the conscience of even the hardest cynic." For five hundred years, land has been the most important struggle facing Indigenous Peoples and will continue to be the primary struggle until there is a meaningful recovery of that which is so deeply intertwined with Indigenous ways of being. In fact, it is difficult, if not impossible, to live as Indigenous Peoples or maintain our Indigeneity without our connection to the land that forms the basis of our identities. As long as Indigenous Peoples are prevented from maintaining this connection to homeland, the injustice will be ongoing.

ACTIVITY:

How has your Indigenous land base been affected by the processes of invasion, conquest, and colonization?

_____

_____

_____

_____

_____

What has been your nation's response to the loss of land or threats to land? How has that loss affected the well-being of your nation?

_____

_____

_____

_____

_____

For many Indigenous Peoples, restoration of land is equated with a resurgence in Indigenous life. This is an important point because the resurrection of nations is a viable possibility. As Thompson argues, "Non-indigenous members of states were responsible for the degradation of indigenous nations, and appropriate reparation in many cases would be to allow and encourage resurrection of nations, so long as indigenous people have distinct communities, want to live according to their law, and have resources over which they can exercise control." From an Indigenous perspective in which cultural traditions, diet, health knowledge, spiritual traditions, and political organizations are all connected to a specific geography, the resurrection of nations is land-dependent. That being the case, why not join the Reparations Movement for black slavery so that Indigenous Peoples might finally receive their just dues?

G. Lessons from the Indian Claims Commission

As mentioned earlier, reparations will be a necessary part of Indigenous healing as well as the achieving of justice, but until there is a public, popular recognition of the wrongs done to Indigenous Peoples, until there is a genuine sense of contrition, Indigenous Peoples are unlikely to get a fair hearing or to receive just reparations. A brief review of the Indigenous experience with the Indian Claims Commission (ICC) offers a historical justification for *not* proceeding with claims in the court system, which has been an instrument of our own subjugation and colonization. In 1946 the Indian Claims Commission was established to settle longstanding grievances held by Indigenous Peoples, largely from inadequate compensation for treaty land cessions. Though $818 million was eventually awarded (a significant chunk of which went to pay attorneys' fees), the ICC is still considered by many to be a failure. For example, in light of the importance of Indigenous relationships with the land, many tribes sought a restoration of their former land base rather than monetary compensation, an impossibility in a claims process that was designed to only offer mone-

tary remuneration. This left a legacy of unresolved claims (the Lakota, for instance, were initially awarded $17.5 million through the ICC but still refuse to sell their land and their award continues to collect interest). In addition, because the ICC was created as termination policies were constructed, the two were intimately connected and "[t]he settlement of claims thus appeared to be, not a bold stroke to correct all past injustices, but simply a necessary preliminary step toward termination."

Perhaps most importantly for the purposes we are discussing here, rather than settling grievances and fostering a sense of finality, the ICC was a frustrating and embittering experience for Indigenous Peoples. Though it was established as a commission, rather than a court, to minimize "adversary proceedings inherent in a judicial format," this goal was not accomplished. As a scholar of Indigenous history, Peter Iverson points out, "[T]he commission gave little credence to the oral histories of the tribes or the testimony of elders based upon such histories. Tribes found themselves mired in protracted proceedings that emphasized contentiousness rather than consensus." One only needs to read through transcripts from these hearings to see how Indigenous Peoples were badgered and their stories discredited, to see that this process ran counter to any notion of Indigenous healing or reparative justice. Instead of having their experiences with loss validated and supported, it might be argued that the ICC further traumatized participants.

To compound the offense, the amount of compensation provided for tribes was offset by "all money or property given to or funds expended gratuitously for the benefit of the claimant," including expenditures for the "civilization" and "education" of Indigenous Peoples, which in themselves are causes of trauma worthy of reparations. Deloria and Wilkins clarify the injustice of this, stating, "Allowance of these expenses freely made as a policy of the government in effect meant that Indians were made to pay for their own cultural destruction." The ironies with the ICC were numerous; the same government that stole Indigenous land in the first place appointed itself to hear the claims, to make the determination on an amount of remuneration, and then to decide that justice had been dispensed. While the commission may have "greatly heightened the legal consciousness" among Indigenous Peoples and increased competency in future legal struggles, as scholar Francis Paul Prucha contends, this process did little to accomplish healing or dispense justice.

In light of this and the sporadic and seemingly arbitrary way in which U.S. Supreme Court rulings do or do not support Indigenous causes, there is little reason to believe support for Indigenous claims for reparations would be given a fair hearing in a courtroom. In addition, this route would be extraordinarily expensive, with legal fees running into the millions for Indigenous Peoples, an expense few tribes could afford. As Archbishop Tutu explained about their decision to pursue a truth commission in South Africa, "We have had to balance the requirements of justice, accountability, stability, peace, and reconciliation." Thus, even in the face of recent and brutal human rights violations, they sought not to seek punishment of the perpetrators (and possible compensation) through the criminal courts because "[a] criminal court requires the evidence produced in a case to pass the most rigorous scrutiny and satisfy the criterion of proving the case beyond reasonable doubt." In this process all efforts would be made to discredit witnesses, destroy or cover up evidence, and deny governmental responsibility, making true healing a challenge even if courts eventually ruled in our favor.

What then are Indigenous Peoples to do to promote our own healing and just reparations for past injustices? A United States truth commission, federally funded and supported, will not occur without considerable domestic support and international pressure. However, there are actions we can take as Indigenous Peoples along with our non-Indigenous allies to estab-lish a truth commission of our own making, for which we can eventually compel a United States response. I suggest we prepare our testimony and evidence, while participating in a major domestic educational campaign about the injustices, and use our materials to seek support from the international community. In essence, we would follow the example currently being set by the Canadian truth commission, perhaps to collaboratively create a continental-wide investigation.

> "Imperialism is still the enemy of human kind and any blow against imperialism whether in the Philippines, El Salvador, Chile, South Korea is clearly a blow for democracy and change."
> —Ngugi wa Thiong'o

H. The Canadian Example

After much initial investigation, in 2001 the Truth Commission into Genocide in Canada released a 280-page report entitled, *Hidden from History: The Canadian Holocaust*, which documents the crimes perpetrated against the Indigenous Peoples of Canada, such as murder, torture, and forced sterilizations. While church and state have thus far refused to answer the charges of genocide posed against them, the truth commission is counting on support from the international community. In 1998, a United Nations–affiliated group, the International Human Rights Association of American Minorities (IHRAAM), formally heard the testimony of Indigenous witnesses in an organized tribunal. Though their report and nineteen hours of eyewitness videotape was supposed to be sent to UN Human Rights Commissioner Mary Robinson, it appears that IHRAAM never took the necessary action because of pressure from the Canadian government. The members of the truth commission are now pursuing international support on their own, appealing to the UN secretary general and the International Criminal Court to establish an international war-crimes tribunal for crimes of genocide that violate the UN Convention on Genocide, the International Convention of the Rights of the Child, and the International Human Rights Convention.

As Indigenous Peoples, however, we have to examine the best route for international appeal. As Indigenous professors Gerald Taiaiake Alfred and Jeff Corntassel have recently pointed out, in highlighting the dismal failure of the International Decade of the World's Indigenous Peoples (1995–2004), "The real important question centres on how Indigenous peoples can promote state accountability to high principal and to Indigenous peoples' rights within the UN system." Time will tell how the international community responds to the Canadian truth commission. In the meantime, its advocates have been physically assaulted, harassed, threatened, and some, such as Kevin Annett, have been stripped of their livelihood.

In spite of difficult obstacles, Indigenous Peoples continue to take a courageous stand and some groups are issuing their own appeal. For example, 350 delegates to the Conference of the Kainaakiiks recently gathered and unanimously passed a resolution that recognized the forced confinement of Indigenous Peoples in the residential schools and the lifelong damage caused to the survivors and their descendants, while rejecting as inadequate the Canadian settlement process, which they say has added to the "shameful conduct of the government." Their final resolution stated:

"We, the women of the Blood Tribe, Kainaakiiks, living on and off reserve, assembled in Conference on December 8, 2003, state....WE THEREFORE RESOLVE to take the Canadian Government to the world court of the United Nations to answer for its breach of our political, civil and human rights which are treasured values of this country and in International Conventions to which the country of Canada is a signatory."

I. Obstacles to and Strategies for U.S. Truth Commission Work

In trying to advocate for justice in the United States, we face the additional struggle of trying to make a country accountable when it has defiantly and routinely broken, not signed, or only conditionally signed international agreements. While touting moral superiority, the United States for forty years refused to ratify the UN genocide convention and then did so conditionally, seriously weakening the convention and requiring U.S. consent for any dispute to which the United States is party. More recently, the United States refused to endorse the Durban Declaration and Programme of Action resulting from the 2001 World Conference against Racism, Racial Discrimination, Xenophobia and Related Intolerance, as well as the International Criminal Court.

The Durban Declaration would be especially useful for establishing a U.S. truth commission or reparations movement, which is precisely why the United States was not one of the 168 nation signatories. While adherence to and enforcement of declaration tenets remains problematic, the declaration does address "[r]emedies, reparations, compensation," and urges states to protect against discrimination by "ensuring that all persons have access to effective and adequate remedies and enjoy the right to seek from competent national tribunals and other national institutions just and adequate reparation and satisfaction for any damage as a result of such discrimination." The United States remains belligerent in this area because it is not yet ready to face up to its past, despite its glaring history of oppression. Laurence Armand French, a scholar writing about reparations, describes this sad state of denial and desire for historical amnesia: "These policies and practices of slaughter, slavery, wars, physical and cultural genocide (ethnic cleansing), death marches, and concentration camps have not sufficiently shamed the federal government into providing meaningful reparations. The United States is even reluctant to offer an apology for these practices."

The human injustices perpetrated in federally run boarding schools have yet to be acknowledged or addressed by the United States government. However, as the sexual abuse scandal in the Catholic Church has split open in recent years, so too have testimonies emerged among Indigenous People who were abused by church workers and teachers in United States–run boarding schools. Class-action lawsuits concerning boarding-school abuses are now under litigation, and organizations have formed to facilitate healing and justice regarding these gross human rights violations. Indigenous intellectual Andrea Smith has spearheaded the Boarding School Healing project, a coalition of organizations seeking to document boarding-school abuses, develop strategies for healing, and demand justice from the federal government and churches. This important project provides a formal outlet for channeling testimony collected regarding boarding-school experiences.

These networks will continue to build and gain momentum as we open the floodgates of memory and provide new avenues for seeking justice. If justice has been hard to achieve domestically or through the most visible international arenas, in the meantime we can continue to facilitate the process of healing that is within our power. Furthermore, we can reach out to Indigenous Peoples globally who are also struggling with the consequences of colonization, to build Indigenous unity.

What We Can Do

We can now begin to articulate how to initiate these efforts among our peoples today. First and foremost, this has been conceptualized as a grassroots effort that would begin with small discussions in our communities and work toward consensus building. Because we are not declaring that individuals who testify are relinquishing their right to sue or file charges (we have no state-sanctioned commitment to reparations), our primary goal will be revealing the truth about the extent of our suffering from injustice, so that we can facilitate healing and social justice.

There are four major steps in working toward a truth commission.
1. Collecting testimonies and researching data
2. Engaging in a public education campaign
3. Instituting aggressive healing measures
4. Seeking a forum for hearing and addressing grievances

This is a project that cannot be engaged in by only a few individuals. This will require community support, effort, and skills as well as collaboration with other Indigenous nations. Fortunately, a pathway is being forged in this area, largely through the work of Kevin Annett and others working on the Canadian truth commission. Many of his ideas and suggestions are reflected here in the following step-by-step suggestions that detail how individuals, tribal communities, student groups, and organizations can participate in working toward a United States truth commission. No one person or group need be responsible for every step in the process because any and all efforts will help us achieve stronger, more unified cases.

Collecting Testimonies and Researching Data

1. Host a community/organization/group discussion on the topic of a truth commission. After making a list of injustices perpetrated against your Indigenous community or nation, discuss some of the following questions:
- Has your community or nation acknowledged these injustices and grieved over them?
- Has your community or nation healed from these injustices or are the people still suffering from them?
- Have injustices discontinued, or are they ongoing?
- Is everyone in your community or nation aware of these injustices, or have they been silenced and suppressed?
- What might be gained from participation in a truth commission process? Are there any possible negative repercussions?
- Does it seem like a worthwhile and important project?
- Are there reparations that could be made to help your

community or nation overcome the suffering and restore a sense of well-being?

- Can you identify people willing to help move the process into the next stage and strategize about ways to document testimonials?
- If your community or nation has agreed that pursing a truth commission would be beneficial to your community, are there ways that this process can fit into your cultural framework (how might you indigenize the process)? For example, what term or terms would you use to describe a truth commission in your language?

2. Announce your intention to collect evidence for a truth commission through community outlets (tribal newspapers, newsletters, flyers in community facilities). Invite people to tell their stories.

3. Find a pleasing, comfortable place where people can give their testimony, or if they prefer, visit them in their homes. Encourage at least one of their loved ones to sit with them as they share painful stories. Solicit the help of community spiritual leaders, as well as community professionals experienced in dealing with issues of grief to participate in this process. Learn about compassionate listening, or deep listening (you can read about this in Thich Nhat Hanh's book *Creating True Peace*). Practice this. Record eyewitnesses' stories, preferably on video, but at least on audiocassette tape, and develop a careful system that records the names of eyewitnesses, as much contextual information about date and place of assaults (even approximate years), the date of recording, and the name of the recorder. Transcribe these statements into affidavits that are duly signed, dated, and witnessed, preferably with notary publics. Maintain originals and submit copies to your community's or nation's designated repository. Are there secondary witnesses who can corroborate the story? Try to find these individuals and, if they are willing, collect their testimony as well.

4. Gather corroborating evidence that supports the oral testimony and/or other acts of injustice. Visit tribal, private, and public archives, libraries, and Internet sources; copy data; and create a body of evidence to demonstrate the history of injustice. Incorporate these activities into tribal college classrooms or community/reservation projects. Contact historians, anthropologists, sociologists, psychologists, and social workers (either Native or non-Native) who have done research on your nation and solicit their help in collecting data. If possible, scan this material into a digital format for widespread Internet distribution and create a truth commission website for your community or nation. Identify which testimony the documentary evidence supports, creating an organization/archival system that can be used by national and international bodies in examination of the materials. Submit this data to your designated repository.

Engaging in a Public Education Campaign

1. Share your evidence with your local community. Have community forums to discuss the evidence emerging. Print eyewitness accounts in tribal newspapers and community newsletters.

2. Share your evidence with the local non-Native community. Submit letters to the editor in local newspapers, provide news releases to newspapers, and invite reporters to write stories on the issue.

3. Engage in a dialogue with non-Native neighbors about the extent to which they were aware of these injustices. Solicit their support as a matter of ethical responsibility. This activity should be engaged in very cautiously as emotions and anger may arise on both sides.

4. Forward all materials to your designated community's or nation's repository.

5. Work with other Indigenous nations or communities to coordinate your truth commission efforts, and plan to distribute your collaborative reports to an international body concerned with human rights abuses. Also, submit your reports to a variety of publication outlets.

6. If resistance is encountered with institutions, question why they would facilitate the cover up of injustices or why they would support injustices perpetrated against Indigenous Peoples. If necessary, peacefully demonstrate to draw attention to their resistance.

7. In your community, strategize about what to do if there is no public response or if no one seems to care. Identify what this might indicate and how you might address it.

Instituting Aggressive Healing Measures

1. Host community discussions about how to proceed with aggressive healing practices for the community.
- Identify traditional cultural practices for healing, whether they be grieving processes in instances of loss, or ceremonies for healing physical, spiritual, and psychological ailments.
- Discuss how, or whether, trauma has been transmitted intergenerationally. If it has, discuss how that process might be interrupted and how anger in the community might be transformed into compassion.
- Are there culturally appropriate ways to facilitate this process?

2. Work with community spiritual leaders to institute healing practices.
- Special support should be arranged for those witnesses who come forward to tell their stories as well as their families.
- Be prepared to support them, especially if there is non-Native backlash to revealing the truth about the injustices they experienced.
- Abide by traditional protocol for requesting help from spiritual leaders, and make sure a relationship of reciprocity is maintained so our spiritual leaders are also supported.

Seeking a Forum for Hearing and Addressing Grievances

1. If collaborating with other Indigenous communities or nations, exchange materials and work at creating a unified truth commission case.
2. Host community discussions about possible forums for international (or national) redress and discuss reparations and what they might look like. This would be a good opportunity to engage in a deep questioning of community values and goals as part of a broader decolonization agenda.
- What is it that your community wants?
- Economic remuneration? If so, why? Would that bring happiness and restore well-being to your people?
- Land? What would your nation hope to regain with a recovery of land? Why is that important?
- Are there measures your community can take to return to your traditional values or relationship with the land and the rest of the world? Is that desirable?

This is a project that will be extremely labor-intensive as well as significantly physically, emotionally, and spiritually draining. However, it is also has the potential to be extremely rewarding, unifying, and, ultimately, healing. One of the profound statements made by Archbishop Tutu at the conclusion of the truth commission in South Africa was that "[n]o one in South Africa could ever again be able to say, 'I didn't know,' and hoped to be believed." Like the families who suffered from the violence of 9-11, we know we are worthy victims and we know how we have suffered at the hands of violence. Can we create an American society in which people can no longer legitimately claim they didn't know? Can we create a society of well people, where justice has prevailed and healing has occurred? Critics of a truth commission might dismiss it as idealistic and impractical because of the magnitude of the reparations necessary to make amends, just as they have argued about the Reparations Movement; however, as Martha Biondi, a reparations advocate, points out, "The objections simply describe the enormity of the task rather than delegitimize it." As intellectual workers, activists, students, teachers, and compassionate human beings, we have tremendous work ahead of us.

J. Suggested Readings

Kevin Annett, *Love and Death in the Valley: Awakening to Hidden Histories and Forgotten Crimes on the West Coast of Canada* (1st Books Library, 2002).

Kevin Annett, "Research tasks for the Truth Commission into Genocide in Canada" (January 7, 2004).

Kevin Annett, "Statement of Claim made before the United Nations and the World Community" (http://canadiangenocide.nativeweb.org/, May 4, 2005).

Martha Biondi, "The Rise of the Reparations Movement," *Radical History Review* 87 (Fall 2003).

Roy L. Brooks, "The Age of Apology." In *When Sorry Isn't Enough: The Controversy over Apologies and Reparations for Human Injustice*, edited by Roy L. Brooks (New York: New York University Press, 1999).

Vine Deloria Jr. and David E. Wilkins, *Tribes, Treaties, & Constitutional Tribulations* (Austin: University of Texas Press, 1999).

Bonnie Duran and Eduardo Duran, *Native American Postcolonial Psychology* (Albany: State University of New York Press, 1995).

Bonnie Duran, Eduardo Duran, and Maria Yellow Horse Brave Heart, "Native Americans and the Trauma of History." In *Studying Native America: Problems and Prospects*, edited by Russell Thornton (Madison: University of Wisconsin Press, 1998).

"Durban Declaration and Programme of Action from the World Conference against Racism, Racial Discrimination, Xenophobia and Related Intolerance"

Frantz Fanon, *The Wretched of the Earth* (New York: Grove Press, 1963).

Laurence Armand French, "Native American Reparations: Five Hundred Years and Counting." In *When Sorry Isn't Enough: The Controversy over Apologies and Reparations for Human Injustice*, edited by Roy L. Brooks (New York: New York University Press, 1999).

Tim Harper, "9/11 Families Reject 'Bribe,' Sue U.S.," *Toronto Star* (December 23, 2003).

Judith Herman, *Trauma and Recovery: The Aftermath of Violence—from Domestic Abuse to Political Terror* (New York: Basic Books, 1992).

Peter Iverson, *"We Are Still Here": American Indians in the Twentieth Century* (Wheeling, IL: Harlan Davidson, 1998).

Albert Memmi, *The Colonizer and the Colonized*, expanded edition (Boston: Beacon Press, 1991).

Thich Nhat Hanh, *Creating True Peace: Ending Violence in Yourself, Your Family, Your Community, and the World* (New York: Free Press, 2003).

"Probe of Canadian residential schools to be reported at UN," *Globe & Mail* (June 20, 1998).

Francis Paul Prucha, ed., *Documents of United States Indian Policy*, third edition (Lincoln: University of Nebraska Press, 2000).

Francis Paul Prucha, *The Great Father: The United States Government and the American Indians*, abridged edition (Lincoln: University of Nebraska Press, 1986).

"Resolution by the Blood Women, the Kainaakiiks, December 8th, 2003": For further information, support, or participation in this initiative, contact Lois Frank or Rhonda Ruston at the Kainaakiiksi Women's Society at kainaakiiksi@netscape.net.

Janna Thompson, *Taking Responsibility for the Past: Reparation and Historical Justice* (Malden, MA: Blackwell Publishers, 2002).

Desmond Tutu, *No Future Without Forgiveness* (New York: Doubleday, 1999).

"Victim Compensation Fund Frequently Asked Questions," U.S. Department of Justice (www.usdoj.gov/victimcompensation).

www.taiaiake.com: A website created by Mohawk intellectual, Gerald Taiaiake Alfred, to provide information to and promote exchange among Indigenous People interested in the struggle toward Indigenous liberation.

Michael Yellow Bird, "The Model of the Effects of Colonialism" (Office for the Study of Indigenous Social and Cultural Justice, University of Kansas, 1998).

Index